Top Federal Tax Issues
FOR 2014 | CPE COURSE

CCH Editorial Staff Publication

Contributors

Technical Reviewer .... George G. Jones, J.D., LL.M
Contributing Editors .... Brant Goldwyn, J.D.
Adam R. Levine, J.D., LL.M
Larry Perlman, CPA, J.D., LLM
Jennifer J. Rodibaugh, J.D.
Leo V. Roinila, JD, LL.M
Raymond G. Suelzer Jr., J.D., LL.M
George L. Yaksick, Jr., J.D.
Production Coordinator .... Gabriel E. Santana
Design/Layout .... Laila Gaidulis
Production .... Lynn J. Brown

ISBN: 978-0-8080-3563-3

4025 W. Peterson Ave.
Chicago, IL 60646-6085
800 344 3734
CCHGroup.com

Printed in the United States of America

TOP FEDERAL TAX ISSUES FOR 2014 CPE COURSE

Introduction

Each year, a handful of tax issues typically require special attention by tax practitioners. The reasons vary, from a particularly complicated new provision in the Internal Revenue Code, to a planning technique opened up by a new regulation or ruling, or the availability of a significant tax benefit with a short window of opportunity. Sometimes a developing business need creates a new set of tax problems, or pressure exerted by Congress or the Administration puts more heat on some taxpayers while giving others more slack. All these share in creating a unique mix that in turn creates special opportunities and pitfalls in the coming year and beyond. The past year has seen more than its share of these developing issues.

CCH's *Top Federal Tax Issues for 2014 CPE Course* identifies those recent events that have developed into the current "hot" issues of the day. These tax issues have been selected as particularly relevant to tax practice in 2014. They have been selected not only because of their impact on return preparation during the 2014 tax season but also because of the important role they play in developing effective tax strategies for 2014 and beyond. Some issues are outgrowths of several years of developments; others have burst onto the tax scene unexpectedly. Among the latter are issues directly related to the recent economic downturn and tax legislation designed to assist in a recovery. Some have been emphasized in IRS publications and notices; others are just being noticed by the IRS.

This course is designed to help reassure the tax practitioner that he or she is not missing out on advising clients about a hot, new tax opportunity; or that a brewing controversy does not blindside their practice. In addition to issue identification, this course provides the basic information needed for the tax practitioner to implement a plan that addresses the particular opportunities and pitfalls presented by any one of those issues. Among the topics examined in the *Top Federal Tax Issues for 2014 CPE Course* are:

- IRS Gears Up for Health Care Reform
- Net Investment Income Tax: Issues and Strategies
- Implementing Accounting Method Changes
- Income Tax-Deferral Techniques
- Innocent Spouse Relief
- Identity Theft: Due Diligence and Remedies
- Boomer Retirement Strategies
- FATCA: New Rules for International Disclosure and Account Reporting
- Public Charities and Private Foundations: Current Compliance Issues

Study Questions. Throughout the course you will find Study Questions to help you test your knowledge, and comments that are vital to understanding a particular strategy or idea. Answers to the Study Questions with feedback on both correct and incorrect responses are provided in a special section beginning on page 10.1.

Index. To assist you in your later reference and research, a detailed topical index has been included for this course beginning on page 11.1.

Quizzer. This course is divided into four Modules. Take your time and review all course Modules. When you feel confident that you thoroughly understand the material, turn to the CPE Quizzer. Complete one, or all, Module Quizzers for continuing professional education credit.

October 2013

Save money and get immediate results with no Express Grading fee when you order all modules together online at **CCHGroup.com/PrintCPE.** Further information is provided in the CPE Quizzer instructions on page 12.1.

CCH'S PLEDGE TO QUALITY

Thank you for choosing this CCH Continuing Education product. We will continue to produce high quality products that challenge your intellect and give you the best option for your Continuing Education requirements. Should you have a concern about this or any other CCH CPE product, please call our Customer Service Department at 1-800-248-3248.

COURSE OBJECTIVES

This course was prepared to provide the participant with an overview of specific tax issues that impact 2013 tax return preparation and tax planning in 2014. These are the issues that "everyone is talking about;" each impacts a significant number of taxpayers in significant ways.

Upon course completion, you will be able to:

- Discuss some of the continuing legal challenges to PPACA since the 2012 Supreme Court decision;
- Describe the requirements for the individual mandate (individual shared responsibility payment);
- Understand the rationale behind Congress's enactment of the net investment income tax and the IRS' response to writing rules and regulations to implement this new tax;
- Determine the income levels at which the 3.8 percent net investment income tax is triggered;
- Explain what an accounting method is and when it is adopted;
- Articulate the scope limitations that prevent filing for an accounting method change or limit audit protection under the advance and automatic change procedures;
- Understand the asset/liability method of accounting;
- Discuss taxable and deductible temporary differences and understand their significance;
- Compare the different types of innocent spouse relief;
- Identify situations in which innocent spouse relief may and may not be granted;
- Understand the severity of taxpayer identity theft;
- Identify common schemes used by thieves to obtain personal information;
- Understand key considerations in rebalancing assets with an eye toward retirement, including strategies for capital gains within investment portfolios as well as the sale of a residence;
- Describe some of the special rules for retirement savings vehicles applicable to boomers;

- Articulate the connection between the FBAR and FATCA requirements;
- Discuss Intergovernmental Agreements and understand their significance;
- Explain the class of practitioners on which private foundations may rely when determining foreign charitable status; and
- Determine whether an organization improperly intervened in a political campaign.

One **complimentary copy** of this course is provided with certain copies of CCH publications. Additional copies of this course may be downloaded for free from **CCHGroup.com/PrintCPE** or ordered by calling 1-800-248-3248 (ask for product 10024491-0001).

TOP FEDERAL TAX ISSUES FOR 2014 CPE COURSE

Contents

MODULE 1: HEALTH CARE LAW: NEW REQUIREMENTS

MODULE 2 — TIMING RULES: CAPITALIZATION AND INCOME DEFERRAL

4 Income Tax-Deferral Techniques

MODULE 3: INDIVIDUALS: RELATIONSHIPS AND THE TAX LAW

5 Innocent Spouse Relief

6 Identity Theft: Due Diligence and Remedies

7 Boomer Retirement Strategies

MODULE 4: COMPLIANCE ISSUES FOR FOREIGN ACCOUNTS AND EXEMPT ORGANIZATIONS

MODULE 1: HEALTH CARE LAW: NEW REQUIREMENTS — CHAPTER 1

IRS Gears Up for Health Care Reform

Health care reform was enacted in 2010 to expand the provision of health insurance to more Americans. Reform comprises two major laws: the *Patient Protection and Affordable Care Act* (PPACA), and the *Health Care and Education Reconciliation Act* (HCERA). Although some provisions of these laws took effect in the years 2010–2013, two important provisions will not take effect until 2014: the individual mandate and the premium tax credit. Another major provision—the employer mandate—was scheduled to take effect in 2014, but the IRS effectively delayed it until 2015. The IRS and other federal agencies (notably the Departments of Labor and Health and Human Services (HHS)) have been issuing important guidance on health care reform. This chapter reviews some of the important tax provisions in PPACA, including these three major provisions, and the IRS guidance.

LEARNING OBJECTIVES

Upon completion of this chapter, you will be able to:

- Discuss some of the continuing legal challenges to PPACA since the 2012 Supreme Court decision;
- Describe the requirements for the individual mandate (individual shared responsibility payment);
- Identify the requirements for the employer mandate (employer shared responsibility payment);
- Determine the eligibility requirements for the health insurance premium assistance tax credit;
- Understand the role of affordable health insurance exchanges;
- Explain other important provisions of PPACA, such as the rules for wellness programs; and
- List and describe important revenue-raising provisions in PPACA, including the tanning services excise tax; the branded prescription drug fee; the medical device excise tax; and the tax on health insurance providers.

INTRODUCTION

PPACA is a lengthy and complex law, with many requirements and features. The IRS has been issuing detailed guidance since the law's enactment in 2010. Some of the law's complexity reflects the law's jumble of effective dates, but by 2014, most of the major provisions of the law will have taken effect, except for the employer mandate and the tax on "Cadillac" health plans. Most individuals and employers are affected by these provisions. They include the *individual mandate* (individual shared responsibility payment), which requires most individuals and their families to carry health insurance or face a penalty; the health insurance premium assistance tax credit, which the IRS will administer to help low- and middle-income Americans pay for health insurance; and the *employer mandate* (employer shared responsibility payment), which requires most employers to provide essential, affordable health insurance coverage or face a penalty.

SHARED RESPONSIBILITY FOR INDIVIDUALS

Beginning in 2014, PPACA requires individuals to:

- Be covered by a health plan that provides basic health insurance coverage (known as *minimum essential coverage* or MEC);
- Qualify for an exemption from the coverage requirement; or
- Pay a shared responsibility payment.

This shared responsibility provision for individuals is also known as the *individual mandate.*

COMMENT

PPACA gives "shared responsibility" to improve access to health insurance to the federal government, state governments, insurers, employers, and individuals. Nevertheless, the government, citing Congressional Budget Office research, claims that less than 2 percent of Americans will owe a shared responsibility payment.

The provision applies to individuals of all ages, including children and other dependents. U.S. citizens living in the United States or abroad are covered by the requirement, but U.S. citizens living abroad for the entire year are treated as having MEC and therefore do not owe a payment. Foreign nationals who live in the U.S. long enough to qualify as resident aliens are covered. Residents of U.S. territories are treated as having MEC.

The adult or married couple who can claim a dependent is held responsible for making the payment if the child or dependent adult does not have coverage or an exemption. A married couple is jointly liable for the payment. Under the proposed regulations, a taxpayer is liable for an individual who may be claimed as a dependent, whether or not the taxpayer actually claims the dependent.

COMMENT

Who should be responsible for children's coverage is an issue for divorced couples and other adults. Commentators have noted that a divorced noncustodial parent who cannot claim the exemption may be ordered to pay for health insurance for a child, but the current rules hold the custodial parent liable for the payment.

The individual mandate applies on a monthly basis. The amount of the payment is based on the number of months in the calendar year that an individual lacks MEC or an exemption. Under the proposed regulations (NPRM REG-148500-12), an individual is treated as having MEC for the month if the individual is covered for at least one day during the month.

Minimum Essential Coverage

An individual who is covered by health insurance that provides MEC will not owe the payment. MEC includes the following:

- Coverage under a specified government-sponsored program;
- Coverage under an eligible employer-sponsored plan, including COBRA continuation coverage and retiree health coverage;
- Coverage under a health plan offered in the individual market;
- Coverage under a grandfathered health plan; and
- Other health benefit coverage recognized as MEC by the Treasury Department and HHS.

Government programs. Government-sponsored programs that provide MEC include Medicare, Medicaid, the Children's Health Insurance Program (CHIP), the TRICARE program, veterans' health care programs, coverage for Peace Corps volunteers, and certain coverage provided by the Defense Department. The proposed regulations exclude certain programs with limited coverage from MEC. These are similar to programs providing excepted benefits.

Employer programs. An eligible employer-sponsored plan is a group health plan or group health insurance coverage. *Group health plans* include both third-party insured health plans and self-insured health plans. Most employer-provided coverage will qualify as MEC. If an employee enrolls his or her family in an employer-sponsored plan, the covered family members will have MEC.

Marketplaces. The federal government encourages individuals who lack coverage, who may discontinue current coverage, or who may want to look for cheaper coverage, to go to a health insurance marketplace (also known as an *affordable insurance exchange*). These are established at the state level either by the state government or by the federal government acting in place of the state. The federal government advises that marketplaces will help individuals find affordable MEC and can determine whether the individual will qualify for financial assistance, such as the health insurance premium tax credit.

Excepted benefits. MEC does not include coverage that consists of certain excepted benefits, including:

- Accident and disability coverage;
- Supplemental coverage to liability insurance;
- Liability insurance;
- Workers' compensation;
- Automobile medical payment insurance;
- Credit-only insurance;
- Coverage for on-site medical clinics; and
- Other similar insurance coverage under which medical benefits are secondary or incidental to other insurance benefits.

  Other excepted benefits are not MEC if offered under a separate policy:

- Long-term care;
- Limited dental and vision benefits;
- Coverage for a disease or specified illness;
- Hospital indemnity or other fixed indemnity insurance; and
- Medicare supplemental health insurance.

Required Contribution

The proposed regulations reiterate that MEC is not affordable if the individual's required contribution (on an annual basis) exceeds 8 percent of the taxpayer's household income for the year. For an individual with employer coverage, the test applies to the cost of the lowest self-only coverage. However, for a related individual eligible for employer coverage, the proposed regulations apply the affordability exemption by looking at the employee's required contribution for the cost of family coverage.

Under the proposed regulations, the taxpayer's household income must be increased by any portion of the required contribution made under a salary reduction arrangement. After 2014, this 8 percent figure will be increased by the excess of the rate of premium growth between the preceding year and 2013, over the rate of income growth for the same period, as determined by HHS.

Health plans are categorized by level (bronze, silver, gold, or platinum), based on their actuarial value, which is the percentage of the plan's share of the full actuarial value of the benefits provided under the plan. The actuarial values are as follow:

- For a bronze plan, 60 percent;
- For a silver plan, 70 percent;
- For gold, 80 percent; and
- For platinum, 90 percent.

For individuals not eligible for employer-sponsored MEC, the minimum required contribution is the premium for the lowest cost bronze plan offered in the health insurance exchange, reduced by the maximum amount of any premium assistance credit, determined as if the individual were covered by a qualified health plan through the exchange for the entire year

EXAMPLE

The annual premium for the lowest cost bronze plan offered by the exchange is $10,000. Based on his family size and income, Elliot Campbell, a married taxpayer, would be entitled to a credit of $3,100. Elliot's required contribution is $6,900. His household income is $80,000 for the year. The coverage is not affordable because the required contribution ($6,900) exceeds 8 percent of his household income ($6,400). Therefore, he is not liable for the individual shared responsibility payment.

The proposed regulations clarify that if both members of a couple are eligible for employer-sponsored coverage, each individual determines the affordability of coverage using the premium for self-only coverage offered by the individual's employer. Neither individual may use the premium for family coverage. As a result, the IRS stated, each employed individual's self-only coverage may be treated as affordable, even though the aggregate cost of covering all employed individuals may exceed 8 percent of the family's household income. HHS is proposing rules to provide a hardship exemption in these circumstances.

Exemptions

Exemption categories. The statute exempts nine categories of individuals from the requirement to carry MEC or make a payment. These statutory exemptions include the following:

- Religious conscience—members of a religious sect that is recognized as conscientiously opposed to accepting any insurance benefits. The Social Security Administration recognizes these sects;
- Members of a health care sharing ministry;
- Indian tribes—members of a federally recognized Indian tribe;
- No filing requirement—individuals whose household income is below the threshold for filing a tax return;
- Short coverage gap—individuals who go without coverage for three consecutive months or less during the year;
- Hardship—a health insurance marketplace, also known as an affordable insurance exchange, certifies that the individual suffered a hardship and cannot obtain coverage or would have to pay an excessive amount for coverage;
- Unaffordable coverage—the individual cannot afford coverage because the minimum amount owed for premiums is more than 8 percent of the individual's household income;

- Incarceration—the individual is in prison after the disposition of charges; and
- Not lawfully present—the individual is not a U.S. citizen or a resident alien.

An individual is exempt for a month if the individual is exempt for at least one day in the month, such as an incarcerated individual. An individual whose household income is below the return filing threshold is exempt for the entire year.

Claiming an exemption. The health insurance marketplaces will provide exemption certificates for many of the exemption categories, such as religious conscience or hardship. Some individuals will be able to claim an exemption on their federal income tax return (such as the 2014 return filed in 2015), for unaffordable coverage, short coverage gaps, and individuals outside the United States. Some categories of individuals may either go to a marketplace or claim the exemption on their return: members of Indian tribes or health care sharing ministries, and incarcerated individuals.

Calculating the Payment

The required payment is determined on a monthly basis. Under the proposed regulations, it equals the lesser of:

- The monthly penalty amounts for each individual in the family (up to three individuals); or
- The monthly national average bronze plan premiums for the family.

The monthly penalty amounts are the greater of:

- The flat dollar amount; or
- The excess income amount.

The flat dollar amounts are $95 in 2014, $325 in 2015, or $695 in 2016. (After 2016 the amount is to be indexed for inflation.) For individuals under age 18, these amounts are reduced by half. The excess income amounts are the excess of the taxpayer's household income over the taxpayer's filing threshold, multiplied by a percentage:

- 1.0 percent for 2014;
- 2.0 percent for 2015; and
- 2.5 percent for years after 2015.

The monthly national average bronze plan premium is based on the annual national average premium for qualified health plans with a bronze level of coverage, offered through the exchanges.

Reporting of Health Insurance Coverage

Reporting requirements on insurers and employers were scheduled to take effect in 2014 for coverage in 2014, but the IRS has delayed these requirements until 2015. Under Code Sec. 6055, health insurers (which includes employers that self-insure) that provide MEC to any individual during the year must report certain information to the individual and to the IRS. The information includes:

- The name, address and Social Security number of the primary insured, as well as others covered by the plan;
- The dates of coverage;
- Whether the coverage is offered through an exchange; and
- The amount of any premium tax credit or cost-sharing reduction.

For an employer-sponsored plan, the insurer must also report the name, address and employer identification number of the employer, and the portion of the premium paid by the employer.

Reporting the Liability

A taxpayer is supposed to report his or her liability for the payment on the taxpayer's federal income tax return for the year. The payment is payable upon notice and demand by the IRS. However, the IRS cannot seek any criminal penalties and cannot place a lien or levy on the taxpayer's property for nonpayment. Accordingly, the IRS expects to collect the payment primarily through offsets to refunds.

STUDY QUESTION

1. Which of the following is included in MEC for individuals?

   a. Medicare supplemental health insurance
   b. Coverage for on-site medical clinics
   c. COBRA continuation coverage
   d. Coverage for a disease or specified illness

HEALTH INSURANCE EXCHANGES

Health insurance exchanges, also known as American Health Benefit Exchanges, play an essential role in PPACA's goal of expanding health insurance coverage. Under the health reform laws' plan, exchanges should be established in each state and be up and running by October 1, 2013, so that they can begin offering insurance for 2014 and beyond. Their role is to act as a marketplace for individuals and families who may lack insurance coverage or who are seeking less expensive coverage. Working with private health insurers, exchanges ideally will provide access to comprehensive health insurance at lower prices.

COMMENT

The exchanges play an important role in providing insurance. The Congressional Budget Office estimated that 7 million people will enroll in insurance through the individual marketplace in 2014.

COMMENT

PPACA also requires the establishment of a *Small Business Health Options Program Exchange* (SHOP Exchange) for small businesses that are looking for help launching plans because they find health insurance too expensive to offer to their employees.

Federal Government

HHS is primarily responsible for developing the rules for the exchanges and for the health plans they offer. Many states have chosen not to provide an exchange. For those states, the federal government will establish the exchange by the same October 1, 2013, deadline and will administer the exchange. The federal government and the state may enter into a partnership to administer the exchange.

COMMENT

During 2013, only 16 states and the District of Columbia reportedly applied to run their own exchanges. The federal government was responsible for exchanges in the other 34 states, although state governments were expected to assist in 15 of the states.

Key Provisions

Although exchanges are not a creature of the tax code, they are necessary for the operation of the key tax provisions of PPACA described in this chapter: the individual mandate (or individual shared responsibility payment), the health insurance premium assistance tax credit, and the employer mandate (or employer shared responsibility payment).

COMMENT

These key PPACA provisions were all supposed to take effect in 2014. Although the employer mandate has been postponed, the individual mandate and the premium assistance tax credit will still take effect in 2014. The IRS has promised that the employer mandate will take effect in 2015.

Individuals and families do not owe a penalty under the individual mandate if they have minimum essential (health insurance) coverage; exchanges will provide this insurance. Individuals and families buying insurance through an exchange may qualify for the premium assistance tax credit, depending on their income level; exchanges will determine who is eligible for the credit. Employers will owe a penalty under the employer mandate if they fail to provide affordable, minimum value comprehensive health coverage, *and* if one or more employees purchase insurance through an exchange and qualify for the credit.

Employers are supposed to notify their employees about the following:

- That health insurance coverage is available through an exchange;
- The services provided by the exchange;
- Contact information for the exchange;
- That the employee may be eligible for the premium assistance tax credit; and
- That the employee may lose his or her employer contribution for employer-provided benefits.

The Department of Labor has provided model language for the notices. DOL requires employers to start providing notices by October 1, 2013, when the exchanges were supposed to begin operating.

Information Sharing

Individuals are supposed to provide information to an exchange so that the exchange can enroll them in health insurance and determine their eligibility for the tax credit or for cost-sharing reductions (the latter administered by HHS). HHS determined that much of this information could be obtained from the IRS, rather than requiring individuals to fill out burdensome applications. In response, the IRS issued proposed regulations (NPRM REG-119632-11) in 2012 on the disclosure of return information to HHS to verify eligibility for the premium tax credit (including advance payments), state Medicaid programs, or other insurance offerings such as CHIP. HHS will then provide the information to the exchange or state agency processing an application for health insurance coverage. The IRS rules would limit disclosure to the year, the taxpayer's identity, filing status, dependents (family size), and adjusted gross income (or modified AGI if available).

COMMENT

The IRS has also issued proposed regulations (NPRM REG-140789-12) on the information that exchanges must report to the IRS on the premium assistance tax credits provide to individuals and families.

STUDY QUESTION

2. All of the following are key health insurance exchange provisions of the PPACA related to federal tax revenue ***except:***

   a. The health insurance premium assistance tax credit
   b. Employer mandate
   c. Premium discounts for participants in wellness programs
   d. Individual mandate

HEALTH INSURANCE PREMIUM ASSISTANCE TAX CREDIT

PPACA provides for the establishment of American Health Benefit Exchanges, as just described, in 2014. Individuals who do not have employer coverage or government coverage, for example, can shop at an exchange to purchase health insurance for themselves and their families. Health insurance offered through an exchange must offer "essential health benefits."

Beginning in 2014, an individual or family who purchases insurance through an exchange and whose income is below certain levels may apply and qualify for the premium assistance tax credit under Code Sec. 36B. The credit is refundable to the taxpayer. Alternatively, the credit may be paid in advance directly to the insurer; the taxpayer then must pay the difference between the premium and the credit. Individuals without group health insurance who want to satisfy the individual mandate will look to the exchanges for insurance and to the credit to help them pay for the insurance.

COMMENT

The Congressional Budget Office has estimated that the credit will provide an average annual subsidy of about $5,500 per year per subsidized individual or family who enrolls in insurance offered by an exchange.

COMMENT

Under the IRS regulations, an exchange includes a state exchange, a federally facilitated exchange, and a partnership exchange run by both a state and the federal government. Thus, individuals purchasing insurance through a federal exchange are potentially eligible for the credit. As discussed in the section on litigation, so opponents of PPACA are challenging the application of the credit (and the employer mandate) to federal exchanges, claiming that Congress only authorized the credit and the mandate for insurance purchased through a state exchange. Although the precise number may change, it appears that 34 state governments have opted not to provide an exchange, thus requiring the federal government to establish the exchange in those particular states.

Eligibility

The credit is available on a sliding scale for individuals and families with household incomes between 100 percent and 400 percent of the federal poverty level (FPL) for the family size. The family includes the taxpayer, spouse, and dependents. Individuals who are not subject to the individual mandate can also be counted as part of the family. However, taxpayers cannot count a child who cannot be claimed as a dependent, echoing concerns about the treatment of dependents of divorced individuals. Individuals who are not lawfully in the U.S. cannot be counted. The credit amount is based on the percentage of income that the individual or family's share of premiums represents, rising from 2 percent of income for taxpayers at 100 percent of FPL, to 9.5 percent of income for those at 400 percent of FPL.

Household income is the taxpayer's modified adjusted gross income (MAGI) (including tax-exempt interest and untaxed Social Security benefits) plus the MAGI of any other household member who must file a return. Married taxpayers must file a joint return. Dependents are not eligible for the credit themselves but will enter into the calculation of the family's credit. An individual applying for the credit must provide information on income, family size, and changes in marital or family status. Initial eligibility for the credit is based on income for the year ending two years prior to the enrollment period.

Interlocking Provisions

An individual is not eligible for the credit if he or she is eligible for MEC, other than coverage available in the individual market. MEC is an important concept affecting several of the PPACA requirements. The individual mandate and the premium assistance tax credit are both tied to the concept of MEC.

The proposed regulations under Code Sec. 5000A (pertaining to the individual mandate) define MEC. An individual who has health insurance qualifying as MEC will not owe the penalty under the individual mandate; thus, many commentators have asked the IRS to treat particular insurance coverage as MEC.

An individual who does not have MEC may be entitled to claim the premium assistance tax credit. Again, the issue is whether particular coverage held by an individual or offered to the individual is MEC. In this context, an individual may not want available coverage to be treated as MEC, so that the individual retains eligibility for the credit.

EXAMPLE

Disability coverage is not MEC. An individual who obtains disability coverage but who lacks comprehensive health insurance coverage does not have MEC and will owe the payment under the individual mandate (unless an exemption applies). At the same time, because the individual's disability coverage does not qualify as MEC, the individual lacks MEC and may be eligible for the premium assistance tax credit (assuming the individual's employer does not offer affordable, minimum value MEC).

IRS guidance. In Notice 2013-41, the IRS discussed whether an individual who otherwise may be eligible for the credit is being offered MEC. HHS may designate health benefits not specified in the tax code as MEC. In final regulations, HHS designated state high-risk pools and self-funded student health coverage as MEC, but only for a one-year transition period for plan years beginning before January 1, 2015. Starting January 1, 2015, sponsors of these plans must apply to HHS if they want them designated as MEC.

The IRS also clarified that individuals eligible for the following programs will not be treated as entitled to MEC unless they are in fact enrolled in one of them: Medicare Part A, TRICARE programs, state high-risk pools, and self-funded student health plans.

Employer Coverage

There are two additional requirements for employer-provided coverage that affect whether an individual may qualify for the credit. The employer coverage must provide MEC. In addition, the employer coverage must provide "minimum value" and must be affordable. *Minimum value* means that the plan's share of the cost of providing benefits is at least 60 percent of the total costs. Coverage is not affordable if the employee's share of the premium for self-only coverage would exceed 9.5 percent of the employee's household income. If the employer coverage does not satisfy all three requirements, the employee can choose not to enroll in the employer's plan, select coverage through an exchange, and attempt to qualify for the credit.

COMMENT

In 2013 final regulations, the IRS affirmed that in applying the affordability test for MEC for family members the credit depends on whether the employee's share of the cost of *self-only* coverage exceeds 9.5 percent of household income, a standard that is easier to satisfy. Thus, the test makes it more difficult for an employee to qualify for the credit. This determination was controversial; many commentators thought that the affordability test should be based on the cost of *family* coverage. The IRS explained that PPACA requires that the test for related individuals be based on the cost of self-only coverage.

In Notice 2012-31 and in proposed reliance regulations (NPRM REG-125398-12) issued in 2013, the IRS clarified the minimum value requirement. The IRS provided several methods for determining minimum value, including:

- A minimum value calculator;
- A safe harbor;
- Actuarial certification; and
- Plan level for small group market plans.

The IRS proposed additional safe harbors that do not require use of the calculator. The safe harbors would specify parameters like the deductible level (for medical services and drugs), a cost-sharing percentage, and an out-of-pocket maximum.

Reporting and Excess Payments

An exchange must report information—both to the IRS and to the individual—on coverage provided to an individual, including identifying information for the insured, the level of coverage provided, the total premium before the credit, the amount of any advance premium, information to determine eligibility for the credit, and information to determine whether the individual received excess advance payments. The IRS issued proposed regulations (NPRM REG-140789-12) in 2013 on these requirements. Exchanges would have to report to the IRS on a monthly basis, by the 15th day following the month of coverage, and to the individual on an annual basis.

If the advance premium credit exceeds the credit amount that the taxpayer is entitled to, the taxpayer must show the excess on his or her income tax return. The excess that is owed to the IRS is subject to a limit, as the table shows.

Table 1. Ceiling on Excess Payments with the Advance Premium Credit

Household Income	Limit
< 200% of FPL	$600
200%–299%	$1,500
300%–399%	$2,500

COMMENT

Taxpayers receiving an advance premium credit thus must file a return.

STUDY QUESTION

3. Eligibility requirements for the health insurance premium assistance tax credit are determined using all of the following ***except:***

   a. Tax-exempt income and untaxed Social Security benefits
   b. Dependents who claim the credit themselves
   c. Household income level
   d. Federal poverty level

SHARED RESPONSIBILITY FOR EMPLOYERS

PPACA's shared responsibility provision for employers (the employer mandate) requires employers to provide their employees with comprehensive health insurance that qualifies as MEC. The coverage must be affordable and must provide minimum value.

If the employer does not offer health insurance or offers health insurance that does not meet the requirements for MEC, affordability, and minimum value, the employer may be responsible for a shared responsibility payment (an *assessable payment*). For an employer to be liable, one or more of its employees must purchase health insurance through a health insurance exchange, and the employee must qualify for the health insurance premium assistance tax credit.

Like many other major provisions of the health care reform laws, the employer mandate was scheduled to take effect January 1, 2014. However, in mid-2013, the federal government announced that it was delaying the effective date of the employer mandate for one year, until January 1, 2015. For some parties, this unexpected delay ignited calls to delay the individual mandate and suggested that the employer mandate was not an essential part of PPACA.

Nevertheless, the employer mandate remains a major provision designed to encourage employers to provide insurance or to help pay for the costs of health care reform. This provision is also known as the "pay or play" requirement. Employers are not relieved of the "shared responsibility" of the employer mandate, but the delayed implementation grants them more time to assess their employment practices and provision of health benefits so that the employers are better prepared to comply with the law when it first applies in 2015. The IRS has pledged to institute the employer mandate at the beginning of 2015 and not to postpone it further.

Large Employers

The employer mandate applies to an *applicable large employer* (ALE), which is an employer that employed an average of at least 50 full-time employees and full-time equivalent (FTE) employees during the preceding calendar year. If an employer employs 50 or more full-time and FTE employees in 2014, the employer will be an ALE for 2015. The statute defines a *full-time employee* as an employee who on average was employed for at least 30 hours per week. Proposed reliance regulations (NPRM REG-138006-12) issued at the beginning of 2013 also treat 130 hours of service in a calendar month as full-time.

Solely for determining an ALE, the regulations count FTE employees as full-time employees. The proposed regulations determine FTEs by calculating the aggregate hours worked in a month by nonfull-time employees (counting up to 120 hours per employee) and dividing the total by 120.

A new employer is an ALE if it reasonably expects to employ an average of at least 50 full-time employees (including FTEs) during the current calendar year. Although the regs decline to exempt new employers from the employer mandate, the IRS indicated it would consider whether to provide safe harbors or presumptions to help new employers determine their status.

All entities treated as a single employer under Code Sec. 414 are treated as a single employer to determine whether the group is an ALE. If the group is an ALE, the penalty provisions apply to each member of the group separately.

COMMENT

The IRS stated that the application of the employer mandate to temporary staffing agencies may be particularly challenging, especially the determination of what constitutes the employer for tax purposes. The IRS indicated that the final regulations on the employer mandate will provide an antiabuse rule to address the use of staffing agencies to evade Code Sec. 4980H.

Assessable Payments

An ALE owes an assessable payment if an employee obtains insurance through an exchange, is certified to receive a premium tax credit, and either:

- Under Code Sec. 4980H(a), the employer does not offer to all of its full-time employees and their dependents the opportunity to enroll in MEC (as defined in Code Sec. 5000A, the individual mandate) under an employer-sponsored plan; or
- Under Code Sec. 4980H(b), the employer offers its full-time employees and their dependents the opportunity to enroll in MEC, but, for an employee entitled to the premium tax credit, the coverage is either unaffordable (based on the employee's household income or fails to provide minimum value.

COMMENT

The requirements for determining the employer's liability apply to full-time employees, not to FTE employees. In Questions and Answers on the employer mandate, the IRS indicated that the proposed regulations provided a lookback measurement method for employers to determine who is a full-time employee, based on previous hours of service. This method is also described in Notices 2012-17 and 2012-58.

The proposed regulations clarify that employers may satisfy Code Sec. 4980H(a) by offering MEC to at least 95 percent of their full-time employees. This provides relief to an employer who inadvertently fails to offer coverage to one or more employees. The regulations affirm that the offer of coverage must be provided to both employees and their dependents. A *dependent* is defined as any child under 26 years of age; it does not include a spouse.

The penalty under Code Sec. 4980H(b) applies if the employee premium for coverage is unaffordable. Coverage that costs more than 9.5 percent of the employee's household income is unaffordable. To determine household income, the proposed regulations provided three safe harbors:

- The Form W-2 safe harbor, based on employee wages;
- The rate of pay safe harbor (based on hourly or monthly pay rates); and
- The federal poverty line safe harbor.

A plan provides minimum value if the plan covers at least 60 percent of the total cost of benefits that are expected to be incurred under the plan.

Calculation of the payment. For liability under Code Sec. 4980H(a), the employer would figure the payment using this equation:

$2,000 for the year × (Number of full-time employees for the year – 30).

If coverage is offered for some months but not for others during the calendar year, the employer's liability per month is:

$\frac{1}{12}^{th}$ of the annual amount (or $167 per month) × (Number of employees – 30).

For liability under Code Sec. 4980H(b), the employer would owe $3,000 times the number of full-time employees for the year who received a premium tax credit. If coverage is offered for some months but not others, the employer's liability per month is $\frac{1}{12}^{th}$ of the annual amount (or $250 per month) times the number of employees receiving the credit.

COMMENT

An employer cannot be liable under both Code Secs. 4980H(a) and (b). The penalty that is imposed cannot exceed the payment under Code Sec. 4980H(a).

Procedure. The IRS will contact employers to inform them of their potential liability for the payment, and give them an opportunity to respond before any liability is assessed and before notice and demand for payment is made. There will not be self-reporting; employers will not make the payment on any tax return that they file. The IRS will act after employees' individual tax returns are due that claim premium tax credits, and after ALEs file information returns identifying their full-time employees and the coverage they were offered.

COMMENT

The postponement of the employer mandate until 2015 was accompanied by the postponement of reporting by employers and insurers under Code Sec. 6055 and by employers under Code Sec. 6056. Because this information would not be reported for 2014, the IRS concluded that it would not be practical to enforce the employer mandate for 2014.

Transition Rules

The proposed regulations had provided several transition rules for 2014, when 2014—rather than 2015—would have been the first year for the employer mandate. One rule allows employers with plans on a fiscal year to wait to apply the standards until the first day of the plan year that begins in 2014. Another rule exempts employers from penalties in 2014 if they must add dependent coverage to their health plans. Other rules affected health plans offered through cafeteria plans and multiemployer plans.

COMMENT

The IRS is expected to update these transition rules in light of the postponement of the employer mandate until 2015.

Delay of the Employer Mandate

In Notice 2013-45, the IRS announced that the employer mandate would not apply for 2014. Because a reported 90 percent or more of employers provide MEC to their employees, the government has expressed the belief that the vast majority of employees will not be harmed by this postponement. Furthermore, the delay of the employer mandate does not affect the application of the individual mandate and the availability of health insurance premium tax credits for 2014. Individuals may still obtain insurance through an exchange and qualify for the credit.

COMMENT

Individuals will be asked to self-certify their eligibility. There is the potential for individuals to incorrectly claim the credit, driving up the cost of providing the credit. The government also will not receive any employer payments for 2014 to help offset the cost of offering the tax credits.

The reporting requirements for 2014 were also postponed. (In fact, the employer mandate itself was postponed primarily because businesses were having difficulty complying with the reporting requirements.) The IRS sought more time to work with stakeholders and the regulated community to develop reporting requirements that would not be duplicative and would be less burdensome. Code Sec. 6055 requires reporting of individuals receiving coverage. The reporting would be made by anyone providing health insurance, including health insurers and employers providing self-insured coverage. Code Sec. 6056 goes to the employer mandate and requires employers to report coverage provided to full-time employees. With these two provisions, there may be the potential for duplicative reporting by employers.

COMMENT

Although reporting is not required for 2014, the government has encouraged employers and insurers to provide voluntary reporting for 2014, to give all parties experience with the reporting requirements.

Some of the rules prescribed for the employer mandate (30 hours per week for a full-time employee; 50 employees for an ALE) have been controversial, with unions and other interested parties claiming that employers may try to reduce their employees' work hours and may be discouraged from bringing in new employees if they are near the 50-employee threshold. However, these rules are in the statute and would have to be changed by Congress. The IRS developed the administrative standards for these rules after comments and hearing testimony from interested parties. There is no indication that the IRS intends to change these rules.

STUDY QUESTION

4. ALEs are offered relief from assessable payment obligations under the proposed regulations if they offer 95 percent of their full-time employees:

a. Silver level plans
b. Minimum essential coverage
c. Dependent coverage for employees' children younger than age 23
d. Group-plan coverage that is unaffordable

WELLNESS PROGRAMS

The IRS defines *wellness programs* as programs of health promotion and disease prevention. Employers and health insurers are turning to wellness programs as a mechanism to improve employee health. Wellness programs are voluntary for sponsors, insurers, and participants. An employer can choose whether to offer a program. Some employers start by offering a reward (such as a gift certificate) without linking the reward to the employer's health plan. This introduces the notion of health awareness to employees. Over time, employers tend to link their programs to their group health insurance coverage by offering premium reductions. A $350 annual reduction in premiums is not unusual.

If a self-insured employer offers a wellness program, any premium reduction offered by the employer will reduce the amount that the employee pays the employer. An employer and a third-party insurer may enter into a program to collect information on employee health and to provide reports for use by the employer. The insurer's program is offered in concert with the employer, not on a standalone basis, although an insurer in the individual market can also choose to offer a wellness program. If the employer reduces the employee's premium, the employer has to make up the different to the insurer. However, if the program increases employee health and leads to a reduction in the cost of claims, the insurer may reduce the premium that otherwise would have been charged to the employer.

Wellness programs can offer penalties as well as rewards. Either way, wellness programs are considered beneficial and are becoming increasingly popular. Studies indicate that providing incentives for employees to be healthier results in greater productivity and less absenteeism. Wellness programs may also reduce health costs and insurance costs, but studies are less clear about the link between wellness and reduced costs..

The IRS, together with the Departments of Labor (DOL) and HHS, jointly issued final regulations (TD 9620) on the design of wellness programs. The rules for wellness programs are effective for plan years beginning on or after January 1, 2014. The wellness program rules apply to all group health plans that offer wellness programs, including grandfathered and nongrandfathered plans. The rules give employers an opportunity to offer wellness programs to their employees.

COMMENT

Wellness programs may also be offered in the individual market. For example, the *Public Health Service Act,* which includes wellness provisions administered by HHS, provides for a 10-state wellness demonstration program to be established in 2014.

HIPAA

The *Health Insurance Portability and Accountability Act of 1996* (HIPAA) prohibits group health plans and issuers from discriminating, based on a health factor, against individual participants and beneficiaries in eligibility, benefits, or premiums. There are eight health status-related factors:

- Health status;
- Medical condition;
- Claims experience;
- Receipt of health care;
- Medical history;
- Genetic information;
- Evidence of insurability; and
- Disability.

However, HIPAA excepts from the discrimination rules programs that allow premium discounts, rebates, or modifications to cost-sharing amounts, such as copayments and deductibles, in return for adhering to a wellness program. PPACA amended HIPAA mainly to incorporate nondiscrimination and wellness provisions previously adopted in 2006 regulations issued under HIPAA.

Goals

The federal agencies recognize that each wellness program is unique. Thus, the regulations provide general guidance on the elements of wellness programs, not specific requirements. The rules set forth criteria that must be satisfied for a plan or issuer to qualify for an exception to the rules that prohibit discrimination based on a health factor. The agencies' intention is that the rules allow every individual participating in a wellness program to be able to receive the full amount of any reward or incentive, regardless of any health factor. There must be an equal opportunity to obtain the incentive or avoid the penalty. An employer must respond with reasonable alternatives, rather than just impose an initial standard.

COMMENT

In the final regulations, the IRS provided a mechanism for an employer to offer an incentive or charge a penalty for the employee's share of an insurance premium, depending on whether the individual complies with the wellness program requirements. The IRS also provided reasonable alternatives that wellness programs must offer to avoid violating the nondiscrimination rules. The agency designed the rules to provide flexibility and to encourage innovation and experimentation.

Program Categories

The regulations divide wellness programs into participatory wellness programs and health-contingent wellness programs. The regulations further divide health-contingent programs into activity-only programs and outcome-based programs. Plans and issuers with health-contingent wellness programs may vary benefits, premiums, or contributions based on an individual's meeting the standards of the program.

Participatory programs. *Participatory programs* either do not provide a reward or do not include any condition for obtaining a reward based on a standard related to a health factor. Participatory programs provide an incentive to participate; there are no conditions for the reward. These programs are not required to meet the five criteria that apply to health-contingent programs.

Participatory programs comply with the nondiscrimination requirements as long as participation is made available to all similarly situated individuals, regardless of health status. This compliance ensures that the general HIPAA prohibition against discrimination based on a health factor is not triggered. Distinctions are allowed based on employment classifications, consistent with the employer's usual practice, such as different treatment for part-time versus full-time employees. Unlike health-contingent programs, which have a general 30 percent cap, there is no limit on the financial incentives that may be provided for participatory wellness programs.

EXAMPLE

Participatory programs include:

- Reimbursement for all or part of the cost of a fitness membership;
- Diagnostic testing programs that reward participation and do not base any reward on test outcomes;
- Programs that reimburse costs of participating or provide a reward for participating, as in smoking cessation programs, regardless of whether the employee quits smoking;
- Programs that reward employees who complete a health risk assessment, without requiring any further action; and
- Programs that encourage preventive care by waiving copayments or deductible requirements, such as for the costs of prenatal care or well-baby care

Health-contingent programs. A *health-contingent wellness program* requires an individual to satisfy a standard related to a health factor in order to obtain a reward. An important change in the final regulations increased the maximum permissible reward under a health-contingent program from the prior 20 percent limit to 30 percent of the cost of coverage. This limit increases to 50 percent if the additional amount is for programs designed to prevent or reduce tobacco use.

The IRS imposed five requirements for health-contingent programs:

- Individuals must have an opportunity to qualify for the reward at least once a year;
- The total reward cannot exceed the specified limits;
- The program must be reasonably designed to promote health or prevent disease;
- Programs must be available to all similarly situated individuals. For both types of health-contingent programs, a reasonable alternative standard (or a waiver) must be made available to any individual for whom it is unreasonably difficult, due to a medical condition, to satisfy the standard; and
- The plan must disclose the availability of alternatives to qualify for the reward (or a waiver).

For *activity-only programs,* individuals must perform an activity to obtain a reward. They do not have to attain a specific health outcome.

EXAMPLE

Walking, diet, and exercise programs are classified as activity-only.

Individuals who cannot participate because of a health factor (e.g., they are unable to walk because of surgery or pregnancy) must be provided a reasonable opportunity to qualify for the reward. Plans may seek verification from an individual's doctor that a health factor makes it unreasonable or inadvisable to attempt to satisfy the standard.

Under an *outcome-based program,* an individual must attain or maintain a specific health outcome, such as not smoking or attaining certain test results. These programs generally have two steps: a screening or test as part of an initial standard, and a larger program that targets individuals who do not meet the initial standard. For individuals who do not meet the specific health outcome, the program may offer compliance with an educational program or activity to achieve the same reward.

EXAMPLE

Ongoing testing for high cholesterol or blood pressure is an outcome-based program in that it rewards employees in a healthy range and requires employees outside the healthy range to take additional steps to obtain the reward. If an individual requests an alternative, the plan must accommodate recommendations from the individual's physician.

EXAMPLE

For a program with a goal to quit smoking, a reasonable alternative in Year 1 may be an educational seminar. For the succeeding year, the plan may require a different alternative, such as nicotine replacement therapy.

The specified cost-of-coverage percentages are based on the total costs of employee-only insurance coverage, including both employer and employee contributions. If dependents may participate in the wellness programs, the specified percentages are applied to the cost of family coverage.

A program is reasonably designed if it has a reasonable chance of improving health, is not overly burdensome, and is not a subterfuge for discrimination. Reliance on studies or evidence is not required, but is encouraged as a best practice. An outcome-based program must provide a reasonable alternative to individuals who do not meet the initial standard.

Tax Consequences

The IRS has not addressed the tax consequences of wellness programs. Compliance with the requirements in the regulations does not affect the tax treatment of receiving a benefit. The benefits provided will be taxable or tax-free under general tax principles, such as the fringe benefit rules. A reduction in the insurance premium would not be taxed, but a cash reward that can be used for any purpose would be taxable income.

PPACA TAXES

PPACA enacted a number of new taxes to help pay for the cost of expanding health insurance coverage. The taxes are designed to raise billions of dollars per year. As part of PPACA's implementation, the IRS has been providing guidance on these fees and taxes. These taxes include:

- The tax on indoor tanning services, effective beginning in the second half of 2010;
- The branded prescription drug fee, effective as of 2011;
- The medical device excise tax, effective beginning in 2013; and
- The annual fee on health insurance providers, effective starting in 2014.

EXAMPLE

Generally, the taxes are treated as nondeductible excise taxes.

Tanning services. The 10 percent tax on indoor tanning services took effect July 1, 2010. The tax applies to the individual paying for the services and to amounts paid by insurance. The IRS issued temporary (T.D. 9486) and proposed regulations in June 2010; it issued final regulations (T.D. 9621) in June 2013.

The final regulations maintained an exemption from the tax for qualified physical fitness facilities that do not charge separately for indoor tanning services, do not offer tanning services to the general public, and do not offer different membership rates based on access to tanning services. The IRS declined to impose the tax on free services. If the tanning services are included in bundled services, the taxpayer must determine the amount attributable to tanning.

Branded prescription drugs. This fee applies to manufacturers and importers of branded prescription drugs sold in the U.S., if those organizations have receipts of more than $5 million a year. The fee is based on prior year sales. The aggregate fee imposed on all entities was $2.5 billion for 2011; $2.8 billion for 2012 and 2013; $3 billion for 2014 and 2015, with continued increases for future years. The fee is credited to the Medicare Part B trust fund.

The IRS will apportion the fee based on each entity's market share. In Notice 2012-74, the IRS set the parameters for calculating the 2012 fee. The IRS determines the fee by determining a ratio, equal to the entity's drug sales for the preceding calendar year over the aggregate drug sales for all entities. The IRS notified entities of its preliminary calculations by April 1, 2013, entities could submit error reports, but had to pay the fee by September 30, 2013.

Medical devices. The tax took effect 2013 for sales after December 31, 2012. The tax is 2.3 percent of the price for sales of certain medical devices by manufacturers, producers, or importers. The IRS issued final regulations (T.D. 9604) on the tax at the end of 2012.

The tax applies to any device regulated by the Food and Drug Administration and meant for humans. The tax does not apply to products for animals, eyeglasses, contact lenses, hearing aids, and retail sales, that is, other medical devices generally purchased by the public at retail for individual use, including purchases from a store, by telephone, or over the Internet.

EXAMPLE

The regulation also exempts adhesive bandages, snake bite kits, denture adhesives, pregnancy test kits, blood glucose monitors and test strips, prosthetic legs, wheelchairs, portable oxygen concentrators, and adjustable home-use beds.

Health insurance providers. This tax will take effect in 2014. It is designed to raise $8 billion in 2014, increasing to $14.3 billion in 2018, and increasing after that by the rate of insurance premium growth. The fee is based on the ratio of the individual insurer's net premiums written on health insurance, divided by the total premiums of all insurers. The total tax to be raised is multiplied by this ratio, to determine each insurer's fee. The IRS issued proposed regulations (NPRM REG-118315-12) on the fee in March 2013.

The tax applies to health insurance premiums earned by health insurance issuers, health maintenance organizations, insurers providing Medicare Advantage or Medicaid, and nonfully insured multiple employer welfare arrangements. Health insurance includes dental, vision, and retiree health care. It does not include accident, disability, long-term care, or Medicare supplemental insurance. The tax does not apply to employers that self-insure their employees' health risks, to governmental entities (including Indian tribes), certain nonprofits, voluntary employee beneficiary associations (VEBAs) not established by employers, and universities charging health insurance fees to students.

Entities must report premiums by May 1 of each year. Like the branded prescription drug fees, the IRS will send preliminary bills, entities may submit an error report, and the IRS will then provide a final bill.

STUDY QUESTION

5. The PPACA amended HIPAA primarily to:

   a. Revise nondiscrimination rules to comply with wellness provisions of PPACA
   b. Expand HIPAA's health status-related factors
   c. Cancel the premium discounts and rebates allowed under HIPAA
   d. Cancel allowed alternatives to wellness programs

SMALL EMPLOYER HEALTH CARE CREDIT

Small employers may take a credit for a percentage of health care premiums paid for their employees. The credit took effect in 2010 and continues through 2015. The credit is refundable and is available to employers with 25 or fewer FTE employees, when the average annual wages of its employees are no more than $50,000 per FTE.

For 2010 through 2013, the maximum credit has been 35 percent of health care costs for taxable employers. For 2014 and 2015, the maximum credit increases to 50 percent. For nonprofit employers, the maximum credit was 25 percent for 2010–2013, and 25 percent for 2014 and 2015. For tax years that begin after 2013, an employer must participate in an insurance exchange in order to claim the credit. The credit is no longer available after 2015.

MORE COURT CHALLENGES

In 2012, the Supreme Court issued an important decision that upheld PPACA (***National Federation of Independent Business, et al. v. Sebelius,*** 2012-2 USTC Par. 50,423). In a 5–4 decision, the court concluded that the individual mandate, which requires individuals either to carry health insurance or pay a shared responsibility payment, was a proper exercise of Congress's taxing power. The court declined to uphold PPACA based on Congress's powers over interstate commerce or powers under other Constitutional provisions. The court did overturn PPACA's expansion of the federal Medicaid program for low-income individuals, concluding that the federal government could not withhold existing funding to force states to expand their Medicaid coverage. States, however, could voluntarily extend Medicaid benefits.

Despite the Supreme Court decision, certain states, organizations, and individuals continue to challenge PPACA in court. These cases are contesting other portions of PPACA or raising new objections to the individual mandate. Some of the cases were filed before the Supreme Court ruled and were put on hold until the court issued its decision. Now, these cases are being resumed.

COMMENT

Obviously, the federal government continues to implement PPACA administratively while the U.S. Department of Justice fights these cases in court.

EXAMPLE

Liberty University sued the federal government in 2010. Liberty and two individuals argued that the employer mandate (which was not the subject of the Supreme Court's decision) was unconstitutional because it was not supported by either the taxing power or the Commerce Clause. Liberty and the individuals also claimed that both the employer mandate and the individual mandate violate their religious freedom. In a July 2013 decision, the U.S. Court of Appeals for the Fourth Circuit affirmed a lower court's dismissal of the lawsuit (***Liberty University, Inc. v. Lew,*** CA-4, 2013-2 USTC Par. 50,432). The appeals court cited the Commerce Clause in upholding the employer mandate; it also determined that the mandates did not violate religious freedom.

Another legal challenge to PPACA focuses on the health insurance exchanges. The exchanges act as a marketplace within a state, at which uninsured people can shopfor health insurance from private insurers, perhaps at reduced prices. PPACA authorizes each state to set up its own exchange, but the state is not required to do so. If a state declines, PPACA authorizes the federal government to set up a federal exchange for that state, presumably to offer the same features as a state exchange.

The premium assistance tax credit is available to qualifying individuals and families, but only if they purchase insurance through an exchange. The employer mandate is also tied to an exchange, because an employer does not owe payments under the employer mandate unless one or more of its employees purchases insurance through an exchange and qualifies for the credit.

The state of Oklahoma and others are claiming that Congress did not authorize the application of the premium tax credit and the employer mandate unless the exchange is set up by the state. Oklahoma claims that, under PPACA, the credit, and therefore the employer mandate, do not apply if the exchange is established by the federal government. Others argue that PPACA applies in the same manner whether the exchange is federally or state administered. The lawsuits are focusing on the IRS regulations issued under Code Sec. 36B (T.D. 9590), which treat federal and state management of exchanges the same.

STUDY QUESTION

6. The health care credit for small employers is scheduled to:

a. Decrease starting in 2014
b. Apply at 50 percent in 2014 and 2015
c. Continue at the same rate through 2016 for nonprofit employers
d. End after 2016

CONCLUSION

PPACA is having a major impact on the provision and expansion of health insurance in the United States. The federal government, state governments, employers, individuals, and families are all affected by the law. In many cases, individuals and families will retain their existing insurance and will not have insurance plans changed by the law. However, several important provisions take effect in 2014; and one major provision—the employer mandate—is now scheduled to take effect in 2015. Individuals may need to consult with their employer, insurance company, or state government, to learn more about the law's requirements and its impact. Employers also need to review their responsibilities under the employer mandate, as well as plan compliance deadlines, options, and available credits.

MODULE 1: HEALTH CARE LAW: NEW REQUIREMENTS — CHAPTER 2

Net Investment Income Tax: Issues and Strategies

The net investment income tax, with its flat 3.8 percent rate, is the first tax imposed outside of the regular income tax in several decades. The impact of this surtax will be felt most often, but not always, by higher-income individuals, as well as certain trusts and estates. Those with moderate incomes will also feel the sting of the tax, however, if income suddenly spikes in any one year.

Although the net investment income tax has been part of the tax law since its enactment within the *Patient Protection and Affordable Care Act of 2010* (PPACA), it had a delayed effective date of tax years beginning after December 31, 2012. As a result, the tax is now effective for most taxpayers for the first time in 2013. The net investment income tax unfortunately has also had a delayed response from the IRS in issuing the guidance needed to comply fully with the law—and to fully plan effectively to avoid the tax when possible.

Stop-gap "proposed" regulations were not issued until less than a month before the tax took effect. Some practitioners have complained that the IRS has made a complex statute (Code Sec. 1411) even more complex through its dense set of regulations. Others have recommended that Congress rewrite Code Sec. 1411 itself before the tax can become manageable both for taxpayers and the IRS. Nevertheless, until better guidance is issued or a new version of Code Sec. 1411 is enacted, taxpayers must deal with the rules as they now exist in assessing their liability for this new tax that is now in effect.

LEARNING OBJECTIVES

Upon completion of this chapter, you will be able to:

- Understand the rationale behind Congress's enactment of the net investment income tax and the IRS' response to writing rules and regulations to implement this new tax;
- Determine the income levels at which the 3.8 percent net investment income tax is triggered;
- Identify the particular groups of taxpayers that are subject to, and those that are exempt from, the net investment income tax;
- Identify the three categories of net investment income that are subject to the net investment income tax;
- Explain the interrelationships between the passive activity loss rules of Code Sec. 469 and the net investment income tax of Code Sec. 1411;
- Understand when rental income is subject to net investment income tax and when it may be exempt; and
- Determine circumstances under which losses and other deductions are allowed to offset only net investment gain and when offset of all three categories of net investment income may be allowed.

INTRODUCTION

Code Sec. 1411 imposes a 3.8 percent net investment income tax (also known as the "unearned income Medicare contribution tax") on the lesser of an individual's:

- Net investment income for the tax year; or
- The excess, if any, of modified adjusted gross income (MAGI) for the tax year, over an applicable threshold amount.

The 3.8 percent net investment income tax is similarly imposed on trusts and estates, but under a different set of rules in connection with the net investment income base and threshold amounts.

IMPLEMENTATION OF THE NII TAX

Effective Date

Although approved in 2010 as part of the PPACA, the net investment income tax (NII tax) did not become effective until 2013. However, the NII tax is fully effective for all tax years beginning after December 31, 2012.

COMMENT

Net investment income is assessed on an annual basis. Therefore, a taxpayer whose income level ordinarily may not be subject to the NII tax may owe the tax during a year in which he or she experiences a spike in income, such as receiving a salary bonus, selling a large capital asset or business, or rolling over retirement funds to a Roth IRA. Planning that includes installment sales and other strategies to "even out" such income should be considered in such cases.

Short Tax Years

The applicable threshold amount is generally not prorated in the case of a short tax year; for example, because of a taxpayer's death (Prop. Reg. § 1.1411-2(d)(2)). However, if the short year is the result of a change of annual accounting period, the regulations generally require reduction of the applicable threshold amount to an amount that bears the same ratio to the full threshold amount as the number of months in the short period bears to 12.

COMMENT

Individuals who are subject to the NII tax must report such income on their Form 1040, with accompanying new Form 8960, *Net Investment Income Tax—Individuals, Estates, and Trusts*. Estate and trusts attach Form 8960 to their Form 1041.

COMMENT

If items of net investment income (including properly allocable deductions) pass through a partnership or S corporation, the passthrough entity must separately state the items on Schedule K-1s issued to investors, a potentially burdensome requirement.

COMMENT

Interpretation of certain provisions of the NII tax as set forth under Code Sec. 1411 continues to be subject to debate. Specifically, certain positions taken under the Code Sec. 1411 proposed regulations have been subject to criticism and await final regulations for anticipated resolution. To the extent a taxpayer chooses to rely upon the proposed regulations during 2013, however, the IRS will not challenge their use even if final regulations alter a particular rule. Areas within the regulations of particular concern to practitioner groups include the inclusion of some rental income in NII when used in a trade or business, the application of the Code Sec. 469 passive loss rules to NII, and the computation of NII in the case of the sale of S corporation stock or a partnership interest by an owner who materially participates in the business.

THRESHOLD AMOUNTS

The taxpayer's overall income, whether wages, net investment income, or other amounts that make up MAGI, must exceed a certain dollar level based on filing status before the NII tax may be imposed. The threshold amounts (which are not adjusted for inflation) are:

- $250,000 in the case of a taxpayer making a joint return or a surviving spouse;
- $125,000 in the case of a married taxpayer filing a separate return; and
- $200,000 in the case of any other individual (most notably, single unmarried individuals other than surviving spouses).

EXAMPLE

Assume that Joe Richards, a single filer, has income consisting only of wages of $180,000 and $15,000 of dividends and net capital gains. Because Joe's MAGI of $195,000 falls below the $200,000 threshold amount, none of his dividends and net capital gain is subject to the NII tax.

EXAMPLE

Assume that Herve and Alicia Rodriguez, a joint-filing married couple, earn combined salaries of $240,000 and have $30,000 in net capital gains. Because their total MAGI of $270,000 exceeds their $250,000 threshold by $20,000, $20,000 of their $30,000 net capital gain is subject to the 3.8 percent NII tax.

COMMENT

These threshold amounts are not indexed for inflation. Consequently, the number of affected taxpayers is expected to increase over time because of inflation. Congress could revise the thresholds in the future to reflect inflation or choose to index the thresholds for inflation. At the time of this writing, however, there appear to be no plans in Congress or the Obama Administration to index the thresholds for inflation.

Trusts and Estates

The threshold amounts for 2013 are $11,950 of adjusted gross (AGI) income in the case of trusts and estates, representing the threshold of the 39.6 percent income tax bracket for trusts and estates, and adjusted for inflation each year. Also, estates and trusts are only subject to the NII tax to the extent they have undistributed net investment income. Net investment income that is distributed and flows through to beneficiaries is considered the net investment income of those individuals, rather than NII of the trust or estate. Grantor trusts under the tax code also are considered to pass through NII to their grantors and are not themselves taxed.

Adjusted Gross Income of Residents Abroad

For purposes of the NII tax, an individual's AGI for the tax year is increased by otherwise-excludable foreign earned income or foreign housing cost offset (as reduced by any deduction, exclusions, or credits properly allocable to or chargeable against such foreign earned income). This adjustment will only apply for U.S. citizens or residents who live abroad. Additional adjustments to AGI may be required because of ownership interests (for example, investments) in controlled foreign corporations or passive foreign investment companies.

COMMENT

Although the tax on NII is based on *netting* income and expenses, the threshold amounts do not take into account "below-the-line" itemized or standard deductions, personal exemptions, or credits, so that a taxpayer's taxable income may fall below a threshold dollar level yet still be subject to NII tax because MAGI exceeds the threshold. Deductible contributions to qualified pension plans and to IRAs do count, however, because they are deducted "above the line." These contributions also do double duty because distributions from such plans or IRAs do not count as net investment income, being specifically excluded under Code Sec. 1411.

STUDY QUESTION

1. When a taxpayer has a short tax year resulting from a change of annual accounting period, liability for net investment income is determined by:
   - **a.** Lumping items with the next accounting period's income
   - **b.** Figuring a reduced threshold based on the same ratio of months as a full year's NII threshold would have to 12
   - **c.** Reporting on Form 8960 without a Form 1040 or 1041 at the end of the short year
   - **d.** Lumping items with the prior accounting period's income and reporting on an amended return

TAXPAYERS SUBJECT TO THE NET INVESTMENT INCOME TAX

The NII tax applies only to individuals, trusts, and estates. It does not apply to corporations. Although passthrough entities such as partnerships and S corporations are not directly subject to the NII tax, income passed through to individual partners or shareholders may be subject to the NII tax depending upon the individual's active participation in the business of the partnership or S corporation. Exceptions to being subject to the NII tax are also carved out for certain individuals, trusts, and estates *(see further explanation, below)*.

COMMENT

The most significant factor that effectively exempts many individuals from the NII tax is the imposition of the tax only above certain threshold dollar amounts (as noted earlier). The NII tax is generally imposed only on "higher-income individuals."

Individuals

The NII surtax applies to all individuals whose income exceeds the threshold, with the exception of nonresident aliens.

Joint returns: U.S. citizen or resident married to nonresident alien. For purposes of applying the NII tax to U.S. citizens or residents married to nonresident aliens, the spouses generally must be treated as married filing separately. Under normal rules, the nonresident alien's investment income will be exempt from NII tax, whereas the U.S. citizen or resident alien will be subject to the lower $125,000 threshold amount and must determine his or her separate net investment income and MAGI. However, if these married taxpayers have elected under Code Sec. 6013(g) to file jointly by treating the nonresident alien as a resident of the United States, the regulations allow the couple to elect to be treated as making the same election for purposes of Code Sec. 1411 (under which the threshold amount is $250,000 and all income is combined).

Bona fide residents of U.S. territories. The application of the NII tax to a bona fide resident of a U.S. territory depends on whether the territory has a mirror code system of taxation. Residents of those territories that have a mirror system (Guam, the Northern Mariana Islands, and the United States Virgin Islands) generally are not subject to the NII tax. Bona fide residents of nonmirror code jurisdictions (American Samoa and Puerto Rico) are subject to NII tax if they have U.S. reportable income that gives rise to both NII and MAGI exceeding the threshold amount. However, a different result may apply to bona fide residents who are nonresident alien individuals.

Minors. The amounts of net investment income included on the parents' Form 1040 by reason of filing Form 8814, *Parents' Election to Report Child's Interest and Dividends,* are included in calculating the parents' net investment income. However, the calculation of NII does not include amounts excluded from their Form 1040 due to the threshold amounts on Form 8814.

Bankruptcy estates. A bankruptcy debtor under Chapter 7 or Chapter 11 of the Bankruptcy Code who is an individual may be subject to the NII tax. In that case, the bankruptcy estate is subject to the same lower $125,000 threshold amount as a married taxpayer filing a separate return.

Trusts and Estates

Trusts and estates are subject to the NII tax on the *lesser* of:

- Undistributed net investment income, *or*
- The excess of AGI over the dollar amount at which the highest tax bracket begins (which, for 2013, is $11,950).

Tax-exempt trusts. The NII tax does not apply to any trust, fund or special account exempt from tax under Code Sec. 501 (exempt plans or organizations) or Sec. 664(c)(1) (charitable remainder trusts). This exemption includes any unrelated business taxable income comprised of NII.

Electing small business trusts. Special NII computational rules apply to electing small business trusts (ESBTs). Code Sec. 641(c)(1) provides that:

- The portion of any ESBT consisting of stock in one or more S corps must be treated as a separate trust; and
- The amount of tax imposed on such separate trust is determined under certain Code Sec. 641(c)(2) modifications.

The proposed reliance regs preserve this treatment of the ESBT as two separate trusts for computational purposes. However, the regulations consolidate the ESBT into a single trust for determining the NII adjusted gross income threshold bracket amount "so as to not inequitably benefit ESBTs over other taxable trusts."

Foreign estates and trusts. Acknowledging that Code Sec. 1411 does not specifically address the treatment of foreign estates and foreign nongrantor trusts, the IRS has stated that it intends to tax NII of a foreign estate or foreign trust only to the extent the income is earned or accumulated for the benefit of, or distributed to, U.S. persons.

STUDY QUESTION

2. When a U.S. citizen is married to a nonresident alien:
    - **a.** The citizen's income is subject to the $125,000 threshold for the NII tax liability
    - **b.** The nonresident alien spouse's income is automatically combined with the citizen spouse's income subject to the $250,000 threshold for joint filing couples
    - **c.** Each spouse's income is totaled individually using the $125,000 threshold for incurring the NII tax liability
    - **d.** The income of each spouse is assessed NII tax only is both spouses have net investment income exceeding $250,000 for the year.

NET INVESTMENT INCOME

The congressional intent behind the tax on net investment income under Code Sec. 1411 was basically to tax unearned, passive-type income, generated within a typical investment portfolio and from business income in which the taxpayer is a passive owner. However, the statutory language under Code Sec. 1411 used to realize this intention, to which many pages of regulations were added by the IRS to further explain Code Sec. 1411, has proven that a simple concept does not necessarily translate into simple rules. The complexity has been due largely to efforts to prevent "loopholes" on the one hand and a concern not to be "overly inclusive" on the other.

Net Investment Income for the Majority of Taxpayers

Although issues remain for precisely defining net investment income, the "typical" taxpayer should not lose sight of those common types of income that will ordinarily constitute net investment income. Common types of investment income subject to the NII tax include:

- Interest from bank accounts, certificates of deposits, and debt instruments held for investment;
- Dividends paid on stocks and mutual funds;

- Gains from the sale of stocks, bonds, and mutual funds (irrespective of whether such gain is long-term or short-term);
- Capital gains distributions from mutual funds;
- Income passed through to an inactive/passive partner or S corporation shareholder;
- The income portion of each annuity payment;
- Royalties held as investments;
- Rents from properties held but not actively managed; and
- Gain from the sale of investment real estate, particularly second homes.

COMMENT

Primary residences may also generate NII if gain exceeds the amount allowed under the Code Sec. 121 home sale exclusion of $500,000 for joint filers and $250,000 for most single taxpayers.

What Net Investment Income Is Not

Net investment income does not include wages, unemployment compensation, operating income from a nonpassive business in which the taxpayer is a nonpassive participant, Social Security benefits, alimony, tax-exempt interest, self-employment income, Alaska Permanent Fund Dividends, and distributions from qualified retirement plans. Although defining net investment income based upon what it is not incurs the same difficulties as providing a comprehensive definition, as do shorthand attempts at explaining what it is, it can help taxpayers understand the parameters of the NII tax more readily, with the "gray areas" left to a relatively small group of taxpayers to whom they may apply.

Use of other tax code provisions. The IRS has stated in its introduction (Preamble) to the proposed regulations under Code Sec. 1411 that, except as otherwise provided in the proposed reliance regs, the following Internal Revenue Code Chapter 1 regular income tax principles apply:

- Gain that is not recognized under Chapter 1 for a tax year is not recognized for that year for purposes of Section 1411, including:
  - Installment sales gain under Code Sec. 453,
  - Deferred gain on like-kind exchanges under Code Sec. 1031,
  - Deferred gain in involuntary conversion under Code Sec. 1033, and
  - Gain on the sale of a principal residence excluded under Code Sec. 121;
- Deferral or disallowance provisions of Chapter 1 that the proposed reliance regs interpret as applying to a determination of NII include:
  - Limitation on investment interest under Code Sec. 163(d),
  - Limitation of expense and interest relating to tax-exempt income under Code Sec. 265,

— At-risk limitations under Code Sec. 465(a)(2),
— Passive activity loss (PAL) limitations under Code Sec. 469(b),
— Partner loss limitations under Code Sec. 704(d),
— Capital loss carryover limitations under Code Sec. 1212(b), and
— S corp shareholder loss limitations under Code Sec. 1366(d)(2).

Further, carryover deductions in connection with these deferral or disallowance provisions otherwise allowed in determining AGI are also allowed in determining NII.

Exceptions to general tax code principles. "To prevent circumvention of the purposes of the statute," the proposed reliance regs modify the Chapter 1 rules in certain cases. Examples include treating substitute interest and dividends as investment income even though not technically considered dividends or interest under Chapter 1; and treating distributions under Code Secs. 959(d), 1293(c), and 1291 as net investment income. Also carved out from general Chapter 1 treatment is the definition of AGI as it relates to investments in controlled foreign corporations and passive foreign investment companies.

NII Under Code Sec. 1411's Statutory Scheme

The complexity in determining exactly what constitutes net investment income in all cases arises from the language of the core subsections to Code Sec. 1411(c) itself, as shown in Figure 1.

Figure 1. Text of Code Sec. 1411(c) Subsections for Determining NII

1411(c)(1) ... The term "net investment income" means the excess (if any) of—

(1)(A) The sum of—

(i) Gross income from interest, dividends, annuities, royalties, and rents, other than such income which is derived in the ordinary course of a trade or business not described in paragraph (2),

(ii) Other gross income derived from a trade or business described in paragraph (2), and

(iii) Net gain (to the extent taken into account in computing taxable income) attributable to the disposition of property other than property held in a trade or business not described in paragraph (2),

over—

(B) The deductions allowed by this subtitle which are properly allocable to such gross income or net gain.

(2) A trade or business is "described in paragraph 2" if such trade or business is—

- A passive activity (within the meaning of Code Sec. 469) with respect to the taxpayer, or
- A trade or business of trading in financial instruments or commodities (as defined in Code Sec.475(e)(2)).

COMMENT

Code Sec 1411(c)(1)(i), (ii), and (iii) are often referred to by practitioners as Categories (i), (ii), and (iii).

COMMENT

Present confusion over the computation of net investment income has generally revolved around five issues:

- Determining when the level of activity constitutes a trade or business (particularly relevant to Category (i));
- Determining when the taxpayer's activity within a trade or business goes beyond the status of being a passive investor (particularly relevant to Categories (ii) and (iii));
- Determining in particular how real estate activities fit into the categories or their exceptions;
- Determining the gain subject to Category (iii) in case of the sale of an interest in a partnership or S corporation; and
- Determining what deductions may offset investment income or gain.

Working capital. In addition to Category (i), (ii), and (iii) net income or gain, Congress added income from working capital to NII, irrespective of whether a business is active or passive.

Under Code Sec. 1411(c)(3) and proposed regulations, all gross income and gains derived from the investment of working capital is included in computing NII, regardless of whether such gross income is derived in a trade or business or such net gains are derived from property held in a trade or business. The IRS has stated that working capital for these purposes refers to "the capital set aside for use in and the future needs of a trade or business."

Code Sec. 1411(c)(3) sets forth the NII tax rules for investment income derived from working capital by providing that a rule "similar to" the rule in Code Sec. 469(e)(1)(B) applies for purposes of Code Sec. 1411.

Although Code Sec 469 is a deferral rule, Code Sec. 1411 is not. Identical rules may have the effect of causing businesses to maintain less working capital and may therefore create greater credit risk among small businesses, practitioners have complained. Specific guidelines for safe harbor rules within final regulations or elsewhere may be needed to avoid this additional risk.

EXAMPLE

Adam Birmingham is the sole owner/operator of a restaurant that does business as an S corp. He maintains an interest-bearing checking account with an average daily balance of $2,500 to hold cash receipts and pay ordinary and necessary business expenses. The S corp also has set aside an additional $20,000 for the potential future needs of the business. Both the checking account and $20,000 are considered working capital, with interest earned on them subject to NII surtax imposed on Adam, who is allocated the interest through the S corporation.

Trade or Business

An activity constitutes a trade or business for purposes of determining whether income or gain fits or is excluded from Category (i), (ii), or (iii) generally if it is considered a trade or business under the familiar Code Sec. 162 business expense rules. If the primary purpose for the activity is profit or income and if the activity has continuity and regularity, it is generally considered a trade or business. Nevertheless, case law requires that the determination of whether a trade or business exists from which income is derived must be based upon an examination of the facts of each case. A taxpayer's management of his or her own investments is not considered a trade or business under Code Sec. 162, however, even if the taxpayer engages in investment management activities on a full-time basis.

"Ordinary course." The proposed reliance regs do not provide guidance on the meaning of *ordinary course.* The IRS instructed that taxpayers should rely on case law and other sections of the regulations that address this issue, such as ***Lilly,*** 343 U.S. 90 (Sup.Ct. 1953), and Reg. § 1.469-2T(c)(3)(ii) (providing rules for determining whether certain portfolio income is excluded from the definition of passive activity gross income).

Wages. Wages and other compensation are not subject to the NII surtax. The IRS explained in the Preamble to the proposed reliance regs that amounts paid by an employer to an employee as wages subject to income tax withholding are not NII, because they are derived in the ordinary course of a trade or business of being an employee. In this manner, they qualify for the trade or business exception.

COMMENT

The IRS clarified in the Preamble to the proposed reliance regulations that nonqualified deferred compensation paid to an employee under Code Sec. 409A, 457(f), 457A, or other provisions is not NII.

Trading in commodities and financial instruments. Income from a trade or business is included in net investment income if the trade or business is trading in financial instruments or commodities. The determination of whether trading in financial instruments or commodities rises to the level of a Code Sec. 162 trade or business is a question of fact, determined under the existing rules applicable to federal income taxes. Thus, a trader is engaged in a Code Sec. 162 trade or business if the trading is frequent and substantial, or frequent, regular, and continuous. In contrast, an investor trading on behalf of his or her own portfolio is generally not engaged in a trade or business, regardless of the extent of the investment activity.

A *financial instrument* includes stocks and other equity interests, evidences of indebtedness, options, forward or futures contracts, notional principal contracts, any other derivatives, or any evidence of an interest in any of these items. An evidence of an interest in any of these items includes, but is not limited to, short positions or partial units in any of these items.

STUDY QUESTION

3. Which of the following is ***not*** an indicator for Code Sec. 1411 tax provisions that an activity is a trade or business?

a. Infrequent activity involving financial instruments or commodities
b. Case law and other regulations have documented that the activity is a trade or business
c. The activity is conducted to create profit or income
d. The activity is considered a trade or activity under Code Sec. 162 rules

Taxpayer Activity

Net investment income does not include income from a trade or business in which the taxpayer materially participates. Accordingly, income from a passive activity counts toward net investment income as Category (ii) income (or Category (iii) gain). (Taxpayer participation in a transaction or transactions that do not amount to a trade or business similarly counts toward net investment income as Category (i) income.)

Material participation. Under the PAL rules, a taxpayer's activity is nonpassive if he or she materially participates in it. Material participation in an activity requires that a taxpayer is involved in the operations of the activity on a regular, continuous, and substantial basis. The determination of a taxpayer's material participation in an activity is made for each tax year.

Portfolio Income

The PAL provisions under Code Sec. 469 provide several rules that restrict the ability of taxpayers to artificially generate passive income from certain types of passive activities. One set of these rules—on "portfolio interest"—applies to interest, dividends, annuities, or royalties. The PAL rules governing portfolio income generally apply to the NII tax as well. Portfolio income therefore is included in net investment income as Category (i) income because it is not derived in the ordinary course of a trade or business. Likewise, gross income from self-charged interest is also included in net investment income as Category (i) income from interest.

Real Estate Exceptions and Exclusions

Under Code Sec. 469, a passive activity can be a trade or business activity in which the taxpayer does not materially participate, or it can be a "rental activity" regardless of whether the taxpayer materially participates. A number of exceptions to the "per se" rental rules apply to activities that generate rent that are not considered rental activities under the passive activity rules. For example, rentals of equipment that last seven days or less are not treated as rental activities subject to this rule.

COMMENT

The rules for the NII tax parallel this subset of PAL rules but do not adopt them entirely. This has caused a degree of confusion for which further guidance from the IRS has been requested.

Income from rental property. Whether rents are subject to the NII tax generally depends on several factors, including whether:

- The rents are derived in the ordinary course of a trade or business;
- The rents are derived from an activity the regulations under Code Sec. 469 except from rental activity; and/or
- The taxpayer satisfies the exception in IRC Sec. 469(c)(7) for "qualifying real estate professionals."

COMMENT

The rules for rents may be condensed into two axioms:

- If the rents *are not* derived in the ordinary course of a trade or business, the rents constitute net investment income (under Category (i)).
- If the rents *are* derived in the ordinary course of a trade or business, the rents constitute income from a passive activity included in net investment income unless Code Sec. 469 or its regulations except, exclude, or recharacterize the rents from passive income.

Real estate professional exception. Code Sec. 469 provides an exception for taxpayers in real property businesses (i.e., the real estate professional exception), under which the per-se passive activity classification of rental real estate does not apply. A taxpayer's rental real estate activities in which he or she materially participates are not subject to limitation under the Code Sec. 469 PAL rules if the taxpayer performs more than:

- Half of the personal services he or she performs in trades or businesses in the tax year in real property trades or businesses, including real property development, redevelopment, construction, reconstruction, acquisition, conversion, rental, operation, management, leasing, or brokerage trades or businesses, in which the taxpayer materially participates; and
- 750 hours of services during the tax year in real property trades or businesses in which he or she materially participates.

If a real estate professional engages in a rental real estate activity that qualifies as a Code Sec. 162 trade or business and the real estate professional meets the material participation standard under Code Sec. 469 with respect to such activity, then the rental income from such activity is excluded from NII under the ordinary course of a trade or business exception.

However, if the rental real estate activity does not rise to the level of a trade or business under Code Sec.162 irrespective of material participation (involvement that is regular, continuous, and substantial), the rental income from that activity would apparently not qualify for the Category (i) exception—even if not treated as passive income under Code Sec. 469's material participation test. This issue is expected to be addressed more directly in the final regulations.

Self-rented property recharacterization. The "self-rented property rule" under Reg. § 1.469-2(f)(6) recharacterizes from passive to nonpassive a taxpayer's rents from renting property to a trade or business activity in which the taxpayer materially participates. Under Reg. § 1.469-2(f)(6), the taxpayer's net rental income from the rental of property for use in a trade or business in which the taxpayer materially participates is treated as not arising from a passive activity.

Assuming that the property is rented in the ordinary course of a trade or business, the recharacterized income should be treated as nonpassive under both Code Sec. 469 and Code Sec. 1411, according to the view of most experts. Again, final regulations may address this issue more directly.

Developer recharacterization. The "developer rule" under Reg. § 1.469-2(f)(7) recharacterizes from passive to nonpassive a taxpayer's gain from disposing of rented property if the taxpayer had materially or significantly participated in the trade or business activity of developing the property. If the taxpayer sold the property within 12 months after rental commenced, the gain is generally nonpassive. Gain that the developer rule recharacterizes as nonpassive under IRC Sec. 469 should not be treated as NII based on similar policies of fairness and the need for a bright line measure, according to most commentators.

Passive activity grouping rules. The PAL provisions provide rules for grouping passive activities together. Under the NII regulations, the PAL grouping rules also apply to the scope of a taxpayer's trade or business in determining whether it is a passive activity for the NII tax.

COMMENT

Historically, many taxpayers grouped activities as much as possible in order to maximize passive activity income and absorb PALs. However, because the NII tax applies to passive income, taxpayers may want to rethink their groupings.

Under the proposed regulations, a taxpayer may do a one-time regrouping in the first tax year in which he or she is liable for the NII tax (without regard to the regrouping). The regrouping must comply with the existing PAL requirements, including disclosure requirements.

Interests in Partnerships and S Corps

As stated earlier, net investment income comprises three categories. Category (iii) income is net gain from the disposition of property, "other than property held in a trade or business not described in paragraph (2)" (that is, a trade or business that is not a passive activity with respect to the taxpayer and not a financial instruments/trading business). Thus, Category (iii) net gain includes income from the disposition of property that is used in a passive activity (as well as any asset not used in a trade or business), such as:

- The sale of publicly traded stock by an individual investor is Category (iii) net gain income because it is not associated with holding the stock within the context of a trade or business; and.
- The sale of stock in a closely held corporation also produces Category (iii) net gain for the same reason, unless the owner stock is also an active participant in its business through a partnership interest or S corporation.

Partnership interests and S corp stock are usually not considered property held in a trade or business (although they represent ownership in a trade or business). As a result, gain (or loss) from the disposition of a partnership interest or S corp stock under the general rule would be Category (iii) income and would be subject to the NII tax. *However,* Code Sec. 1411(c)(4)(A) provides an exception, which the proposed regulations (NPRM

REG-130507-11, December 5, 2012) refer to as an "adjustment." This exception is particularly valuable to the owner-employee of the typical small business that elects S corporation tax status or that operates as a partnership.

Exception. The exception applies to active interests in a partnership or S corporation that has a trade or business. The exception provides that the transferor of a partnership or S corporation interest only takes gain from the transfer into account (as net investment income) to the extent that the net gain would be taken into account (as NII) if all of the partnership or S corporation property were sold for fair market value in a deemed sale. (And to recapitulate, the net gain is NII only if the property was not held in a trade or business.)

Thus, the exception is a relief rule. This rule reduces the amount treated as NII. Because gain from property held in a trade or business is not net investment income, the exception reduces income from the transfer of a partnership/S corp interest, by the amount of the gain that would result from a deemed sale of the entity's property.

EXAMPLE

Paul McKenna owns all of the stock in an S corp engaged in a trade or business. Paul is an active participant in the business. He sells all of his stock for a gain of $100,000. This amount would be treated as NII from a passive activity, if not for the exception.

If Paul's S corp had sold all of its property, it would have realized a gain of $100,000. The S corp's property is used in its trade or business; therefore, gain from the deemed sale is not NII because it is derived from "active" assets used in a trade or business. Thus, the adjustment to Paul's NII is $100,000. Although this amount is a gain, the proposed regulations refer to it as a negative adjustment, because it reduces the gain from the sale of the interest.

Under the exception, Paul's gain from the stock sale ($100,000) is adjusted (reduced) by the amount of gain from the deemed sale of the S corp's property (also $100,000). As a result, Paul's NII from the sale of the S corp stock is zero, and Paul does not owe any NII tax on his transfer of the S corp interest.

When adjustment applies. The proposed regulations apply the adjustment if:

- The partnership or S corp is engaged in one or more trades or businesses and at least one of its trades or businesses is not trading in financial instruments or commodities; and
- With respect to the partnership or S corp interest transferred, the transferor is engaged in at least one trade or business that is not a passive activity.

COMMENT

Thus, the adjustment is not available if the entity does not engage in a trade or business. The adjustment also is not available for the disposition of stock in an S corp if the transferor made an election under Code Sec. 338(h)(10) to treat the stock sale as a sale of the corporation's assets.

Installment sales. If a partnership or S corp interest is disposed of in an installment sale occurring on or after January 1, 2013 (the effective date of Code Sec. 1411), any adjustment of the net gain is determined in the year of disposition. The adjustment is taken into account in the same proportion of the total gain as the gain is taken into account under the installment sale rules (Code Sec. 453).

If the installment sale occurs before the effective date of Code Sec. 1411, taxpayers can elect to apply the exception. The taxpayer must file a computational statement with the taxpayer's original or amended return for the first taxable year in which the NII tax applies.

Statement of adjustment. Under the proposed regulations, a transferor that applies the exception must attach a statement for the year of disposition of the interest in the entity. The statement must include:

- A description of the interest;
- The name and taxpayer identification number of the entity transferred;
- The fair market value of each of the entity's property;
- The entity's basis in each property;
- The transferor's allocable share of gain or loss for each of the entity's property;
- Information on whether the property was held in an active trade or business;
- The amount of net gain on the disposition of the interest; and
- The computation of the adjustment.

Deemed sale. To compute the adjustment on the sale of a partnership or S corp interest, the proposed regulations provide the following steps for the deemed sale and adjustment process:

1. A hypothetical disposition of all of the entity's properties (including goodwill) in a fully taxable transaction for cash equal to the fair market value of the properties immediately before the disposition of the interest;
2. The partnership or S corp determines the amount of gain or loss for each property. The gain or loss for each property must be computed separately;

3. The gain or loss from each property is allocated to the transferor. The allocation by a partnership must comply with Code Secs. 704(b) (distributive share) and 704(c) (allocation of gain to the transferor of property contributed to the partnership). The allocation by an S corp does not take into account any hypothetical imposition of tax on the deemed sale;
4. Gains or losses from all the properties are combined to determine whether there is a net gain or net loss from the deemed sale of the assets. The transferor then adjusts the gain or loss from the disposition of the interest by applying the net gain or loss from the property; and
5. If there is a gain from the property, the transferor reduces the gain from the transfer of the interest (a negative adjustment, according to the regulations). The gain cannot be reduced below zero to create a loss.

If there is a loss from the property, the transferor increases the gain from the transfer of the interest (a positive adjustment). The loss cannot be increased above zero to create a gain.

EXAMPLE

Alison McDougall owns 75 percent of the stock of an S corp engaged in a business. Bart Hanney owns the other 25 percent. Alison is an active participant; Bart is passive. The S corp holds three properties used in its trade or business, with an aggregate fair market value of $120,000, an aggregate basis of $100,000, and a gain of $20,000 on a deemed sale. Alison sells her interest to Charles for $90,000, with a basis of $75,000 and a gain of $15,000. Bart sells his interest for $30,000, with a basis of $25,000 and a gain of $5,000. The exception applies to Alison because she is an active participant in the S corp's business. The exception does not apply to Bart because he is a passive participant; his gain of $5,000 is subject to the NII tax.

As a 75 percent interest holder, Alison is allocated 75 percent of the $20,000 gain from the deemed sale of assets, or $15,000 in gain. This gain generates a negative adjustment to Alison's $15,000 gain from the sale of her S corp interest. As a result, her adjusted gain from the sale of the interest is zero, and none of the actual $15,000 gain on the sale of the interest is subject to the NII tax.

Repayment of reduced basis debt held by S corporation shareholder. Under Code Sec. 1367(b)(2), S corporation shareholders can loan money to the corporation and the basis of this debt can be used for the deduction of losses described in Code Sec. 1366. When this type of transaction occurs, the basis of the debt is reduced appropriately, according to Code Sec. 1367(b)(2)(A) *(reduced basis debt)*. When a written reduced basis debt is repaid prior to the basis of that debt being restored under Code Sec. 1367(b)(2)(B) through recognition of income, the repayment is treated as the sale or exchange under Code Sec. 1271(a)(1). Such capital gain or loss, if not considered attributable to the disposition of property held in a trade or business in which the taxpayer materially participates, may be subject to the NII computation of Category (iii) net gain.

If a shareholder of an S corporation with an activity in which the shareholder materially participates holds a reduced basis loan and part of that loan is repaid in a year when basis has not been fully restored, the active interests exception in Code Sec. 1411(c)(4) should apply. Such reduced basis debt should be considered in "an interest in a S corporation" for Code Sec. 1411(c)(4) purposes because this type of debt, with its unique characteristics, exists only when a taxpayer holds both a stock and debt "interest in a corporation."

STUDY QUESTION

4. In an installment sale of a partnership or S corp interest:

a. No adjustment is allowed because payments range across tax periods
b. Adjustment of the net gain is determined in the year of disposition
c. The adjustment is accelerated into the earliest months of installment payments
d. The entire adjustment is taken into account in the year of disposition

Exception for self-employment income. Under Code Sec. 1411(c)(6), net investment income does not include amounts subject to *Self-Employment Contribution Act* (SECA) tax or any item taken into account in determining self-employment income. (For self-employment income, the tax code imposes a separate 0.9 percent additional Medicare tax under Code Sec. 1401(b).) The proposed regulations explain that "taken into account" means income included and deductions allowed in determining net earnings from self-employment. Amounts that are not taken into account may be included in net investment income if the amounts otherwise satisfy the definition of NII.

Traders. Net investment income includes "other" gross income from a trade or business of trading in financial instruments or commodities. Deductions allocable to the trade or business of trading in financial instruments or commodities are taken into account only to the extent they reduce the taxpayer's net earnings from self-employment. Any deductions that exceed net earnings from self-employment are allowed in determining net investment income. The IRS indicated that this treatment of the deductions will apply if the taxpayer is engaged in a trade or business of trading in financial instruments or commodities and does not have any net earnings from self-employment.

EXAMPLE

Andy McClellan is a general partner in a partnership that carries on a trade or business. For the year, Andy's distributive share is $1 million, of which $300,000 is attributable to gain from the sale of partnership capital assets. Code Sec. 1402 excludes from self-employment income gain or loss from the sale or exchange of a capital asset. Andy's $700,000 of self-employment earnings is not treated as net investment income. However, the $300,000 is excluded from self-employment income and is treated as net investment income.

EXAMPLE

Dayle Brogan is engaged in the trade or business of commodities trading. Under Code Sec. 475(f)(2), Dayle elected to mark-to-market her interests in commodities, by recognizing gain or loss at the end of the year, as if the securities were sold. Dayle has $400,000 of income and $150,000 of expenses from the business. None of the income is treated as earnings from self-employment. Therefore, the income is included in net investment income. However, because the $150,000 in expenses was not taken into account to reduce self-employment income, it may be used to reduce Dayle's gross income of $400,000 under Code Sec. 1411.

Exception for Qualified Plan Distributions

Under Code Sec. 1411(c)(5), NII does not include any distribution from a qualified retirement plan or arrangement described in Code Sec. 401(a), 403(a), 403(b), 408, 408A, or 457(b). The proposed reliance regs explain that distributions from qualified plans would encompass:

- A qualified pension, stock bonus, or profit-sharing plan;
- A qualified annuity plan;
- A tax-sheltered annuity plan;
- An individual retirement arrangement (IRA);
- A Roth IRA; or
- A Code Sec. 457(b) plan of a state or local government, or tax-exempt organization.

Distributions or transfers from one of these plans will generally qualify as an exempt distribution. Actual distributions, deemed distributions, rollovers and corrective distributions, permitted distributions to purchase life insurance, or a similar arrangement are all exempt from NII surtax.

COMMENT

Distributions that may be excluded from NII may be included in gross income under the regular Chapter 1 rules of the tax code that tax distributions from retirement plans. This income, therefore, would be taken into account in determining MAGI for purposes of calculating the amount of NII subject to NII surtax.

Dividends from CFCs and PFICs

Under Code Sec. 1411(c)(1)(A)(i), net investment income includes gross income from interest, dividends, annuities, royalties, and rents (unless the income is derived in the ordinary course of an active trade or business that is not trading in financial instruments or commodities). Furthermore, income from investments in foreign corporations generally is treated as net investment income.

In the Preamble to the proposed regulations, the IRS explained that the income tax rules require a U.S. shareholder of a controlled foreign corporation (CFC) or passive foreign investment company (PFIC) to include certain amounts in income currently, even though the amounts are not distributed to the shareholder by the CFC or PFIC. These amounts, although taxable, are not treated as dividends and, therefore, are not treated as net investment income under Code Sec. 1411.

The rules for CFCs and PFICs also prevent amounts that have been included in income by a U.S. shareholder from being taxed again when there is an actual distribution from the foreign corporation. The rules again provide that the actual distributions are not treated as dividends for Chapter 1 of the tax code (Code Secs. 1-1400).

Treatment as dividends. The IRS has advised that, in the absence of these special rules for CFCs and PFICs, the actual distributions would be taxable as dividends. Moreover, the distributions reduce earnings and profits, like dividend distributions. Accordingly, the proposed regulations provide that a previously taxed distribution from a CFC or PFIC remains a dividend for purposes of Chapter 2A (the net investment income tax, Code Sec. 1411). Therefore, these distributions are treated as gross income from dividends that are subject to the NII tax under Code Sec. 1411(c)(1)(A)(i). The IRS noted that the timing of income derived from a CFC or PFIC may be different for Chapter 1 and Chapter 2A purposes (unless an election is made).

COMMENT

To simplify the calculation of the NII tax, treatment of income as a dividend will only apply to distributions of earnings and profits that were previously taxed in a year beginning after December 31, 2012.

STUDY QUESTION

5. All of the following rules apply to the exception under Code Sec. 1411 for qualified plan distributions ***except:***
   - **a.** Code Sec. 457(b) government or tax-exempt organization plan benefits are not included in NII
   - **b.** Distributions permitted for purchasing life insurance policies are eligible for the exception
   - **c.** Net investment income does not include distributions from qualified stock bonus or profit-sharing plans
   - **d.** The exception does not apply to distributions that may be included in gross income under Chapter 1 rules

DEDUCTIONS IN NETTING GAIN AND INCOME

The ability to reduce the investment income and investment gain subject to the NII tax by taking offsetting deductions against them has generated a degree of controversy regarding which deductions may be taken and when. Certain deductions may only be taken in computing Category (iii) net gain. Others may offset any one of the three categories of income or gain. Timing deductions with recognizing income and the ability to carry over certain deductions, including losses, have also prompted either disagreement or recommendation for change.

Category (iii) Netting

Losses from property dispositions (i.e., transactions under Category (iii)) may offset only income and gains from property dispositions. In addition, a Category (iii) amount can never be a negative amount and therefore can never, as a negative amount, reduce NII of Category (i) or (ii). By contrast, Code Sec. 1411(c)(1)(B) provides that the sum of the income or net gain realized from Categories (i), (ii), and (iii) be reduced by "the deductions allowed by this subtitle which are properly allocable to such gross income or net gain."

Net Operating Loss Deductions

In its Preamble to the proposed regulations, the IRS expressly stated that taxpayers are prohibited from applying net operating loss (NOL) deductions against net investment income. It reasoned that the character of each of the various deduction items that compose an NOL is generally not tracked once the item becomes part of a net operating loss. Thus, when an item becomes part of an NOL that is carried to another year, it generally is no longer properly allocable to a specific type of income. Practitioners have asked the IRS to reconsider this rule in drafting final regulations and address ways in which taxpayers may track, carry forward, and apply the portion of NOLs that are properly deductible against net investment income.

Timing Deductions

To be properly allocable to income included in NII, a deduction need not be recognized in the same tax year that gross income or net gain is recognized, according to many practitioners, despite proposed regulations being unclear. These practitioners argue that the situation is no different from a cash-basis individual that has investment income in one year and a related investment expense deduction in the following year. One practitioner group recommends that final regulations go even further, saying that taxpayers should be allowed to defer or capitalize, for NII purposes, income tax deductions that are not used against NII in the tax year in which they are used for income tax purposes because there is insufficient NII in that year.

Suspended Passive Losses

Code Sec. 469(g) provides that, when a taxpayer disposes of his or her entire interest in a passive activity in a taxable transaction, the taxpayer's suspended passive activity losses be applied against his or her active income. However, these losses must first be applied against the taxpayer's net income or gain from passive activities. Any remaining loss is then classified as nonpassive and may be used to offset income from nonpassive activities.

The Treasury/IRS has requested comments on whether the losses triggered under Section 469(g)(1) upon disposition of a passive activity should be taken into account in determining the taxpayer's net gain on the disposition of the activity under Category (iii) or whether the losses should be properly allocable deductions against Category (i) gross income.

STUDY QUESTION

6. Suspended passive losses:

- **a.** Must be applied against the taxpayer's net income or gain from passive activities before offsetting income from nonpassive activities
- **b.** May not be applied against active income when the taxpayer disposes of his or her entire interest in a taxable transaction
- **c.** May never be used to offset income from nonpassive activities
- **d.** May be used to offset income from nonpassive activities if the disposition of the interest was not taxable

CONCLUSION

The 3.8 percent net investment income tax had been envisioned by congressional tax writers in 2010 as a simple, straightforward, single-rate surtax that would be assessed on all passive-type income that did not require the taxpayer's energies to produce over and above perhaps selecting and monitoring an investment. In trying to plug all loopholes before they were found, however, Congress selected statutory language in the form of Code Sec. 1411 that has since challenged many taxpayers to interpret. The IRS in turn saw additional possible loopholes to the statutory language that it felt compelled to address in lengthy regulations.

Some argue that only the "edges" of the rules remain unclear for many taxpayers, with the core base for the net investment income tax clearly identifiable. Others, especially those involved in certain passive activities, hope for future clarification. In the meantime, however, the NII tax as set forth within Code Sec. 1411 and as interpreted in IRS guidance, remains the law that must be dealt with by taxpayers for their 2013 tax year and into the future.

CPE NOTE: When you have completed your study and review of chapters 1–2, which comprise Module 1, you may wish to take the Quizzer for this Module.

Go to **CCHGroup.com/PrintCPE** to take this Quizzer online.

MODULE 2 — TIMING RULES:
CAPITALIZATION AND INCOME DEFERRAL — CHAPTER 3

Implementing Accounting Method Changes

This chapter explores the definition of an accounting method and the differences between automatic accounting method changes under the voluntary advance consent and automatic consent procedures. Scope limitations, Code Sec. 481(a) and cutoff adjustments, and filing requirements are also considered. The chapter explains adverse consequences of an IRS-imposed change, including loss of audit protection,

LEARNING OBJECTIVES

Upon completion of this chapter, you will be able to:

- Explain what an accounting method is and when it is adopted;
- Articulate the scope limitations that prevent filing for an accounting method change or limit audit protection under the advance and automatic change procedures;
- Understand the requirements for a Code Sec. 481(a) or cutoff adjustment;
- Understand filing requirements for Form 3115 under the voluntary advance and automatic consent procedures; and
- Explain the advantages of a voluntary change over an involuntary IRS-imposed change.

INTRODUCTION

Nearly every business taxpayer at one time or another needs to change an accounting method, either voluntarily or, as the result of an IRS audit, involuntarily. For example, compliance with mandated accounting method changes relating to the final repair regulations, which are expected to be effective in tax years beginning after 2013, will require most business taxpayers to file multiple accounting method change requests. Many taxpayer-favorable but nonmandatory accounting methods will also be available under the regulations.

IRS CONSENT REQUIREMENTS

A taxpayer must secure IRS consent to voluntarily change an accounting method (Code Sec. 446(e); Reg. § 1.446-1(e)(2)(i)). Consent is required to change from an impermissible accounting method to a permissible accounting method or from one permissible accounting method to another permissible one.

An accounting method is not permissible unless it clearly reflects income. An accounting method is acceptable if it accords with generally accepted accounting principles, is consistently used by the taxpayer from year to year, and comports with the Income Tax Regulations (Reg. § 1.446-1(c)(1)(2)(C)). Ordinarily, the use of accounting principles and practices that are the accepted norm in a particular type of trade or business will be regarded as clearly reflecting income, provided all items of gross income and expense are treated consistently from year to year (Reg. § 1.446-1(a)(2)).

COMMENT

It is important to distinguish between *adopting* an accounting method and *changing* one. The adoption of an accounting method does not usually require consent of the IRS. For example, a business may adopt the cash or accrual method in its first tax year of operation without IRS consent or a method to account for advance payments in the first year that it receives an advance payment (Reg. § 1.446-1(e)(1)). Once a method is adopted, the taxpayer is required to apply the method consistently from year to year unless the method is changed with IRS consent. Even an adopted method that is impermissible as to the taxpayer may not be changed without IRS consent. Unless specifically authorized by the IRS, a taxpayer may not request, or otherwise make, a retroactive change in method of accounting, regardless of whether the change is from a permissible or an impermissible method.

Voluntary accounting changes may be effected through the *advance consent* procedures provided in Rev. Proc. 97-27 or *automatic consent* procedures provided in Rev. Proc. 2011-14. The automatic consent procedures only apply to changes that are specifically enumerated in the Appendix of Rev. Proc. 2011-14 or in other published IRS guidance as qualifying for automatic consent; all other voluntary changes are effected through the advance consent procedures.

COMMENT

Rev. Proc. 97-27 and Rev. Proc. 2011-14 have been modified by numerous subsequently issued revenue procedures. These subsequently issued modifications will be incorporated into the two revenue procedures that will eventually be issued to supersede Rev. Proc. 97-27 and Rev. Proc. 2011-14. Until then it is critical for taxpayers who refer to the text of Rev. Proc. 97-27 and Rev. Proc. 2011-14 to take into account all subsequent modifications.

Whether the automatic or advance consent procedure applies, a taxpayer files Form 3115, *Application for Change in Accounting Method,* to request consent for the change subject to rare exceptions.

In addition to voluntary changes, the IRS may impose an involuntary change if the taxpayer is under audit and the IRS discovers that the taxpayer is using an impermissible accounting method or has changed its method without receiving consent under the advance or automatic consent procedures.

Exception to Filing Requirement for Change in Form of Business

A taxpayer may change an accounting method without IRS advance or automatic consent if there is a change in the form of running a business. This rule applies to the formation of a new corporation in a transaction described in Code Sec. 338 or Code Sec. 351 or the formation of a new partnership in a Code Sec. 721 or Code Sec. 708(b)(1)(B) transaction.

Accounting Method Change Defined

A *change in method of accounting* includes a change in the overall plan of accounting for gross income or deductions (e.g., cash basis to accrual basis or long-term contract method of accounting) or a change in the treatment of any material item, such as vacation pay or bonuses (Reg. § 1.446-1(e)(2)(ii)(a)).

A change in an overall plan or system of identifying or valuing items in inventory as well as any change in the treatment of any material item used in the overall plan for identifying or valuing inventory items is also an accounting method change (Reg. § 1.446-1(e)(2)(ii)(c)).

A *material item* is any item that involves the proper time for including the item in income or claiming the item as a deduction. Materiality for this purpose does not relate to cost or value.

COMMENT

If the way in which a taxpayer treats an item does not permanently affect the taxpayer's lifetime income but does or could change the tax year in which income is reported, it involves timing and, therefore, involves a method of accounting (Rev. Proc. 91-31). For example, corrections of items that are deducted as interest or salary but that are in fact payments of dividends, and corrections of items that are deducted as business expenses but that are in fact personal expenses. are not changes in method of accounting because they do not relate to timing of the deduction (Reg. § 1.446-1(e)(2)(ii)(b)).

EXAMPLE

Everett Howe, an apartment building owner, fails to claim a $1,200 repair expense as a current deduction on his building in 2013 and instead capitalizes and depreciates the repair expense over 39 tax years at the rate of $31 per year. Everett's capitalization of the repair expense is an improper accounting method because it affects the timing of taxable income. The $1,200 reduction in taxable income that should have occurred in 2013 is spread over 39 years (Reg. § 1.446-1(2)(2)(ii)(d)(2); IRS Chief Counsel Advance Letter Ruling 201231004, April 18, 2012).

COMMENT

An accounting method change may work in favor of or against a taxpayer. A favorable change can save taxes by accelerating deductions or deferring income recognition. On the other hand, an unfavorable change has the opposite effect. Obviously, a taxpayer using a permissible method of accounting would not want to change to another permissible but less favorable method. However, if an impermissible method is in use, the taxpayer should change to a permissible method whether the results are favorable or not. The upside of a voluntary change from an impermissible method is that a taxpayer receives audit protection, as explained below.

When Is an Accounting Method Adopted?

If a taxpayer improperly treats a material item in the same way in determining gross income or deductions on two or more consecutively filed returns, the taxpayer has adopted a method of accounting and an amended return may not be filed to fix the error (Reg. § 1.446-1(e)(2)(ii); Rev. Rul. 72-439). Thus, in the previous example, the taxpayer may file an amended 2013 return to claim a repair expense so long as he has not filed a 2014 return. Once the 2014 return has been filed, he has adopted an accounting method with respect to the repair expenses, albeit an impermissible method, and must obtain IRS permission to change its treatment of the repair expense by filing Form 3115.

When an item is properly treated on even one return, an accounting method has been adopted and an amended return may not be filed to change the treatment. Permission to change from one permissible accounting method to another permissible one must first be obtained (Reg. § 1.146-1(e)(1)).

Mathematical and Posting Errors Are Not Accounting Methods

Mathematical and posting errors may only be corrected by filing an amended return within the limitations period. Also, errors in the computation of tax liability such as errors in computation of the foreign tax credit, net operating loss, percentage depletion, or investment credit may only be corrected on an amended return filed within the limitations period. These errors may not be fixed by changing accounting methods (Reg. § 1.446-1(e)(2)(ii)(b)).

AUDIT PROTECTION

A taxpayer that properly files an advance or automatic consent application on Form 3115, *Application for Change of Accounting Method,* to change from an impermissible accounting method to a permissible method prior to coming under examination receives "audit protection" (Section 7 of Rev. Proc. 2011-14; Section 9 of Rev. Proc. 97-27). The "scope limitations" described below generally prevent a taxpayer under examination from changing accounting methods and receiving audit protection.

Audit protection means that the IRS will not require the taxpayer to change its method of accounting for an item that is the subject of the change for any tax years prior to the year of change. The primary benefit is that interest and penalties may not be imposed for tax years prior to the year of voluntary change with respect to tax underpayments caused by the improper use of the accounting method.

EXAMPLE

Better Solutions, Inc., a calendar year corporation, is not the subject of an audit and files Form 3115 under the advance or automatic consent procedure, as applicable, to change from its impermissible accounting method in 2013. Although Better Solution's taxable income may be increased by a Code Sec. 481(a) adjustment (discussed, below) in 2013, the corporation is not subject to interest and penalties. If Better Solutions were under audit, the IRS would impose an involuntary accounting method change in the earliest open year under audit (e.g., 2010). Interest would be charged on underpayments of tax in 2010, 2011, and 2012 attributable to the accounting method change and penalties such as the substantial underpayment penalty might apply.

Audit protection does not apply if the taxpayer's Form 3115 contains misstatements or material omissions of fact or if the taxpayer is subject to a pending criminal investigation (or becomes subject to a future criminal investigation) concerning any federal tax liability issue for a year prior to the change, including the making of false or fraudulent statements.

COMMENT

Audit protection begins on the date that the Form 3115 is filed with the IRS National Office in Washington, D.C. (Section 7.01 of Rev. Proc. 2011-14). In the case of advance consent, Form 3115 must be filed with the National Office before the last day of the tax year of change. In the case of an automatic change, a taxpayer is given several additional months to file Form 3115 because the filing needs to occur by the extended due date of the return for the year of change. A taxpayer, particularly a taxpayer using the automatic consent procedure, should file the application with the National Office as early as possible to beat out the start of any potential examination that would otherwise end audit protection and result in a service-imposed change.

If a taxpayer's accounting method change relates to a "submethod" of an accounting method (e.g., the method of valuing inventory increments (a *submethod*) under the LIFO inventory method), audit protection does not prevent the IRS from terminating the method (e.g., LIFO) during a prior tax year (Section 7.02(2) of Rev. Proc. 2011-14; Section 9.02 of Rev. Proc. 97-27).

STUDY QUESTION

1. Voluntary changes in accounting method not subject to the automatic consent procedures in Rev. Proc. 2011-14 are:
   - **a.** Effected through permission granted by the Appeals Office or in a National Office conference
   - **b.** Effected through the advance consent procedures of Rev. Proc. 97-27
   - **c.** Made without filing Form 3115
   - **d.** Not eligible for audit protection

SCOPE LIMITATIONS FOR VOLUNTARY ACCOUNTING METHOD CHANGES

Subject to the exceptions described below, a taxpayer may not file an automatic or advance consent accounting method change if the taxpayer is "under examination" (Section 6 of Rev. Proc. 2011-14; Section 6 of Rev. Proc. 97-27).

COMMENT

Taxpayers should carefully read the guidelines that apply to the specific accounting method change. The guidelines for a particular change (usually located in the Appendix of Rev. Proc. 2011-14 in the case of an automatic change) occasionally waive the scope limitation on taxpayers under examination. For example, Rev. Proc. 2012-19 and Rev. Proc. 2012-20, relating to automatic accounting method changes to comply with the temporary repair regulations (T.D. 9564), waive the scope limitations.

Commencement of Examination

An examination begins on the date the IRS contacts a taxpayer in any manner to schedule an examination of its income tax return (Section 3.07 of Rev. Proc. 97-27; Section 3.08 of Rev. Proc. 2011-14).

The following special rules apply in determining when a taxpayer is under examination:

- In the case of a partnership or limited liability company that is subject to the TEFRA unified audit and litigation provisions, an examination begins on the date of the notice of the beginning of an administrative proceeding sent to the tax matters partner (TMP) (Section 3.08(2) of Rev. Proc. 2011-14; Section 3.07(2) of Rev. Proc. 97-27);
- A taxpayer is considered under examination while the taxpayer has a refund or credit in excess of $2 million under review by the Joint Committee on Taxation pursuant to Code Sec. 6405 (Section 3.08(4) of Rev. Proc. 2011-14; Section 3.07(3) of Rev. Proc. 97-27);

- For any tax year for which a consolidated group is under examination, a corporation that was a member of the group during that year is considered under examination (Section 4.02(2) of Rev. Proc. 2011-14; Section 4.02(5) of Rev. Proc. 97-27); and
- A taxpayer participating in the Compliance Assurance Process (CAP) is under examination as of the date a Memorandum of Understanding for the CAP is executed (Section 3.08(5) of Rev. Proc. 2011-14).

COMMENT

Under the CAP program the IRS's Large Business and International Division works with large business taxpayers to identify and resolve issues prior to the filing of a tax return. The objective of the program is to reduce a taxpayer's burden and uncertainty through the contemporaneous exchange of information about completed events and transactions that affect tax liability while assuring the IRS of the accuracy of tax returns prior to filing, thereby reducing or eliminating the need for postfiling examinations. See Announcement 2005-87.

COMMENT

A partnership or S corporation is prohibited from using the automatic or advance consent procedures if the partnership's or S corporation's accounting method is an issue under consideration in an examination of a partner or S corp shareholder on the date the partnership or S corporation would otherwise file Form 3115 (Section 4.02(3) of Rev. Proc. 2011-14; Section 4.02(6) of Rev. Proc. 97-27).

Exceptions to Scope Limitation for Taxpayers Under Examination

The following scope exceptions, which apply to both automatic and advance consent requests unless otherwise noted, allow a taxpayer under examination to voluntarily change accounting methods by filing Form 3115 (Section 6.01 of Rev. Proc. 97-27; Section 6.03 of Rev. Proc. 2011-14).

If any of the exceptions applies, a copy of Form 3115 must be filed with the examining agent.

90-day window with audit protection. A taxpayer under examination for at least 12 months as of the first day of a tax year may file an application to change its accounting method within the first 90 days of the tax year. However, this exception does not apply if the method of accounting relates to the issue that is under examination or an issue that has been placed in suspense by the examining agent.

COMMENT

Some larger taxpayers are effectively under continuous examination for all tax years. These taxpayers may file an automatic or advance consent accounting method change unrelated to an audit issue within the first 90 days of any tax year. The 90-day window does not compromise the IRS's position because it will have had at least one year to identify any accounting method issues before the taxpayer is given the opportunity to voluntarily change its accounting method and obtain audit protection.

EXAMPLE

A calendar-year taxpayer under continuous examination must file an advance accounting method change for the 2014 tax year within the first 90 days of 2014. Without regard to the 90-day window rule the Form 3115 could be filed as late as December 31, 2014, the regular advance consent filing deadline. In the case of an automatic change for the 2014 tax year, Form 3115 would need to be filed within the first 90 days of 2015. Normally, the deadline for a 2014 change would be the extended due date for the 2014 return (e.g., October 15, 2015, for a calendar year individual).

120-day window with audit protection. A taxpayer may file a Form 3115 to change its accounting method under the automatic or advance consent procedure within 120 days after the date an examination ends even though another examination has begun so long as:

- The second examination does not relate to the accounting method change; and
- The accounting method change is not an issue that has been placed in suspense by the examining agent.

The 120-day window is suspended if the Appeals Office refers the case to the examining agent for reconsideration.

Director's consent with audit protection. A taxpayer under examination may obtain consent from the examining agent's director to file an application using the automatic or advance consent procedure. Consent to file the application will normally be granted unless the method of accounting to be changed would ordinarily be included as an item of adjustment for the tax year(s) under examination.

EXAMPLE

Consent would normally be granted to file an application to effect a change from one permissible accounting method to another permissible accounting method. Also, consent would be granted to file an application that changes from an impermissible accounting method adopted subsequent to the tax year under examination to a permissible accounting method or the examiner does not intend to raise a method of accounting issue for the accounting method change requested by the taxpayer.

The director's consent to file the application should be requested through the examining agent or team.

The director will contact the examiner before granting consent to file the application. Once the decision is made, the director will notify the taxpayer using either a "Nonobjection Letter" or an "Objection Letter."

COMPLIANCE POINTER

The director's written consent to file the application must be attached to the Form 3115 required to be filed with the National Office. The consent only allows the taxpayer to file the application; it does not guarantee that the application will be accepted.

Changes described in automatic consent procedure as not having audit protection. A taxpayer under examination may request consent under the automatic procedure for an accounting method change if the description of the automatic change specifically states that it is not subject to the audit protection provisions of Rev. Proc. 2011-14. The rule applies whether or not the change relates to an item under examination (Section 6.03(5) of Rev. Proc. 2011-14).

COMMENT

This exception allows a taxpayer to adopt a proper method in its current tax year without jeopardizing the IRS's right to make the use of the impermissible method an audit issue in prior years.

Issue pending. A taxpayer under examination may request to change a method of accounting that is an issue pending for any tax year under examination. Because the accounting method is already the subject of an audit, the audit protection provisions do not apply (Section 6.01(5) of Rev. Proc. 97-27; Section 6.03(6) of Rev. Proc. 2011-14).

Taxpayer before Appeals Office or federal court. A taxpayer before an IRS appeals office or federal court may request a change in method of accounting under the advance or automatic consent procedures. However, the audit protection provisions do not apply if the method to be changed is an issue under consideration by the Appeals Office or court (Sections 6.02 and 6.03 of Rev. Proc. 97-27, as modified by Rev. Proc. 2011-14; Sections 6.04 and 6.05 of Rev. Proc. 2011-14).

A copy of the application must be filed with the appeals officer or IRS court counsel, as applicable (Section 6.02 and 6.03 of Rev. Proc. 97-27).

Code Sec. 381(a) transactions. For Section 381(a) transactions (relating to certain tax-free reorganizations under Code Sec. 361 or liquidations under Code Sec. 332) occurring before August 31, 2011, a taxpayer was generally prohibited from filing an automatic method change if it engaged in a transaction to which Code Sec. 381(a) applied within the proposed tax year of change. Effective for transactions occurring on or after August 31, 2011, this prohibition has been removed for changes that are otherwise subject to the automatic change procedure (4.02(4) of Rev. Proc. 2011-14, as modified by Rev. Proc. 2012-39). Previously, all changes in accounting method for a year in which a Code Sec. 381(a) transaction occurred (including those described in the appendix of the automatic change procedure) needed to made through the advance consent procedure, assuming the advance consent scope limitations did not prevent use of the advance consent procedure.

Additional Scope Limitations for Automatic Consents

The automatic consent change procedures may not be used to change:

- An accounting method in the final tax year of a trade or business (Section 4.02(5) of Rev. Proc. 2011-14)
- An overall method of accounting or a method of accounting with respect to a specific item if in the previous five years the taxpayer changed (or applied to change) its overall method of accounting or its method of accounting with respect to the specific item (Section 4.02(6) and (7) of Rev. Proc. 2011-14).

COMMENT

The advance consent procedure does not contain these two scope limitations. Accordingly, a taxpayer may use the advance consent procedure to request a change for a final tax year or within the five-year period. Generally, however, these requests are denied unless the method being changed is an impermissible method or the taxpayer can otherwise show a compelling reason.

The automatic consent procedure may be used if the trade or business is terminated as the result of a transaction to which Code Sec. 381(a) applies that occurs on or after August 31, 2011 (Section 4.02(5) of Rev. Proc. 2011-14, as modified by Rev. Proc. 2012-39).

STUDY QUESTION

2. A taxpayer may file a Form 3115 to request a change in accounting method and receive audit protection if:
   - **a.** The method change is an issue before the Office of Appeals or a federal court
   - **b.** The taxpayer files Form 3115 within 120 days after an examination has ended and a second examination regarding the method change has begun
   - **c.** The method change is related to a pending issue for any tax year under examination
   - **d.** The taxpayer files Form 3115 within 90 days of the beginning of the tax year of change, the taxpayer is under continuous examination, and the change does not relate to an issue under examination

CODE SEC. 481(a) ADJUSTMENT

The Code Sec. 481(a) adjustment prevents the duplication or omission of deductions and income attributable to a change in accounting method. When there is a change in method of accounting in which items would be duplicated or omitted, the IRS generally requires the calculation of a Code Sec. 481(a) adjustment. When Code Sec. 481(a) applies, income for the tax year preceding the year of change is determined under the method of accounting that was then employed and income for the year of change and the following tax years are determined under the new method as if the new method had always been used.

EXAMPLE

Business owner Heather Grasso, a taxpayer using the cash basis method, has $100,000 of accounts receivable in 2013. In 2014 the she changes to the accrual accounting method. Heather has a positive Code Sec. 481(a) adjustment of $100,000 that must be included in 2014 income. Without this adjustment the $100,000 would never be taxed because it was not included in her income in 2013 under the cash basis when it was accrued and would not be included in income in 2014 or later under the accrual basis because it was accrued before 2014.

COMMENT

If a Code Sec. 481(a) adjustment is not required by the IRS, the change is made on a "cutoff basis," as described below. The IRS determines when a Code Sec. 481(a) adjustment or cutoff method applies. No election is involved. Most changes are made with a Code Sec. 481(a) adjustment.

When a partnership or S corporation changes its method of accounting, Code Sec. 481(a) adjustments are made at the partnership or S corporation level (Reg. § 1.481-2(c)(5)).

Code Sec. 481(a) Adjustment and Statute of Limitations

The Code Sec. 481(a) adjustment is computed by taking all tax years preceding the tax year of change into account, including tax years closed by the statute of limitations (Chief Counsel Advice 201231004, April 18, 2012; Section 2.05(1) of Rev. Proc. 2011-14).

Code Sec. 481(a) Adjustment Periods for Voluntary Changes

For a voluntary change under the advance or automatic consent procedures, the Code Sec. 481(a) adjustment period is one tax year for a net negative adjustment (i.e., a taxpayer-favorable adjustment that results in a decrease in taxable income) and four tax years for a net positive adjustment (resulting in an increase to taxable income). The negative adjustment is taken into account entirely in the year of change. A net positive adjustment is taken into account ratably over a four-year adjustment period that begins in the tax year of change. A taxpayer, however, may elect a one-year adjustment period in lieu of the four-year adjustment period for a positive adjustment if the adjustment amount is less than $25,000. The election is made by completing the appropriate line on Form 3115 and taking the entire adjustment into account in the year of change (Section 5.04 of Rev. Proc. 2011-14; Section 5.02(3) of Rev. Proc. 97-27).

Any portion of an adjustment that remains in the last year of a taxpayer's business is taken into account in the last year.

Code Sec. 481(a) Adjustment for Involuntary Changes

As explained below the Code Sec. 481(a) adjustment for an IRS-imposed change, whether positive or negative, is one year.

Cutoff Method

As an alternative to requiring a Code Sec. 481(a) adjustment to be taken into account during the applicable adjustment period, the IRS may apply a method change using a cutoff method. For this method the taxpayer continues to account for items that arose prior to the year of change using the old method. Items arising in the year of change and thereafter are accounted for using the new method (Section 2.06 of Rev. Proc. 2011-14; Section 2.06 of Rev. Proc. 97-27).

Whether an accounting change is made with a Code Sec. 481(a) adjustment or on a cutoff basis, the duplication or omission of items is effectively addressed.

EXAMPLE

John Jacob uses the cash basis and has $100 of accounts receivable outstanding in 2013. He obtains consent to change to the accrual basis method in 2014 and the cutoff method applies. The accounts receivable are included in income when received in accordance with the rules that apply to cash method taxpayers even though John is now on the accrual basis. If the change were made using a Code Sec. 481(a) adjustment, John could elect to include $100 in income in 2014 or, without an election, include $25 in income over the four-year spread period.

STUDY QUESTION

3. The Code Sec. 481(a) adjustment period for a voluntary change in accounting method for either an advance or automatic change is ____ for a taxpayer-favorable change and _____ for a change resulting in increased taxable income.

a. One; four
b. Two; four
c. Three; six
d. Four; five

IRS ACCEPTANCE OR REJECTION OF CONSENT REQUESTS

A request for a change in method of accounting under the automatic or advance consent procedure filed on Form 3115 is considered a request for a letter ruling (Section 2.01 of Rev. Proc. 2013-1). A taxpayer filing under the advance consent procedure will receive a written consent or rejection from the IRS in the form of a letter ruling. As explained below, a taxpayer may be able to confer with the IRS before a formal rejection ruling is issued.

A formal ruling in response to automatic consent requests is not issued unless the IRS reviews the automatic request and rejects it or wishes to modify it. A taxpayer who files an automatic request is already deemed to have received consent to change its accounting method. Most automatic requests are not reviewed due to IRS personnel limitations.

If the IRS reviews an automatic consent request and issues a formal rejection, the taxpayer has adopted an "improper" accounting method if two or more returns using the method have been filed. If only one return has been filed using the improper method, the taxpayer may simply file an amended return to undo the change (and pay any applicable interest and penalties). If an improper method has been adopted by filing two returns, the taxpayer will need to change (but not retroactively) to the old method or another proper method. If the taxpayer is placed under examination prior to making the change, the scope limitations may prevent the taxpayer from making the change. As in the case of advance consents, the taxpayer may be able to confer with the IRS prior to a formal rejection.

Advance Consent Requests: Taxpayer's Consent to IRS Consent Required

A letter ruling from the National Office consenting to a taxpayer's proposed change under the advance consent procedure will contain:

- A description of the change, the tax year in which it is effective;
- The Code Sec. 481(a) adjustment (if any); and
- Additional terms and conditions that apply to effect the change (Section 8.11 of Rev. Proc. 97-27; Section 9.17 of Rev. Proc. 2013-1).

In order to implement the change the taxpayer must consent to the change within 45 days of receipt of the letter ruling. Consent is made by returning a signed copy of the letter ruling to the National Office. The National Office provides this "consent agreement" copy with the original ruling. A copy of the signed consent agreement must also be attached to the taxpayer's return.

If a taxpayer does not return a signed or unsigned copy of the consent agreement within the 45-day deadline, the letter ruling is null and void.

If the taxpayer does not wish to implement the change the unsigned consent agreement should be returned with a statement explaining why the change will not be made.

If the reason(s) relate to the Section 481(a) amount or some other term or condition, the National Office will notify the taxpayer whether the IRS will modify the letter ruling. If the ruling is not modified, the taxpayer is given 15 days from the date of notification to accept or reject the original ruling.

COMMENT

If IRS consent to change accounting methods under the advance consent procedure is received, the consent is generally effective on the first day of the tax year in which the Form 3115 was filed even if the consent is received after the due date of the income tax return. Because a return should not be filed until after actual consent is received it is necessary to file an amended return (and quite likely amended state income tax returns) to reflect the change if the consent is received after the return is filed. A taxpayer with an application pending after the return due date may want to request the National Office to delay the effective tax year of the change or, after receiving the consent, decline to sign unless it is modified.

EXAMPLE

Gian Nelson, a cash basis taxpayer using a calendar tax year, files Form 3115 on December 31, 2013, to change the accounting method for his business for the 2013 tax year under the advance consent procedure. December 31, 2013, is the last day for filing Form 3115 under the advance consent procedure. Gian's extended return filing date is October 15, 2014. If the consent is not received prior to October 15, Gian should file his return based on his existing accounting method. If consent is received thereafter, Gian will need to file an amended return using the new method unless the National Office agrees to delay the effective year till 2014.

EXAMPLE

IRS advance consent guidelines provide that a taxpayer changing an accounting method on its income tax return prior to receiving consent may rely on the consent. However, if it turns out that consent is denied or the terms or conditions are different than those expected, the taxpayer remains liable for any interest, penalties, or other adjustments resulting from the improper implementation of the change (Section 9.17 of Rev. Proc. 2013-1).

Opportunity for Conference Prior to Final Adverse Decision

When the National Office reviews a Form 3115 filed under the advance consent rules and determines that the IRS intends to reject a proposed accounting method change, it will offer the taxpayer an opportunity to meet in a "conference of right" prior to issuing a formal rejection. This affords the taxpayer the opportunity to argue its case or make any changes required by the IRS. Critically, however, a conference is not usually offered unless the taxpayer has requested a conference in advance by checking box 16 on Form 3115 or by sending a written request for a conference prior to an adverse determination (Section 8.10 of Rev. Proc. 97-27).

Assuming the National Office reviews a change made under the automatic consent procedure and determines that the change was improper because it did not comply with all applicable provisions of the procedure (for example, the taxpayer changed to a method of accounting that varies from the applicable accounting method described in this revenue procedure or the taxpayer is outside the scope of this revenue procedure), the IRS will notify the taxpayer that consent is not granted to make the change. The taxpayer would then need to file a new application to make the change properly. The change would be effective for the later tax year for which it was filed. However, in its discretion, the National Office may allow the taxpayer to conform its "improper" accounting method effective for the tax year of the improper accounting method change and file amended returns for the year of the change and subsequent tax years to make any appropriate adjustments (Section 10.01(2) and (3) of Rev. Proc. 2011-14).

If the National Office reviews an application filed under the automatic change procedure, a taxpayer who checked box 16 will be given an opportunity to meet in a conference and challenge a tentative adverse determination (Section 10.03(1) of Rev. Proc. 2011-14). Thus, it is important to check box 16 to preserve a right to meet in conference, whether filing under the advance or automatic procedure.

STUDY QUESTION

4. Which of the following is ***not*** a possible National Office response to an improper change made under the automatic consent procedure?

   a. Notification that consent is not granted to make the change
   b. Allowing the taxpayer to conform to the proper accounting method by filing amended returns both for the year of the change and subsequent tax years
   c. Approving the change even though it is improper
   d. Making a conference of right available to the taxpayer even if one was not requested

FORM 3115 FILING REQUIREMENTS

Where to File Form 3115

For changes made pursuant to the automatic consent procedure, the original Form 3115 is attached to the taxpayer's federal income tax return for the year of change and a second, signed copy of the Form 3115 is filed with the IRS National Office unless the guidance in the Appendix of Rev. Proc. 2011-14 relating to the specific accounting method change requires the copy to be filed with the IRS office in Ogden, Utah. In a few instances a signed copy must be filed with both offices.

For a taxpayer seeking advance consent, a Form 3115 is filed with the National Office. There is no need to attach a copy of the Form 3115 to the tax return for the year of change. The change should not be made until actual consent is received from the IRS.

Generally, a separate Form 3115 is filed for each accounting method change. However, in some cases the guidance specific to a particular change may allow or require certain method changes to be requested on the same Form 3115.

Power of Attorney Required

A power of attorney (Form 2848) must be attached to Form 3115 in order for the IRS to contact the taxpayer's representative (e.g., return preparer) or, in the case of an advance consent request, for the representative to receive a copy of the requested ruling (i.e., consent) (Section 9.03(8) and (9) of Rev. Proc. 2013-1).

Due Date for Form 3115

The due date for filing Form 3115 depends on whether the change is requested under the advance consent or automatic consent procedure.

A change under the advance consent rules must be during the tax year in which the change takes effect. Thus, December 31, 2014, is the last day for a calendar year taxpayer to file Form 3115 to effect a change for the 2014 tax year under the advance consent procedure.

COMMENT

The IRS advises a taxpayer to file advance consent requests as early as possible in the tax year of change to give the IRS sufficient time to respond to the request prior to the due date of the taxpayer's return. The IRS normally sends an acknowledgment of receipt of advance change requests within 60 days of receipt. The IRS does not acknowledge receipt of automatic change requests nor does it formally acknowledge that the taxpayer may make the requested change. However, if the National Office or a director reviews the taxpayer's automatic change request (most automatic change applications are not reviewed) the taxpayer will be notified if additional information is needed or if the request is denied. Generally, a taxpayer will simply not know whether it properly changed and implemented an accounting method under the automatic consent procedure. There is always a possibility that the IRS will challenge a change in an audit, for example, because the filing procedures were not followed. For this reason it is essential that a taxpayer making an automatic change follow all procedural guidelines.

A change under the automatic consent procedures only needs to be filed by the due date (including extensions) of the return for the tax year of change. For example, in the case of an individual, the Form 3115 would only need to be filed by October 15, 2014 (the extended due date), to effect a change in the 2013 tax year if a filing extension is filed. This represents a generous cushion for taking advantage of opportunities and correcting improper methods.

CAUTION

The due date for filing a copy of a Form 3115 under the automatic procedure with the National Office is no earlier than the first day of the tax year of change and no later than the date that the original is filed with the federal income tax return for the year of change. For example, if the original Form 3115 is filed on May 15, 2015, for an individual's 2014 calendar year return for which an extension applies, the copy must be filed with the National Office by May 15, 2015, and not the extended due date deadline of October 15, 2015.

Extensions to File Application

A taxpayer who does not file a timely Form 3115 will only be granted an extension of time to file in unusual and compelling circumstances (Reg. § 301.9100-3; Section 6.02(3)(d)(ii) of Rev. Proc. 2011-14; Section 5.03(2) of Rev. Proc. 2013-1). A user fee for the extension request applies:

- $1,000 for a taxpayer with gross income less than $250,000;
- $4,000 for gross income of $250,000 or greater but less than $1 million; and
- $8,000 for gross income of $1 million or greater (Appendix A of Rev. Proc. 2013-1).

In the case of an automatic accounting method change only, an automatic six-month extension is available if the taxpayer filed a timely return (including extensions). The six-month period runs from the original due date of the return without regard to extensions (Reg. § 301.9100-2; Section 6.02(3)(d)(i) of Rev. Proc. 2011-14). There is no filing fee to obtain this automatic extension. If this automatic extension does not apply, an extension would need to be requested under Reg. § 301.9100-3 and a fee paid.

Advance Consent Filing Fees

One practical difference between automatic and advance consent requests that may be of particular importance to a small business taxpayer is that a user fee is charged by the IRS for a nonautomatic change. The fee schedule is the same as above for filing extension requests except that for a taxpayer with gross income of $1 million or greater the fee is $7,000 rather than $8,000..:

- (Appendix A of Rev. Proc. 2013-1).

Reduced fees apply for certain identical requests. The fee is a deductible business expense. No user fee is charged to file Form 3115 under the automatic consent procedure of Rev. Proc. 2011-14.

Accurate and Complete Information Required

The IRS has made a push against "skeletal" Form 3115s that provide minimum information regarding an accounting method change, including the Code Sec. 481(a) computation.

Examples of required information now specifically listed in Rev. Proc. 2011-14 for automatic consent changes include:

- Beginning and ending dates of tax year of change;
- Designated automatic accounting method change number(s);
- The amount and computation of the Code Sec. 481(a) adjustment if the method change is not made on a cutoff basis;
- A full description of the item(s) being changed;
- A full description of the present method(s) of accounting from which the taxpayer is changing and the proposed method(s) to which the taxpayer is changing; and
- Any other information required by Form 3115 (Section 6.02(1)(c) of Rev. Proc. 2011-14).

COMMENT

The instructions for Form 3115 list 180 separate automatic accounting method changes that are either specified in the Appendix to Rev. Proc. 2011-14 (the automatic consent procedure) or in other IRS published guidance. Each automatic change has an assigned number (numbers 1–180) that is entered on line 1 of Form 3115. The IRS telephone number of an IRS expert for most of these changes is listed in the Appendix to Rev. Proc. 2011-14.

When a taxpayer uses the advance consent procedure to change an accounting method, the required information regarding the change is considerably more stringent than under the automatic consent procedures. Changes within the purview of the automatic consent procedure are ones that are commonly made and fall within the IRS's "comfort range" as clearly reflecting income. For other changes the burden is on the taxpayer to fully explain why the proposed method would clearly reflect income in the taxpayer's particular circumstances. The taxpayer is even required to provide any authority, such as cases and rulings that are adverse to the taxpayer's request. The advance consent may be revoked if the IRS later discovers in an audit that the taxpayer failed to disclose all relevant facts. See, for example IRS Technical Advice Memorandum 201030025.

Incomplete Applications: Second Chance for Taxpayers

If upon review of an advance consent application, the IRS determines that the Form 3115 is incomplete or improperly completed, the IRS will notify the taxpayer and allow a 21-day period to provide required additional information. If the additional information is not provided, the IRS will not process the application (Section 8.09 of Rev. Proc. 97-27).

A similar rule applies under the automatic change procedures if the National Office reviews the application except that a 30-day deadline applies (Section 10.02 of Rev. Proc. 2011-14).

COMMENT

Although the National Office does review each advance consent request, it does not review most automatic change requests.

STUDY QUESTION

5. Which one of the following statements regarding Form 3115 is correct?

- **a.** For a change under the advance consent procedure, the form must be filed by the extended due date of the return for the year of change
- **b.** A $7,000 filing fee applies to advance consent procedure changes if the taxpayer has gross income of $1 million or greater
- **c.** A taxpayer who files an incomplete Form 3115 under the automatic consent procedures will be given 60 days to provide any required information
- **d.** An automatic six-month filing extension applies to advance consent requests.

INVOLUNTARY ACCOUNTING METHOD CHANGES

The IRS may require a taxpayer who is under examination to change from an improper accounting method to a method that in the IRS's opinion clearly reflects taxable income (Code Sec. 446(b); 1.446-1(b)(1)).

The following accounting method issues are among the most common subjects of IRS audits (IRM 4.11.6.2(05-13-2005):

- Capitalization issues—Code Secs. 263(a) and 263A relative to inventory, tangible assets, and intangible assets;
- Accounting for liabilities that involve timing (Code Sec. 461(h);
- Accounting for when income is recognized (Code Sec. 451);
- Depreciation method changes involving changes in recovery periods, conventions, or depreciation methods;
- Inventory valuation issues including LIFO inventory (Code Secs. 471 and 472);
- Accrual to cash method for qualifying small business (Rev. Proc. 2002-28); and
- Accounting for long-term contracts (Code Sec. 460).

COMMENT

The procedures relating to involuntary accounting method changes are contained in Rev. Proc. 2002-18.

When, more than one method of accounting is proper, the IRS may decide which method a taxpayer using an improper method must adopt, subject only to an abuse of discretion standard (Section 2.02 of Rev. Proc. 2002-18). Ordinarily the change will be effective for the earliest open tax year under examination.

An examining agent, appeals officer, or other authorized official will provide notice to the taxpayer that an accounting method issue is being treated as an accounting method change and a description of the proposed new method of accounting along with the Code Sec. 481(a) adjustment, if any.

COMMENT

The IRS may not require a taxpayer to change from one proper method of accounting to another proper one even though the other proper method reflects income more clearly (Section 2.02(5) of Rev. Proc. 2002-18)). However, if a taxpayer changes from an impermissible method to a permissible method or another impermissible method without obtaining consent, the IRS may require the taxpayer to return to its impermissible method. The change back may be made to the year of change if that year is not closed by the statute of limitations. Otherwise, the change back may be made effective for the earliest open year (Section 2.06 of Rev. Proc. 2002-18).

Once an IRS-imposed accounting method change that clearly reflects income is finalized through the execution of a closing agreement, the taxpayer receives "audit protection" for future years. That is to say the taxpayer will not be required to change or modify the method provided:

- The taxpayer complies with all provisions of the closing agreement;
- There has been no fraud, malfeasance, or misrepresentation of a material fact; and
- There are no changes in material fact or applicable law.

In the event one of these situations occurs, the IRS can require a change or modification in the accounting method in the earliest open tax year (Section 7.04 of Rev. Proc. 2002-18).

COMMENT

The IRS may not require a taxpayer to change from one proper method of accounting to another proper one even though the other proper method reflects income more clearly (Section 2.02(5) of Rev. Proc. 2002-18)). However, if a taxpayer changes from an impermissible method to a permissible method or another impermissible method without obtaining consent, the IRS may require the taxpayer to return to its impermissible method. The change back may be made to the year of change if that year is not closed by the statute of limitations. Otherwise, the change back may be made effective for the earliest open year (Section 2.06 of Rev. Proc. 2002-18).

Involuntary Change: Code Sec. 481(a) Adjustment Period

An examining agent must impose any Code Sec. 481(a) adjustment (positive or negative) in a single year (subject to Code Sec. 481(b) for positive adjustments in excess of $3,000) (Section 3.04(c)(3) of Rev. Proc. 2011-18). Appeals and counsel for the government, however, have discretion to modify the adjustment period as explained below.

Collateral adjustments. Because the Code Sec. 481(a) adjustment required as the result of an IRS-imposed change is taken into account for a tax year in which a return has already been filed, it may be necessary to make collateral adjustments to items, such as NOLs and credits, affected as a result of increasing or decreasing the taxpayer's taxable income by the adjustment amount (Section 7.03(1) of Rev. Proc. 2002-11). This adjustment is not a consideration in the case of a voluntary change, because such a change is not applied retroactively.

In the case of an IRS-imposed change, the Code Sec. 481(a) adjustment is computed without regard to any pre-1954 tax years (Reg. Sec. 1.481-3).

Code Sec. 481(b) computation. When the IRS imposes an involuntary accounting method change with a positive (unfavorable) Section 481(a) adjustment greater than $3,000, an alternative computation may limit the tax increase attributable to the adjustment amount. Specifically, if the aggregate tax increase that would result by including one-third of the adjustment in the tax year of change and one-third in each of the two preceding tax years is less than the additional tax that results by including the entire adjustment in income in the year of change, the additional tax imposed in the year of the change is limited to the aggregate tax increase (Code Sec. 481(b)(1)). Code Sec. 481(b) provides a second alternative computation based on a precise allocation of the adjustment to prior tax years.

COMMENT

Due to the four-year forward spread period for positive adjustments used when a voluntary change applies, the Code Sec. 481(b) alternative computation normally only has the potential to save a taxpayer money if the change is involuntary with a one-year adjustment period.

Involuntary Change: Audit Protection Lost

If the IRS requires a taxpayer under audit to change its accounting method in the earliest open tax year and the change generates a positive (unfavorable) adjustment to taxable income in that year, the taxpayer will be responsible for penalties and interest resulting from the understatement of income in that earlier year and any subsequent open years. Taxpayers that voluntarily file accounting method changes on the other hand receive audit protection. See the earlier discussion of audit protection.

Involuntary Change: Year of Change

An examining agent is generally required to impose an accounting method change in the earliest open year under examination that the current method is deemed impermissible. However, the agent may defer the change to a later tax year that is under examination if (Section 5.04 of Rev. Proc. 2002-18):

- A Code Sec. 481(a) adjustment cannot be determined or reasonably estimated in the year the change would otherwise be imposed and the examiner determines it would be inappropriate to use a cutoff method;
- The existing method of accounting has no material effect in the year in which the change would otherwise be imposed; or
- The statute of limitations has expired for tax years after the year that the change would otherwise be imposed.

Once the change is imposed, a taxpayer will need to file amended returns for open tax years subsequent to the year of change to reflect items that are affected by the accounting method change and to pay any related interest and penalties. The closing agreement may require that these amended returns be filed prior to the execution of the agreement (Section 7.03 of Rev. Proc. 2002-18).

Resolution of Accounting Method Issues by Appeals and Government Counsel

An examining agent's authority is generally limited to changing a taxpayer's accounting method if the taxpayer's accounting method is impermissible or if the taxpayer changed its accounting method without consent. However, if the taxpayer moves the issue to the IRS Appeals Office or initiates a court proceeding, appeals officers and counsel for the government have much greater discretion in resolving an accounting method issue because they may take the "hazards of litigation" or other interest of the government into account (Section 6 of Rev. Proc. 2012-18).

For example, an appeals officer or counsel for the government may agree to modify the terms and conditions ordinarily applicable to an examination-imposed accounting method change. The year of change may be negotiated, a cutoff method may be used instead of an otherwise required Code Sec. 481(a) adjustment (or vice versa), the amount of a Code Sec. 481(a) adjustment may be reduced, and the spread period may be increased.

An appeals officer or counsel for government is also authorized to resolve an accounting method issue on an "alternative timing" basis or on the basis of the "time value of money."

Alternative timing resolution. Under an *alternative timing resolution,* the IRS and taxpayer agree to alternative timing for all or some of the items arising during, or prior to and during, the tax years before the Appeals Office or a federal court. The taxpayer's method of accounting for items not attributable to years covered by the resolution are not affected and continue to be handled in accordance with the taxpayer's present method of accounting (Section 6.02(3) of Rev. Proc. 2012-18).

EXAMPLE

An examining agent determines that a taxpayer is improperly deducting inventory costs that should be capitalized. The agent is examining the taxpayer's 2011 and 2012 tax years. An appeals officer or government counsel may agree that the taxpayer will capitalize inventoriable costs incurred during 2011 and 2012 that were deducted under the taxpayer's method of accounting. Inventoriable costs incurred in tax years prior to 2011 and subsequent to 2012 are not affected by the resolution and, thus, consistent with the taxpayer's method of accounting may continue to be deducted.

Time value of money resolution. An appeals officer or government counsel may agree to allow the taxpayer to pay the government an amount that represents the *time value of money benefit* the taxpayer derived from using an improper method of accounting for the tax years before appeals or the court reduced by an appropriate factor that reflects the hazards of litigation.

The payment may not be deducted or capitalized. However, the computation may take into account the effect of a hypothetical tax deduction when appropriate and the taxpayer's actual tax rates and tax attributes. The IRS is not allowed to make a payment to the taxpayer under this provision when the time value computation results in a negative amount (Section 6.02(4), of Rev. Proc. 2002-18).

STUDY QUESTION

6. An examining agent may defer an involuntary change to a tax year later than the earliest open one under examination for all of the following reasons ***except:***

a. The Code Sec. 481(a) adjustment cannot be determined or estimated in the year in which the change would be imposed
b. The existing method of accounting has no material effect in the year in which the change would be imposed
c. To reflect the hazards of litigation
d. Expiration of the statute of limitations for tax years after the change would have been imposed

CONCLUSION

The advantages of a voluntary accounting method change over an IRS-imposed change are significant and include audit protection (i.e., no imposition of interest and penalties for prior years), an extended four-year Code Sec. 481(a) adjustment period for unfavorable adjustments, and the opportunity to choose the best permissible accounting method in lieu of an IRS-imposed method. A taxpayer may, of course, also use the voluntary procedures to change from one permissible method to a better permissible method. In either event, the taxpayer will need to determine whether the advance or automatic consent procedure should be used and whether any of the scope limitations applies. Finally, the taxpayer will need to pay strict adherence to all procedural requirements to ensure that the change is effective.

MODULE 2: TIMING RULES: CAPITALIZATION AND INCOME DEFERRAL — CHAPTER 4

Income Tax-Deferral Techniques

For as long as there has been an income tax, taxpayers have sought ways in which to defer payment of that tax. The reason is simple. By deferring payment, taxpayers are able to retain possession of their money for longer periods of time; and, the longer taxpayers can keep their money, the more opportunities they will have to put that money to work for them. In addition, effective tax deferral can allow taxpayers to access their funds at a later time, ideally a time in which they are in a lower tax bracket, and thus, garner a tax savings in real terms. Tax-deferral strategies run the gamut, from the simple to the very complex. Some are favored by the government and represent a policy decision; others are frowned upon. Still others are illegal.

LEARNING OBJECTIVES

Upon completion of this chapter, you will be able to:

- Articulate the difference between tax deferral as an accounting concept and on a cash basis;
- Understand the asset/liability method of accounting;
- Discuss taxable and deductible temporary differences and understand their significance;
- Understand the nature and requirements of individual retirement arrangements;
- Articulate the character and importance of employer-sponsored retirement plans;
- Differentiate such plans from nonqualified retirement plans;
- Relate the tax benefits available through the use of incentive stock options;
- Describe the special tax treatment accorded permanent life insurance and annuities;
- Identify like-kind exchanges and discuss their requirements; and
- Articulate the current tax status of variable prepaid forward contracts and potential workarounds.

INTRODUCTION

It bears mention initially that two different types of tax deferral exist. In the first, available only to business, taxes are deferred as a result of differences in accounting methods. The second involves tax deferral in terms of cash flow. This chapter examines some of the more common tax-deferral strategies in both areas. In the former, tax deferral can occur as a result of temporary differences that arise between financial accounting on the one hand and income tax accounting on the other. Among other features, installment sales, certain treatment of inventory and, in particular, depreciation can all create beneficial temporary differences. Cash flow tax deferral available to individuals, meanwhile, can involve the use of certain types of retirement accounts, real estate transactions, and a variety of investment options.

TAX DEFERRAL IN ACCOUNTING TERMS

Companies are allowed under the law to keep their books in two divergent ways. Entities can employ standard *financial accounting* practices in their bookkeeping and the creation of financial statements, which are often public. These standards are created by the Financial Accounting Standards Board (FASB), a private organization charged with the responsibility for establishing financial accounting and reporting standards in the United States. At the same time, entities may also use a separate set of accounting standards for purposes of figuring and remitting income tax. This second set of standards, known as *income tax accounting,* is borne of much messier political processes and generally incorporates broader public policy concerns.

U.S. GAAP

It should not be surprising, then, that, although the generally accepted accounting principles (GAAP) created by the FASB are intended to ensure uniformity of companies' financial statements and accounting methods, similar activities may be treated very differently for tax purposes. Indeed, it is not only possible, but often probable, for a company's financial reports to differ, sometimes substantially, from the tax returns prepared for the IRS.

Lest one think the result is chaos, various income tax provisions and Schedule M-1 of Form 1120, *Corporation Income Tax Return,* span the gap between financial accounting and income tax accounting. Although a complete exposition of the nuances of these differences is beyond the scope of this chapter, a brief over should prove elucidating.

The Asset/Liability Method

Essentially, accounting for income taxes seeks to recognize:

- The amount of taxes payable or refundable for the current year; and
- Deferred tax liabilities and assets for the future tax consequences of events that have been recognized in an entity's financial statements or on its tax returns.

Principles of tax accounting. To accomplish these goals, the following basic principles are applied in accounting for income taxes at the date of the financial statements:

- A *current* tax liability or asset is recognized for the estimated taxes payable or refundable on tax returns for the current year;
- A *deferred* tax liability or asset is recognized for the estimated future tax effects attributable to temporary differences and carryforwards;
- The measurement of current and deferred tax liabilities and assets is based on provisions of the enacted tax law. The effects of future changes in tax laws or rates are not anticipated; and
- The measurement of deferred tax assets is reduced, if necessary, by the amount of any tax benefits that, based on available evidence, are not expected to be realized.

CAUTION

Exceptions to these four basic principles, including ones for investments in foreign subsidiaries and the amortization of goodwill, exist.

Taxable and deductible temporary differences. The difference between the carrying amount of an asset or liability on the balance sheet and its tax base is referred to as a *temporary difference.* An important distinction in applying the procedures required to account for income taxes by the asset/liability method is the difference between taxable and deductible temporary differences:

- A *taxable temporary difference* is one that will result in the payment of income taxes in the future when the temporary difference reverses; and
- A *deductible temporary difference* is one that will result in reduced income taxes in future years when the temporary difference reverses.

Taxable temporary differences give rise to deferred tax liabilities; deductible temporary differences give rise to deferred tax assets. The table below further illustrates this important difference between taxable and deductible temporary differences.

The expanded definition of *temporary differences* includes some items that do not appear in the company's balance sheet. For example, a company may expense organization costs when they are incurred but recognize them as a tax deduction in a later year. Between the two events, no balance-sheet item exists for this type of temporary difference.

When a company has a *net* deferred tax asset, it will pay more tax now than in the future on the accounts that create the net deferred tax asset.

This is because the company is precluded from recognizing current tax deductions or it is recognizing more in taxable income in the current year than in the future with respect to the sum of the accounts that compose the net deferred tax asset. On the other hand, if the company has a net deferred tax liability, it is paying less tax now than it would in the future if these items were treated the same as for book purposes. Thus, the effect of a deferred tax liability is a deferral in paying taxes. With adequate planning, particularly through the use of depreciation, the results can be a significant deferral of tax.

COMMENT

A valuation allowance is recognized if, based on the weight of available evidence, it is *more likely than not* that some portion or all of the deferred tax asset will not be realized.

NOTE

Developing a system for identifying and tracking the amounts of all temporary differences and carryforwards is an important implementation issue. In theory, differences should be identified by comparing items and amounts in the entity's balance sheets for accounting purposes and for tax purposes. Many companies do not maintain tax-basis balance sheets, though this may be the most logical way to identify and track temporary differences in relatively complex situations.

The following major categories of temporary differences refer to events that result in divergences between the tax bases of assets and liabilities and their reported amounts in the financial statements:

- Revenues or gains that are taxable after they are recognized in accounting income, for example, receivables from installment sales;
- Expenses or losses that are deductible for tax purposes after they are recognized in accounting income, such as a product warranty liability;
- Revenues or gains that are taxable before they are recognized in accounting income, including subscriptions received in advance; and
- Expenses or losses that are deductible for tax purposes before they are recognized in accounting income, including depreciation expense.

Other less common examples of temporary differences are:

- Investment tax credits accounted for by the deferred method.
- Business combinations accounted for by the acquisition method.

Table 1. Taxable and Deductible Temporary Differences

Nature of Temporary Difference	Explanation	Deferred Tax
Taxable Temporary Differences		
Depreciable assets	Use of modified accelerated cost recovery system (MACRS) for tax purposes and straight-line for accounting purposes makes the tax basis of the asset less than the accounting basis	Liability, to be paid as MACRS deduction becomes less than straight-line depreciation
Installment sale receivable	Sales recognized for accounting purposes at transaction date and deferred for tax purposes until collection, resulting in a difference between the tax and accounting basis of the installment receivable	Liability, to be paid when the sale is recognized for tax purposes
Deductible Temporary Differences		
Warranty liability	Expense recognized on accrual basis for accounting purposes and on cash basis for tax purposes, resulting in a liability that is recognized for financial reporting purposes but has a zero basis for tax purposes	Asset, to be recovered when deduction is recognized for tax purposes
Accounts receivable/ allowance for doubtful accounts	Expense recognized on an accrual basis for accounting purposes and deferred for tax purposes	Asset, to be recovered when uncollectible account is written off for tax purposes

COMMENT

Certain differences between the tax basis and the accounting basis of assets and liabilities will not result in taxable or deductible amounts in future years, and no deferred tax asset or liability should be recognized. These differences are often referred to as *permanent differences,* although that term is not used in the tax code.

Installment sales. Installment sales of personal or real property by non-accrual method nondealers are reported using the installment method unless taxpayer elects out. An *installment sale* is a sale or disposition of property in which at least one payment is received after the close of the tax year in which the disposition occurs. The installment method generally permits the reporting of payments in the year of receipt in same proportion that the gross profit on sale bears to the contract price. In other words, the amount of the gain that must be reported as income in a particular year is the percentage of the payments received in that year that is the same percentage of the total contract price that represents the total gain on the sale.

STUDY QUESTION

1. A deferred tax liability results in:

   a. Higher accrued taxes due
   b. Avoiding use of the asset/liability method
   c. A deferral in paying taxes
   d. A deferral in recognizing net tax assets

TAX-DEFERRED INDIVIDUAL RETIREMENT ARRANGEMENTS

Individual retirement accounts represent a very common tax-deferral technique and are available to a majority of individual taxpayers.

There are four kinds of *individual retirement arrangements* (IRAs):

- Traditional individual retirement accounts;
- Individual retirement annuities;
- Individual retirement bonds; and
- Roth IRAs.

Individual retirement accounts and individual retirement annuities are collectively referred to as *traditional IRAs.* Both types provide an opportunity to defer taxation.

COMMENT

Individual retirement bonds are still outstanding, but none are currently being issued and the governing statute has been repealed.

Most IRAs are established by individuals, but, as discussed below, they can also be established by employers and by employee associations. The accounts must be administered by a trustee, and the assets generally can not be commingled.

Until the year in which they turn 70½, individuals can contribute annually up to the lesser of their compensation or an applicable dollar limit. For 2013, the maximum that a taxpayer can contribute to all of his or her traditional and Roth IRAs is the smaller of:

- $5,500, plus an additional "catch-up contribution" of $1,000 for those age 50 or older; or
- The individual's taxable compensation for the year.

The maximum contribution amount is indexed for inflation.

COMMENT

Contributions to Roth IRAs are never deductible, though any gains in a Roth IRA will be tax-free.

CAUTION

The deduction for traditional IRAs is phased out as income increases for individuals who are active participants in a qualified retirement plan.

COMMENT

Taxpayers unable to deduct their contributions to a traditional IRA because they are active participants in a qualified plan and are above the AGI limit may contribute to a nondeductible traditional IRA, which will provide tax-deferred growth, but not current deductibility of contributions.

Deductible contributions may be made to a spouse's IRA, even if the spouse has no compensation for the year. Individuals can also make *nondeductible* contributions to traditional IRAs.

Traditional Deductible Individual Retirement Accounts

One of the most common investment vehicles available to most Americans, traditional IRAs offer tax-deferred growth potential, in addition to deductibility of all or part of their contributions from pretax income, so long as certain conditions are met. Individuals who are under age 70½ throughout the tax year and that receive compensation that is includible in gross income, including alimony, are entitled to make contributions to traditional IRAs. Amounts earned in a traditional IRA are not taxed until distributions are made.

CAUTION

Contributions that exceed the annual limit on contributions are subject to an excise tax, although this tax can be avoided by a timely withdrawal of the excess contributions.

Roth IRAs

An individual may be able to contribute to a Roth IRA if his or her AGI does not exceed the annual limit. Taxpayers who have reached age 70½, and can no longer contribute to a traditional IRA, but have earned income, may still contribute to a Roth IRA. Contributions to Roth IRAs are phased out for taxpayers whose AGIs exceed certain limits. Taxpayers unable to contribute to a Roth IRA because of their AGI may still be able to contribute to a traditional IRA. Rollover contributions may be made to Roth IRAs from other Roth IRAs. Rollovers from traditional IRAs and other types of retirement plans are subject to tax at the time of transfer.

CAUTION

IRAs are subject to restrictions on withdrawals and early distributions are subject to a penalty tax.

Required minimum distributions (RMDs) from traditional IRAs must be made after the IRA owner reaches the age of 70½, with an excise tax being imposed on excess accumulations caused by a failure to take these required distributions. RMD features of the traditional deductible or nondeductible IRA differentiate it from terms of the Roth IRA, from which the contributor need never take a distribution.

Distributions from traditional IRAs are subject to the general rules governing the taxation of distributions from retirement plans, subject to certain modifications.

IRAs may receive rollover distributions from other retirement arrangements. IRA distributions also can be rolled over into another IRA, and in some situations, into an employer's retirement plan.

Inherited IRAs

An *inherited IRA* is one which the individual for whose benefit the account is maintained acquired the account by reason of the death of another individual. Specific distribution rules apply to inherited IRAs.

STUDY QUESTION

2. When an IRA owner reaches age 70½, he or she must do all of the following ***except:***

- **a.** Stop contributing to a traditional IRA, even if still earning income
- **b.** Begin to take required minimum distributions from a traditional IRA
- **c.** Pay income tax on distributions of contributions and earnings from a traditional deductible IRA
- **d.** Begin to take distributions from a Roth IRA

EMPLOYER-SPONSORED QUALIFIED TAX-DEFERRED RETIREMENT ACCOUNTS

Another very common method of achieving tax deferral is via an employer-sponsored tax-deferred retirement account. Though labyrinthine in appearance, these accounts are really quite simple in operation. Employers choosing to provide retirement benefits for employees in this manner may establish a pension, profit-sharing, or stock bonus plan, all of which qualify for certain tax benefits, such as:

- Tax deferral for the employee on the employer's contributions and earnings;
- A tax exemption for the trust that is established to provide benefits; and
- A current deduction by the employer for contributions made to the trust.

The Two Types of Qualified Retirement Plans

Generally, two broad categories of qualified retirement plans exist: defined benefit plans and defined contribution plans. Traditionally, employer-sponsored retirement benefits were provided under guaranteed benefits plans, known generally as *defined benefit pension plans.* Under these plans, workers were assured of receiving a set dollar amount or fixed percentage of earnings at retirement. As the plans became more and more costly, however, defined contribution plans became the dominant employer-sponsored plan type. As noted, contributions under plans of this type are tax-deferred, that is to say, deducted from employees' paychecks on a pretax basis and later taxed (along with earnings on the investment) to the employee upon withdrawal, often when the taxpayer is in a lower tax bracket. Moreover, any earnings realized from the investments in these accounts, including interest, dividends or capital gains, are also tax-deferred.

Defined benefit plans include pension and annuity plans that offer a specific retirement benefit to employees, usually in the form of a monthly retirement pension that is based on the employee's wages and years of service with the employer. An employer's annual contributions to the plan are based on actuarial assumptions and are not allocated to individual accounts maintained for the employees.

Defined contribution plans, on the other hand, include profit-sharing, stock bonus, and money purchase plans in which a separate account is provided for each employee covered by the plan and the employee's retirement benefit is based on the contributions to the account, as well as any income, expenses, gains, losses, and forfeitures of other accounts that may be allocated to the account.

A brief overview of these plans follows.

Defined Benefit Plans

Traditional pension. Traditional pension plans promise a certain benefit to employees at retirement. Contributions are determined based on the funding needs of the plan to enable it to deliver these benefits.

CAUTION

The annual benefit paid to any employee may not exceed the lesser of ($205,000 in 2013), or 100 percent of the participant's average compensation for his or her highest three income years.

Cash balance plan hybrid. Though, in a legal sense, a *cash balance plan* is a defined benefit plan, in operation, it is really a hybrid of both types of plans. This because instead of defining an employee's accrued benefit as a stream of payments based on years of service and final salary, a cash balance plan defines an employee's accrued benefit as an account balance that annually accumulates pay credits based on the employee's current annual salary and interest credits on the previous year's balance, similar in operation to a defined contribution plan.

COMMENT

One particularly attractive feature of cash balance plans is the amount of contributions allowed, which significantly exceed the 401(k) maximum. Indeed, up to $51,000 ($56,500 in 2013 with catch-up) may be contributed.

Keogh plan. *Keogh plans* operate much like a traditional pension except, notably, they are self-funded, often by high-income self-employed individuals, so they serve as both a defined benefit and defined contribution plan.

CAUTION

Although Keogh plans were quite popular, a change in the tax law in 2011 significantly reduced their attractiveness as a savings and tax-deferral vehicle. They have largely been replaced by SEP IRAs.

Defined Contribution Plans

Payroll deduction IRA. Under a payroll deduction IRA, employees establish an IRA with a financial institution and authorize a payroll deduction amount for it. A business of any size, even self-employed individuals, can establish a payroll deduction IRA program.

SEP plan. A *simplified employee pension* (SEP) plan provides business owners with a simplified method to contribute toward their employees' retirement, as well as their own retirement savings. Contributions are made to an individual retirement account or annuity (IRA) set up for each plan participant (a SEP-IRA). Distributions are governed by the same rules applicable to traditional IRAs and employer contributions represent deferred income to the employee. Noteworthy, however, is the feature that contributions may be made to participants older than age 70½, although participants at that age must take required minimum distributions. Employers using a fiscal tax year have until their annual income tax filing date to make contributions for that year (i.e., the deadline differs from regular IRA contribution deadlines of April 15 for the previous tax year).

COMMENT

A SEP-IRA account is a traditional IRA that follows the same investment, distribution, and rollover rules as traditional IRAs. However, employer contributions to the plans have a maximum of 25 percent of an employee's wages or $51,000 for 2013.

SARSEP plan. A *salary reduction simplified employee pension* (SARSEP) plan is a SEP plan that was established before 1997 and permits employee salary reduction contributions and meets certain participation requirements. Although new accounts are now prohibited, employers can continue to make contributions to SARSEPs that existed before 1997. Under these grandfathered SARSEP plans, employers may contribute the lesser of 25 percent of an employee's compensation or $17,500 (for 2013), subject to annual cost of living adjustments.

CAUTION

Employers using model *SARSEP* plans that hope to avail themselves of the latest *law changes* must adopt the latest model Form 5305A-SEP.

SIMPLE IRA. A savings incentive match plan for employees plan provides employees and employers the ability to contribute to traditional IRAs set up for employees. It is ideally suited as a start-up retirement savings plan for small employers not currently sponsoring a retirement plan.

The employer is required to contribute each year either a:

- Matching contribution up to 3 percent of compensation; or
- 2 percent nonelective contribution for each eligible employee.

Maximum salary reduction contributions increased to $12,000 for 2013, with a catch-up contribution limit for SIMPLE IRA plans for 2013 of $2,500.

401(k) plan. A 401(k) plan comprises several varieties:

- Qualified profit-sharing;
- Stock bonus;
- Pre-ERISA money purchase pension; or
- Rural cooperative plan.

Using a 401(k), an employee can elect to have the employer contribute a portion of the employee's cash wages, on a pretax basis, to the plan. These deferred wages are not subject to federal income tax withholding at the time of deferral and are not reflected as taxable income on the employee's Form 1040, *U.S. Individual Income Tax Return.* Gains also accumulate in the account in a deferred manner until distribution.

With a *traditional 401(k) plan,* eligible employees to make elective, pretax deferrals of income via payroll deductions. In a traditional 401(k) plan, moreover, employers may make contributions on behalf of all participants, make matching contributions based on employees' elective deferrals, or both.

COMMENT

Employer contributions are often subject to a vesting schedule that provides an employee's right to employer contributions becomes nonforfeitable only after a period of time, or be immediately vested.

CAUTION

Rules relating to traditional 401(k) plans require that contributions made under the plan meet specific nondiscrimination requirements. In order to ensure that the plan satisfies these requirements, the employer must perform annual tests, known as the actual deferral percentage (ADP) and actual contribution percentage (ACP) tests, to verify that deferred wages and employer matching contributions do not discriminate in favor of highly compensated employees.

A *safe harbor 401(k) plan* is similar to a traditional 401(k) plan, but, among other differences, it must provide for employer contributions that are fully vested when made. These contributions may be made via employer matching contributions, limited to employees who defer, or employer contributions made on behalf of all eligible employees, regardless of whether employees make elective deferrals.

COMMENT

Safe harbor 401(k) plans are not subject to the complex annual nondiscrimination tests applicable to traditional 401(k) plans.

COMMENT

Safe harbor 401(k) plans that do not provide any additional contributions in a year are exempted from the top-heavy rules of Code Sec. 416.

CAUTION

Employers sponsoring safe harbor 401(k) plans must satisfy certain notice requirements. These requirements are satisfied if each eligible employee for the plan year is given written notice of his or her rights and obligations under the plan, and certain content and timing requirements are met. To satisfy the content requirement, the notice must describe the safe harbor method in use, how eligible employees make elections, any other plans involved, etc. The notice must be provided within a reasonable period before each plan year.

Both the traditional and safe harbor plans are for employers of any size and can be combined with other retirement plans.

The *SIMPLE 401(k) plan* was created so small businesses would have an effective, cost-efficient way to offer retirement benefits to their employees. These plans are not subject to the annual nondiscrimination tests that apply to traditional 401(k) plans. As with a safe harbor 401(k) plan, the employer is required to make employer contributions that are fully vested. This type of 401(k) plan is available to employers with 100 or fewer employees who received at least $5,000 in compensation from the employer for the preceding calendar year. Employees who are eligible to participate in a SIMPLE 401(k) plan may not receive any contributions or benefit accruals under any other plans of the employer.

CAUTION

A 401(k) plan cannot require, as a condition of participation, that an employee complete more than one year of service.

The IRS sets the maximum contribution amount each year after indexing for inflation. For the 2013 tax year, individuals can contribute up to $17,500 as an elective deferral to their employer's 401(k) plan. In addition, individuals age 50 or older can make an additional catch-up contribution of $5,500.

Contributions to a profit-sharing plan are discretionary. There is no set amount that an employer need make. If contributions are made, however, they must be made in accord with a set formula for determining how the contributions are divided. This money goes into a separate account for each employee.

COMMENT

One common method for determining each participant's allocation in a profit-sharing plan is the "comp-to comp" method. Under this method, the employer calculates the sum of all of its employees' compensation (the "total comp"). To determine each employee's allocation of the employer's contribution, the employee's compensation ("employee comp") is divided by the total comp. Then each employee's fraction is multiplied by the amount of the employer contribution to find each employee's share of the employer contribution.

COMMENT

The lesser of 25 percent of compensation or an inflation indexed amount of $51,000 for 2013, may be contributed to a profit-sharing plan.

A *Roth 401(k) plan* may permit an employee who makes elective contributions under a qualified cash or deferred arrangement to designate some or all of those contributions as designated Roth contributions. Designated Roth contributions are elective contributions under a qualified cash or deferred arrangement that, unlike pretax elective contributions, are currently includible in gross income. However, a qualified distribution of designated Roth contributions is excludable from gross income.

Money purchase plan. *Money purchase plans* differ from profit-sharing plans in that the former requires that contributions be made by the employer. Employers are thus required to make a contribution, on behalf of the plan participants, to the plan each year. The money purchase plan states the required contribution percentage. A maximum of the lesser of 25 percent of compensation or an inflation indexed amount of $51,000 in 2013, may be contributed annually.

EXAMPLE

Edgy Employer has a money purchase plan with a required contribution of 5 percent of each eligible employee's pay. As the employer, Edgy must contribute 5 percent of each eligible employee's pay to his or her separate account each plan year. A participant's benefit is based on the amount of contributions to their account and the gains or losses associated with the account at the time of retirement.

COMMENT

In years past, money purchase plans had higher deductible limits than profit-sharing plans. This is no longer the case.

Target benefit plan. As the name would suggest, *target benefit plans* are designed to pay a targeted payment at retirement. They are funded by annual contributions. Indeed, an employer *must* contribute the required contribution amount on time or face paying penalties to the IRS.

CAUTION

Proposed regulations threaten to make target benefit plans, which have never been popular, virtually obsolete.

403(b) tax-sheltered annuity plan. A *403(b) tax-sheltered annuity* (TSA) plan is a retirement plan very similar to a 401(k) plan, offered by public schools and certain 501(c)(3) tax-exempt organizations. An individual may only obtain a 403(b) annuity under an employer's TSA plan.

COMMENT

The basic limit on elective deferrals is $17,500 in 2013 (adjusted for inflation) or 100 percent of the employee's compensation, whichever is less. The elective deferral limit for SIMPLE plans is 100 percent of compensation or $12,000 in 2013, subject to future cost-of-living increases.

STUDY QUESTION

3. All of the following are ways SEP-IRAs differ from other traditional IRA types ***except:***

a. Employer contributions may total 25 percent of employee salary or $51,000 for 2013
b. Contributions may be made up to the employer's income tax return filing date
c. Distributions from SEP-IRAs are not subject to federal income tax
d. Contributions may be made after an employee reaches age 70½

NONQUALIFIED DEFERRED COMPENSATION

To be distinguished from deferred compensation, and income taxation, through the use of a qualified retirement plan, the term, *nonqualified deferred compensation plans*, governed by Code Sec. 409A, refers to compensation that workers earn in one year, but that is paid in a future year. Nonqualified deferred compensation arrangements defer payment of salary, bonuses, incentive compensation, or supplemental retirement benefits. Significantly for purposes of this chapter, moreover, an employee's income tax on payment is also deferred. Employers deduct the deferred payment when the employee is taxed on it.

Prior to 2008, deferred compensation arrangements gained great popularity, particularly among executives who used these arrangements to defer current taxation of substantial amounts of income. Believing that certain nonqualified deferred compensation arrangements had been developed that allowed the improper deferral of income, however, Congress enacted legislation to curb the abuse. In so doing, however, Congress provided a roadmap to use of these arrangements by delineating specific rules for determining whether deferral of income should be permitted.

COMMENT

Compensation can be deferred under a plan or through individualized arrangements. Nonqualified deferred compensation arrangements provide employees and independent contractors with a method of deferring income tax by postponing the receipt of compensation. They may also be used to provide employees with additional retirement benefits or incentive compensation.

In general, the determination of when amounts deferred under a nonqualified deferred compensation arrangement are includible in the gross income of the individual will depend on the facts and circumstances of the arrangement. Myriad tax principles and tax code provisions may be relevant in making this determination, including the doctrine of constructive receipt, the economic benefit doctrine, the provisions of Code Sec. 83 relating generally to transfers of property in connection with the performance of services, and, in certain circumstances, provisions relating specifically to nonexempt employee trusts and nonqualified annuities.

Inclusion in Income

Generally, however, timing income inclusion of nonqualified deferred compensation revolves around whether the arrangement is unfunded or funded. If the arrangement is funded, the income will be includible in the year in which the individual's rights are transferable, or not subject to a substantial risk of forfeiture. If, on the other hand, the arrangement is unfunded, the compensation will generally be includible in income when it is actually or constructively received, that is, deferred. In general, an arrangement will be considered funded if there has been a transfer of property as determined under the rules of Code Sec. 83. Under that section, a transfer of property occurs when a person acquires a beneficial ownership interest in such property.

COMMENT

Property is defined very broadly for purposes of Code Sec. 83. Property includes real and personal property other than money or an unfunded and unsecured promise to pay money in the future. Property also includes a beneficial interest in assets, including money, that are transferred or set aside from claims of the creditors of the transferor, for example, in a trust or escrow account.

EXAMPLE

If, in connection with the performance of services, vested contributions are made to a trust on Vice-President Anita Durbin's behalf and the trust assets may be used solely to provide future payments to her, the payment of her employer's contributions to the trust constitutes a transfer of property to Anita that is currently taxable under Code Sec. 83.

On the other hand, deferred amounts are generally not includible in current income if nonqualified deferred compensation is payable from general corporate funds that are subject to the claims of general creditors; such amounts are treated as unfunded and unsecured promises to pay money or property in the future.

As discussed above, if the arrangement is unfunded, the compensation will be generally includible in the employee's income when it is actually, or constructively, received, that is, when it is credited to an individual's account, set apart, or otherwise made available so that it may be drawn on at any time.

COMMENT

Income is not constructively received if the taxpayer's control of its receipt is subject to substantial limitations or restrictions. A requirement to relinquish a valuable right in order to make withdrawals is generally treated as a substantial limitation or restriction.

COMMENT

Executives often use arrangements that allow deferral of income, but also provide security of future payment and control over amounts deferred.

CAUTION

Nonqualified plans need not meet discrimination or other rules applicable to qualified plans, though they must meet certain election, distribution, funding, and certain other requirements.

INCENTIVE STOCK OPTIONS

An *incentive stock option* (ISO) is an option granted to an employee under a plan that meets the requirements of Code Sec. 422. These options bring very favorable tax consequences to employees. Under an incentive stock option plan, a corporation awards an employee the right or option to purchase company stock in the future at a fixed price at least equal to the market value on the award date. The primary purpose for granting ISOs is the favorable tax treatment accorded them under the tax code. Specifically, neither the grant nor the exercise of an ISO award results in tax consequences to the company or the employee/optionee. This deferral of tax consequences occurs even though the optionee exercised the option at a price that is significantly less than the market value of the stock at the time of exercise. The employee recognizes taxable income only at the time of the sale of the stock acquired through the option and then at the long-term capital gains rate, subject to compliance with certain minimum holding period requirements.

However, to qualify for this favorable tax treatment, the ISO must meet the following requirements:

- Holding period—the employee must hold the option
  - For two years from date of grant, and
  - One year from date of share transfer;
- Employment period—the employee must be employed
  - At the time of option, and
  - Throughout three months before exercise, or one year if the person is disabled;
- Plan requirements—the plan must
  - State the maximum aggregate number of shares that will be issued pursuant to options,
  - State those employees or class of employees eligible, and
  - Obtain shareholder approval within 12 months before or after plan is adopted;
- Option requirements—the options must
  - Be made within 10 years from earlier of plan adoption or approval,
  - Be exercisable no later than 10 years from date of grant, or 5 years if made to individual already holding more than 10 percent of combined voting power,
  - Be exercisable at no less than fair market value at time of grant or 110 percent of fair market value if made to individual already holding more than 10 percent of combined voting power,
  - Not be transferable, except by will or the laws of descent and distribution,
  - Not exceed $100,000 in aggregate value of the stock options that are exercisable, and

- If these conditions are satisfied, the option will not fail to be an ISO merely because
  - It provides for cashless exercise,
  - The optionee has the right to receive additional compensation, in cash or in property, when the option is exercised, provided such additional compensation is includible in income, or
  - The option is subject to a condition, or grants a right, that is not inconsistent with the ISO regulations;
- Gain or loss from the sale of the stock received in an ISO will be capital in nature, if:
  - The taxpayer does not dispose of the stock for at least two years from the date on which the option is granted, and
  - The stock is held for at least one year after the option is exercised.

COMMENT

The amount of gain or loss is the difference between the amount the employee paid for the stock—that is, the option price—and the amount the employee received when he or she sold the stock.

CAUTION

If the employee sells the stock before the required holding period ends, gain on the sale is ordinary income equal to the fair market value of the stock when the option was exercised, less the exercise price. Any excess gain is capital gain, and any loss is a capital loss. The gain is recognized for the tax year in which the sale occurs and any gain from a disqualifying disposition is excluded from wages for FICA and FUTA tax purposes and is not subject to income tax withholding.

Basis of an ISO

An employee's basis in an ISO is the amount that the employee paid for the option. If the employee did not pay for the option and the option lapses, the employee does not have a deductible loss because he or she does not have basis in the option. An employee's basis in stock purchased through an ISO is the amount he or she paid for the stock when the option was exercised (plus any amount he or she paid for the option).

Annual Dollar Limit

As noted, the maximum value of stock with respect to which ISOs may first become exercisable in any one year is $100,000. Stock is valued when the option is granted. Options are ordered in the order in which they are granted, and options issued under ISO plans of any parent, subsidiaries, or predecessor corporations are taken into account.

CAUTION

The favorable tax treatment of ISOs does not apply for purposes of the alternative minimum tax (AMT). Instead, the excess of the fair market value of the stock received upon the exercise of the option, over the amount paid for the stock, plus any amount paid for the ISO, must generally be recognized as an AMT adjustment. Consequently, individuals who have exercised ISOs to purchase stock with a high fair market value that declined before they could sell will be left with large AMT liabilities and no cash proceeds to pay them.

STUDY QUESTION

4. Tax consequences of an ISO award are:

a. Tax paid on the stock's market value by the employer when the ISO is granted
b. Tax paid on the market value of stock when the employee receives the option
c. Tax paid on income realized when selling the stock acquired through the option
d. Capital loss claimed for a lapsed option for which the employee has no adjusted basis

PERMANENT LIFE INSURANCE POLICIES AS A TAX-DEFERRAL TECHNIQUE

In essence, there are two types of life insurance:

- Term life insurance; and
- Cash value, also called permanent, life insurance.

Term life, consisting of life insurance coverage for a particular period of time in exchange for the payment of a specific premium, is the most basic type of life insurance. All life insurance policies contain at least a term component. *Cash value policies,* on the other hand, also include an investment component. These policies, which include whole life and universal life among others, are generally designed to provide long-term life insurance coverage, usually for the insured individual's entire life.

The premium paid on any permanent (or cash value) life insurance policy can be divided into three components:

- A pure insurance component;
- A loading component; and
- An investment or savings component.

During any period, the pure insurance component of a policy serves to redistribute funds from policyholders who pay for insurance protection to the beneficiaries of policyholders who pass during that time period. The loading component covers the insurance company's expenses and provides the insurer's profit. The investment component of a policy arises from the fact that the company can invest the funds paid by the policyholders between the time the funds are received by the company and the time they are paid out to beneficiaries. The insurance company, in turn, credits fixed or variable amounts to the cash value of the policy, thus increasing that cash value and providing a return to the policy holder on her investment in the policy. This element is referred to as the *inside build-up.*

Substantial tax advantages are bestowed upon products meeting the definition of life insurance under the tax code and applicable state law. For example, the cash value buildup inside the policy will be tax-deferred, and, accordingly, accumulate more rapidly than a taxable investment. In addition, no income tax will generally be owed when a policyholder borrows against the cash value of the policy. Policy dividends are also generally treated as tax-free returns of capital. Policies can be exchanged tax-free. And perhaps most importantly, death benefits are income tax-free to beneficiaries unless the policy has been transferred for value.

A policy will meet the definition of *life insurance* for income tax purposes, and thus benefit from preferred income tax treatment, if it is defined as a life insurance contract under state law and satisfies one of two alternative tests:

- A cash value accumulation test; or
- A test consisting of a guideline premium requirement and a cash value corridor requirement.

Cash Value Accumulation Test

Under the cash value accumulation test, the cash surrender value of the contract by the terms of the contract cannot exceed the *net single premium* that would have to be paid at such time to fund *future benefits* under the contract at any time. The overall purpose of the cash value accumulation test is to exclude contracts with an innate investment orientation, such as endowment contracts, from treatment as life insurance contracts.

Guideline Premium Plus Cash Value Corridor Test

The second test for life insurance contract status has two components, a "guideline premium" requirement and a "cash value corridor" requirement, both of which must be satisfied if the contract is to qualify. The *guideline premium* requirement essentially distinguishes between contracts under which the policyholder makes traditional levels of investment through premiums, and those involving larger investments, whereas the *cash value corridor* requirement seeks to disqualify contracts that permit excessive amounts of cash value to build up in regard to the life insurance risk.

CAUTION

Whichever test is chosen, that test must be met for the entire life of the contract for the contract to be treated as life insurance for tax purposes

A life insurance contract will not include that portion of any contract that is treated under state law as providing any annuity benefits, other than as a settlement option. Thus, although a life insurance contract may provide by rider for annuity benefits, the annuity portion of the contract will not be part of the life insurance contract for tax purposes, and the annuity benefits may not be reflected in computing the guideline premiums.

EXAMPLE

Irving Insurance-Beyer is considering the purchase of an insurance arrangement written as a combination of term life insurance with an annuity contract, or with a premium deposit fund. These arrangements will not be deemed a life insurance contract for purposes of the guidelines because all of the elements of the contract are not treated under state law as providing a single integrated death benefit. As a result, only the term portion of any such contract can meet the tests and be treated as life insurance proceeds upon Irving's death.

On the other hand, any life insurance contract treated under state law as a single, integrated life insurance contract that satisfies these guidelines will be treated as a single contract of life insurance for federal tax purposes and not as a contract that provides separate life insurance and annuity benefits.

EXAMPLE

If, instead of the arrangements described in the previous example, Irving purchases a whole life insurance contract that provides for the purchase of paid-up or deferred additions, this arrangement will be treated as a single life insurance contract.

In the case of variable life insurance contracts, the determination whether the contract meets the cash value accumulation test or the guideline premium requirements, and falls within the cash value corridor shall be made whenever the amount of the death benefits under the contract changes, but not less frequently than once during each 12-month period. In addition, if a contract is evaluated yearly to ascertain whether it satisfies the requirements, the determination must be made at the same time each year.

CAUTION

According to the IRS, the tax-deferral element of life insurance and annuity contracts is being abused by some taxpayers. One particular perceived abuse that has proliferated in recent years involves the sale of life insurance and annuity contracts that are "wrapped" around other investments. These arrangements seek to defer tax on the investment earnings. As long as holders do not have direct or indirect control over the separate account or any subaccount asset, they will lack sufficient indicia of ownership to be deemed the owners of the assets funding the contracts for tax purposes. Thus, any interest, dividends, or other income derived from those assets should not be includible in the holders' gross income in the year earned, but only if such direct or indirect control does not exist.

Life Insurance Dividends

Dividends paid on life insurance policies generally are not subject to income tax except to the extent that they cumulatively exceed the amount paid in premiums on the policy. The payments are not considered true dividends but rather a return of the policyholder's investment in the contract. This is the case whether the dividends are paid in cash, used to reduce premiums, or used to purchase additional paid-up coverage.

CAUTION

If left with the insurance company to accumulate interest, the interest is taxable. Dividends are taxable, however, if paid after redemption of the policy.

Withdrawals and Loans of Insurance Proceeds

A particularly attractive feature of individually owned life insurance policies is the ability of the insured or owner of the policy to borrow from the insurer against the policy's value at relatively low interest rates without taxation.

COMMENT

Deductibility of interest paid on the loan depends on the purpose for which the loan proceeds are used.

Withdrawals made against the policy, whether by loan or otherwise, are generally not taxable unless and until the insured has fully recaptured his or her investment in the contract. In other words, withdrawals are generally accorded first-in, first-out treatment (FIFO).

For a further discussion of the efficacy of loans as a tax-deferral technique, see the discussion of "variable prepaid forward contracts" below.

Transfers for consideration. If a life insurance policy is transferred for consideration, the amount of death proceeds excludable from the income of the beneficiary generally is limited to the amount paid for the transfer of the policy plus the premiums and other amounts later paid by the transferee.

CAUTION

The transfer-for-value limitation does not apply when:

- The transferee's basis in the policy is determined in whole or in part by reference to the transferor's basis; or
- The policy is transferred to the insured, a partner of the insured, a partnership in which the insured is a partner, or to a corporation in which the insured is a shareholder or officer.

Life settlements. *Life settlements* offer an option for some insured individuals who no longer want or need a life insurance policy. Rather than selling the policy back to the originating insurance company at less than market value, or allowing it to lapse and forfeiting the value, life settlements provide a potentially more gratifying exit strategy for the policy owner.

COMMENT

Although there is a historical connection between the life settlement and the viatical settlement markets, there is a definite distinction between the two concepts. *Viatical settlements* are related to terminally ill insured parties, whereas life settlements involve insureds who are not suffering from any terminal illness or chronic or catastrophic medical conditions.

Insurance, endowment, and annuity policies are "property," so that an exchange of one such policy for another ordinarily is taxable. However, the general rule of taxability does not apply to certain exchanges. Specifically, no gain or loss is recognized on the exchange of:

- A life insurance contract for another life insurance, endowment, annuity, or qualified long-term care insurance contract;
- An endowment contract for another endowment contract that provides for regular payments beginning at a date not later than the date payments would have begun under the contract exchanged;
- An endowment contract for an annuity contract;
- An endowment contract for a qualified long-term care insurance contract;
- An annuity contract for another annuity or qualified long-term care insurance contract; or
- A qualified long-term care insurance contract for another qualified long-term care insurance contract.

CAUTION

Gain realized on the exchange of an endowment contract or annuity contract for a life insurance contract or an exchange of an annuity contract for an endowment contract must be recognized.

STUDY QUESTION

5. The _____ prevents endowment contracts from being treated as life insurance contracts.

a. Savings component
b. Cash value accumulation test
c. Cash value corridor test
d. Loading component

LIKE-KIND EXCHANGES

Under the most basic of basic tax principles, gain or loss realized upon the sale or exchange of property must be recognized for tax purposes unless a specific nonrecognition rule provides otherwise. The like-kind exchange rules are one such provision. These rules generally provide that no gain or loss is recognized, and hence will be tax deferred, when appreciated business or investment property is exchanged solely for other business or investment property of like kind. If the like-kind exchange provisions are satisfied, nonrecognition of gain and loss is mandatory, not elective. Thus, a transferor expecting to realize a loss should not dispose of his or her property in a like-kind exchange. For those seeking to defer taxation of gain, however, the like-kind exchange rules provide an outstanding opportunity.

Nonrecognition is allowed under the like-kind exchange rules only if:

- There is an exchange of property;
- The property transferred and the property received are of like kind;
- The property transferred and the property received are both held for productive use in the transferor's trade or business or for investment;
- The property exchanged is eligible for like-kind exchange treatment; and
- If like-kind properties are not exchanged simultaneously, two timing requirements regarding identification and receipt of the replacement property are satisfied.

Exchange of Property

The tax on realized gain is deferred only if there is a transfer or exchange, as opposed to a sale, of property. Essentially, a *sale* is a transfer of property for a price expressed in money or its equivalent, whereas an *exchange* is the tender of one thing for another. In other words, in a sale, property is transferred in consideration of a definite price expressed in terms of money, whereas in an exchange, property is transferred for property without the intervention of money.

Types of Like-Kind Property

Any tax on realized gain will be deferred only to the extent that property is exchanged for property of like kind. In general, the term *like kind* refers to the nature or character of property, rather than its grade or quality.

EXAMPLE

A used automobile and a new one are like-kind property.

For purposes of determining whether the like-kind requirement is met, property can be divided into three types:

- Depreciable tangible personal property;
- Other personal property; and
- Real property.

Held for Productive Use in the Transferor's Trade or Business or for Investment

The term *held for productive use in a trade or business* is nowhere defined in the tax code or in the regulations. Nevertheless, for purposes of the like-kind exchange rules, the IRS has applied the meaning given to the term *property used in the trade or business* under Code Sec. 1231(b).

COMMENT

The determination of whether property is held for productive use in a trade or business or for investment is made at the time of the exchange.

Eligibility for Like-Kind Exchange Treatment

These six types of property are specifically excluded from, and cannot receive, like-kind exchange treatment:

- Stock in trade or other property held primarily for sale;
- Stocks, bonds, or notes, other than an exchange of stock in certain mutual ditch, reservoir, or irrigation companies completed after May 22, 2008;
- Other securities or evidences of indebtedness or interest;
- Interests in a partnership;
- Certificates of trust or beneficial interests; and
- Choses in action.

CAUTION

U.S. real property and foreign real property are also not like-kind.

The dual timing requirements. The property to be received in the exchange must be *identified* within 45 days of the date the property relinquished in the exchange is transferred. The replacement property must be *received* by the earlier of:

- The 180th day after the date the property given up in the exchange is transferred; or
- The due date, including extensions, for the tax return for the year in which the transfer occurs.

COMMENT

If a transfer involves multiple properties that are transferred at different times, the identification and receipt periods begin on the date of the earliest transfer.

Partially tax-deferred exchanges. If both like-kind and nonlike-kind property are received in an exchange, gain is recognized to the extent of the fair market value of any unlike property or money received.

Nonlike-kind property (boot) may consist of cash, unlike property, and obligations of which the transferor is relieved. In a reciprocal assumption of mortgages or reciprocal transfer of properties subject to mortgages, the amount of debt relief may be offset by the amount of debt assumed.

Multiparty Exchanges

It is possible for additional parties to be added to a like-kind exchange, with the ultimate result that each party to the transaction gives property to one party and receives property from a different party. These transactions can be accomplished by placing property with an accommodation party until appropriate replacement property is located.

Tax Cost of Like-Kind Exchanges

A like-kind exchange that involves depreciable property may carry a tax cost even if it avoids current gain recognition. If depreciable property—say, a building, for example—that has appreciated in value is exchanged for depreciable property of like kind, the property received has the same basis as the property given up, with certain adjustments for boot given. If the transferor's basis in the transferred property is less than its value, the depreciation deductions on the replacement property are correspondingly less than if the latter was acquired by purchase.

COMMENT

GoldenStar, Inc., owns an unencumbered office building worth $800,000, built on land worth $200,000. Its basis in the building, reduced by depreciation deductions during ownership, is $400,000. In January of this year, GoldenStar exchanges its property for an unencumbered warehouse worth $800,000, built on land worth $200,000. GoldenStar avoids a current tax on $400,000 of gain. However, the corporation's basis for depreciation is smaller than had the property been acquired by purchase ($400,000 substituted basis versus $800,000 cost basis).

Using straight-line depreciation and the mid-month convention over the 39-year recovery period, GoldenStar has a $9,844 first-year depreciation deduction instead of a $19,688 deduction. In effect, a small part of the benefit gained through deferral of tax on the gain is "paid back" each year by a smaller depreciation deduction.

In such situations, the benefit of gain deferral must be weighed against the concomitant smaller depreciation deductions. Taxpayers with offsetting losses in the tax year in which an exchange is contemplated may find it preferable to sell the depreciable property and recognize gain instead of entering into a like-kind exchange. Another factor for consideration is whether gain on the disposition of depreciable property is subject to recapture.

Special Like-Kind Exchange Rules

If related parties exchange like-kind property, tax deferral ends if either party disposes of property acquired in the exchange within two years after the exchange takes place. In addition, taxpayers that exchange multiple properties must compute recognized gain (if any) and basis of properties received under special rules.

COMMENT

The rationale for current nonrecognition of tax in a like-kind exchange is that the newly acquired property is basically a continuation of the old investment, which remains unliquidated. The new property is viewed as a change in the form, but not in the substance, of the investment. Thus, the gain is not tax-free but deferred until the investment is liquidated.

COMMENT

To preserve the unrecognized gain and subject to certain adjustments, the basis in the property received is equal to the basis in the property transferred.

COMMENT

The holding period of qualifying property transferred in a like-kind exchange is tacked onto the period during which the replacement property is held.

VARIABLE PREPAID FORWARD CONTRACTS

In a trinity of relatively recent cases, the U.S. Tax Court took direct aim at a particularly effective tax-deferral technique, the variable prepaid forward contract (VPFC), but, in the process, may have again provided a roadmap for future success. In these transactions, a taxpayer, who owns appreciated stock in a publicly traded corporation, monetizes his or her position by entering into a VPFC through a *stock purchase agreement* (SPA) with an investment bank. In exchange for an up-front cash payment, generally representing 75 percent to 85 percent of the current fair market value of the stock, the taxpayer agrees to deliver a variable number of shares at maturity, usually three to five years. The VPFC usually has a cash settlement option in lieu of delivering the underlying shares at maturity.

The economic benefits of the VPFC structure are as follows:

- Downside protection represented by the amount of the unrestricted payment to the taxpayer; Limited upside growth participation as reflected by the maximum share value price;
- The potential for diversification by reinvesting the up-front cash advance; and
- Tax deferral of the gain to the maturity date of the VPFC.

Under the terms of an SPA, the taxpayer is required to deposit the maximum number of shares that may be delivered under the VPFC into a pledge account and to grant the investment bank an interest in the pledged securities. The parties to the pledge agreement are the taxpayer as pledgor and the counterparty as pledgee. In most instances, the SPA contains a provision that allows the counterparty to hedge its position under the VPFC by giving it the right to sell, pledge, rehypothecate, invest, use, commingle, or otherwise dispose of or use in its business the pledged securities. During the life of the SPA, the counterparty has the right to transfer and to vote the pledged shares but may be required to pay certain distributions received on the pledged shares to the taxpayer.

The IRS has argued, and the Tax Court has agreed, that VPFCs are actually fully taxable sales in disguise. In determining whether an agreement transfers substantially all of the incidents of ownership and hence results in a sale for federal tax purposes, all of the facts and circumstances surrounding the transfer are relevant. In particular, several nonexclusive factors are evaluated in determining whether a particular transaction transfers the accoutrements of stock ownership:

- Whether the taxpayer has legal title or a contractual right to obtain legal title in the future;
- Whether the taxpayer has the right to receive consideration from a transferee of the stock;
- Whether the taxpayer enjoys the economic benefits and burdens of being a shareholder;
- Whether the taxpayer has the power to control the company;
- Whether the taxpayer has the right to attend shareholder meetings;
- Whether the taxpayer has the ability to vote the shares;
- Whether the stock certificates are in the taxpayer's possession or are being held in escrow for the benefit of that taxpayer;
- Whether the corporation lists the taxpayer as a shareholder on its tax return;
- Whether the taxpayer lists himself as a shareholder on his individual tax return;
- Whether the taxpayer has been compensated for the amount of income taxes due by reason of shareholder status;
- Whether the taxpayer has access to the corporate books; and
- Whether the taxpayer shows by overt acts that he or she believes he or she is the owner of the stock.

What is particularly enlightening about the contracts is that the IRS attacked the transactions on beneficial ownership grounds and not on the grounds that the constructive sale rules of Code Sec. 1259 applied. Accordingly, loans using appreciated securities as collateral can, in essence, monetize the gain without resulting in a sale, or current taxation, as long as the taxpayer retains enough of the indicia of ownership.

STUDY QUESTION

6. Which of the following is a type of property eligible for like-kind exchange treatment?

a. Partnership interests
b. Vehicle trade-ins
c. Mortgaged purchases of real property
d. Notes held for a debt

CONCLUSION

For as long as there has been an income tax, there have been efforts to defer payment of that tax. This chapter examined some of the more common techniques through which this objective is achieved. There are many others, of course. Multinational corporations, for example, are able to defer taxation on profits earned abroad indefinitely—or at least until those profits are repatriated. This rather controversial example proves enlightening because it illustrates the extent to which tax deferral can prove costly; and, with elected officials reluctant to raise tax rates, other ways to raise revenues will be sought. This could put certain tax deferral techniques squarely in officials' sights. Nevertheless, regardless what the government does, creative tax professionals will seek ways in which to achieve a goal as longstanding as the income tax itself.

CPE NOTE: When you have completed your study and review of chapters 3–4, which comprise Module 2, you may wish to take the Quizzer for this Module.

Go to **CCHGroup.com/PrintCPE** to take this Quizzer online.

MODULE 3: INDIVIDUALS: RELATIONSHIPS AND THE TAX LAW — CHAPTER 5

Innocent Spouse Relief

This chapter provides an overview of innocent spouse relief.

Spouses who file a joint return are jointly and separately liable for the tax due, even if one spouse is unaware of inaccuracies in the return. However, a spouse or former spouse may be relieved of responsibility for a joint tax liability if certain conditions are satisfied. A spouse who files a joint return can also seek relief from fraud penalties attributable to the other spouse or from the offset of the couple's joint overpayments against the other spouse's unpaid support obligations or government debts. Spouses who are domiciled in community property states and file separate returns can also seek relief from the application of community property laws.

Despite the general rule of joint and several liability, a spouse can escape liability on a joint return in certain circumstances. *Innocent spouse relief* refers to specific types of statutory relief from tax liabilities that arise from a married couple's joint return, but are generally attributable to only one of the spouses. A similar form of relief is available to spouses who married taxpayers who did not file joint returns with their spouse, but who are liable for an underpaid or understated tax resulting from state community property laws.

LEARNING OBJECTIVES

Upon completion of this chapter, you will be able to:

- Compare the different types of innocent spouse relief;
- Identify situations in which innocent spouse relief may and may not be granted;
- Understand how the IRS evaluates requests for equitable relief; and
- Describe the options for relief that are available to taxpayers in community property states.

INTRODUCTION

Spouses who file joint tax returns are jointly and severally liable for the tax due. Thus, one spouse can be liable for additional taxes, penalties, and interest, even if those items are attributable to the income, deductions, or credits of the other spouse, and even if the spouse is unaware of inaccuracies in the return. The IRS can collect this tax liability even after the spouses have divorced or separated, and even if the divorce or separation decree states that one spouse is solely responsible for unpaid tax liabilities.

In certain cases, however, a spouse or former spouse may be relieved of responsibility for a joint tax liability. This relief is generally referred to as innocent spouse relief.

The term encompasses specific types of statutory relief from tax liabilities that arise from a married couple's joint return but are generally attributable to only one of the spouses. If an innocent spouse is relieved of a tax liability, the IRS will no longer pursue that spouse for payment of the liability.

In general, there are three types of relief that may be available to taxpayers with joint tax liabilities:

- General innocent spouse relief;
- Separation of liability relief; and
- Equitable innocent spouse relief.

Another form of relief may be available to married taxpayers who did not file joint returns with their spouse, but who are liable for an underpaid or understated tax resulting from state community property laws. Taxpayers who qualify may be granted relief based on traditional grounds that are similar to those used for general innocent spouse relief or on equitable grounds that are similar to those used for equitable innocent spouse relief.

The IRS has recently made changes to the procedures regarding requests for equitable innocent spouse relief and equitable relief from liabilities resulting from community property laws. These changes include an expansion of the amount of time that taxpayers have to request such relief and a revision of the criteria that the IRS uses to evaluate those requests. The changes are discussed below.

Innocent spouse relief is sometimes confused with injured spouse relief; however, the two forms of relief are not the same. *Injured spouse relief* may be available to an individual whose share of a joint overpayment is applied to his or her spouse's qualified past-due debt. In such cases, the injured spouse may seek relief to claim his or her share of the refund. To qualify as an injured spouse, generally the taxpayer:

- *Must* file Form 8379, *Injured Spouse Claim and Allocation;*
- Must not be obligated to pay the debt or obligation;
- Must have received income, such as wages or interest or self-employment;
- Must have made tax payments, such as withholding or estimated tax payments, or claimed the earned income credit, additional child tax credit or other refundable credit; and
- Must have filed a joint return that reported the income and tax payments and resulted in an overpayment, all or part of which was applied to the past-due debt of the taxpayer's spouse.

A taxpayer domiciled in a community property state need satisfy only the first two conditions.

JOINT RETURNS AND JOINT LIABILITY

Married taxpayers may elect to file a joint return or file as married persons filing separately. Married couples generally find it advantageous to file a joint return because the tax rates for married couples filing jointly are lower than those that apply to married individuals filing separately. Additionally, certain credits are only available to a married couple if they file a joint return.

COMMENT

The option to file a joint federal income tax return is available only to married couples. In general, whether a marriage is recognized for federal tax purposes depends on state law. If taxpayers are married in compliance with the laws of the state in which they are married, then the marriage is recognized for federal tax purposes, even if they later reside in another state (Rev. Rul. 58-66, 1958-1 CB 60). Despite this general rule, the *Defense of Marriage Act* (DOMA) provided that same-sex domestic unions that were recognized as valid marriages under state law were not treated as marriages for federal tax purposes because federal law recognized a marriage only when it was a legal union between one man and one woman (*Defense of Marriage Act*, P.L. 104-199, Sec. 3).

In June 2013, the United States Supreme Court ruled in ***Windsor v US***, 2013-2 USTC ¶50,400, that Section 3 of DOMA violates the Equal Protection Clause of the Fifth Amendment of the U.S. Constitution, opening the door for same-sex couples who live in states where they can legally marry to file joint federal tax returns. Following the Supreme Court's decision in ***Windsor***, the IRS ruled that same-sex couples who were legally married in a jurisdiction that recognizes same-sex marriages will be treated as married for all federal tax purposes, even if the couple lives in a jurisdiction that does not recognize the validity of same-sex marriages. The ruling applies to any same-sex marriage that was validly entered into in a domestic or foreign jurisdiction whose laws authorize the marriage of two individuals of the same sex. However, it does not apply to registered domestic partnerships, civil unions or similar formal relationships recognized under state law. The ruling is generally effective as of September 16, 2013, but taxpayers may rely on it for the purpose of filing an original or amended return or claim for credit or refund for any prior tax year for which the refund limitation period is still open (Rev. Rul. 2013-17; Answers to Frequently Asked Questions for Individuals of the Same Sex Who Are Married Under State Law).

The filing of a joint tax return has certain ramifications, the most significant of which is that spouses who file jointly are jointly and severally liable for the tax liability arising from the joint return (Code Sec. 6013(d)(3)). As a result, one spouse may be subject to joint liability for the omissions from income or erroneous deductions of the other spouse.

TYPES OF INNOCENT SPOUSE RELIEF

Innocent spouse relief is a specific type of statutory relief from joint and several tax liabilities that arise from a married couple's joint return, but are generally attributable to only one of the spouses. The relief allows a requesting spouse to avoid all or a portion of a tax liability, including interest, penalties, and other amounts, for an understatement of tax arising from a joint tax return.

There are three types of innocent spouse relief under Code Sec. 6015:

- General innocent spouse relief, which is available to all taxpayers who filed joint returns and meet certain conditions (Code Sec. 6015(b));
- Separate liability relief, which relieves the requesting spouse from tax liabilities arising from tax items allocable to the nonrequesting spouse, is available to taxpayers who are no longer married or treated as no longer married (Code Sec. 6015(c)); and
- Equitable innocent spouse relief, which may be available to taxpayers who do not qualify for general innocent spouse relief or separate liability relief (Code Sec. 6015(f)).
- The three types of relief share several common elements, including:
- The requirement of a joint return filing;
- Formal election of relief;
- Notice and participation rights for the other spouse; and
- The opportunity to seek judicial review of decisions to deny relief.

Another form of relief is available to married taxpayers who did not file joint returns with their spouse, but who are liable for an underpaid or understated tax resulting from state community property laws (Code Sec. 66(c)).

The different types of innocent spouse relief and their requirements are discussed in detail below.

General Innocent Spouse Relief

Under the general innocent spouse relief procedures, a *requesting spouse* (a spouse who seeks relief) may be granted relief from a joint tax liability if:

- The liability arises from a joint tax return;
- There is an understatement of tax caused by erroneous items (i.e., omissions of income and/or improper deductions) of the nonrequesting spouse;
- The requesting spouse did not know or have reason to know of the understatement when signing the return;
- Under all the facts and circumstances, it would be inequitable to hold the requesting spouse liable for the understatement; and
- The requesting spouse makes an election for relief no later than two years after the date on which the IRS first attempts to collect the tax liability from him or her.

In order to qualify for innocent spouse relief, a requesting spouse must show that there is an understatement of tax, and that it is due to erroneous items attributable to the nonrequesting spouse.

An *understatement of tax* is the difference between the tax that is required to be shown on a return for the tax year and the amount of tax that is actually shown on that return.

An *item* is anything that is required to be separately listed on an individual income tax return or any required attachments, such as gross income, deductions, credits, and basis. An *erroneous item* is any item resulting in an understatement or deficiency in tax to the extent that the item is omitted from, or improperly reported or characterized on, a return. This includes unreported income from sources such as:

- An investment asset;
- Ordinary income improperly reported as capital gain;
- Deductions for expenses that are personal in nature; and
- Improperly reported items that affect the liability on other returns, such as an improper net operating loss that is carried back to a prior year's return.

Penalties and interest are not erroneous items.

EXAMPLE

A deduction taken for a nondeductible personal expense is an erroneous item.

Generally, an item giving rise to an understatement on a joint return is allocated between the spouses in the same manner as it would have been allocated if they had filed separate returns. In other words, an item is attributable to a spouse if it arose from that spouse's property or activities.

An *understatement* of tax should not be confused with an *underpayment* of tax. An underpayment of tax exists when a taxpayer has properly reported a tax due on a return, but the liability has not been paid. General innocent spouse relief is only available for understatements of tax. However, equitable innocent spouse relief may be available for relief from underpayments of tax.

Knowledge factor. In order to qualify for general innocent spouse relief, the requesting spouse must establish that, at the time the joint return was signed, he or she did not know or have reason to know of the understatement of tax (Code Sec. 6015(b)(1)(C)).

A requesting spouse knows or has reason to know of an understatement if he or she actually was aware of the understatement, or if a reasonable person in similar circumstances would have known of the understatement. All of the facts and circumstances are considered when determining whether a requesting spouse had reason to know of an understatement, including:

- The nature and amount of the erroneous item relative to other items;
- The spouse's financial situation;

- The requesting spouse's educational background and business experience;
- The extent of the requesting spouse's participation in the activity that resulted in the erroneous item;
- Whether the requesting spouse failed to inquire, at or before the time the return was signed, about an item on the return or omitted from the return that a reasonable person would question; and
- Whether the erroneous item represented a departure from a recurring pattern reflected in prior years' returns, such as omitted income from an investment regularly reported on prior years' returns (Reg. §1.6015-2(c)).

Actual knowledge is an actual and clear awareness of the existence of an item that gave rise to the deficiency. In the case of omitted income, the relevant inquiry is whether a requesting spouse had actual knowledge of the omitted item, rather than whether he or she had actual knowledge of the tax consequences of the item. In the case of an erroneous deduction or credit, knowledge of the item means knowledge of the facts that made the item not allowable as a deduction or credit. However, if a deduction or credit is fictitious or inflated, the IRS must establish that the requesting spouse actually knew that the expenditure was not incurred, or not incurred to the extent claimed (Reg. §1.6015-3(c)(2)(i)).

The IRS may rely on all of the facts and circumstances in determining whether a requesting spouse had actual knowledge of an erroneous item at the time he or she signed a return. The factors that the IRS may rely on in making this determination include whether the requesting spouse made a deliberate effort to avoid learning about the item in order to be shielded from liability, and whether the requesting spouse and the nonrequesting spouse jointly owned the property that resulted in the erroneous item. Joint ownership is a factor supporting a conclusion that the requesting spouse had actual knowledge of an erroneous item (Reg. §1.6015-3(c)(2)(iv)).

Mere knowledge of the source of an erroneous item is insufficient in establishing or precluding actual knowledge.

EXAMPLE

Sergio Vianello, an electing spouse, is not assumed to have had actual knowledge of any dividends paid to his wife Paola during the 2013 tax year, even though he is aware that she has invested her savings in IBM stock. However, if Sergio deposited a dividend check in their checking account and thus knows that Paola received income, Sergio has actual knowledge of that income, even if he did not know its source.

Actual knowledge of an erroneous item will not preclude relief if the electing spouse establishes that he or she signed the return under duress (Code Sec. 6015(c)(3)(C)). A return signed under duress is not considered to be that spouse's return, and so the spouse is not jointly and severally liable for the tax on that return (Reg. §1.6013-4(d)). Additionally, if a requesting spouse establishes that he or she was the victim of domestic abuse during a time before the return was signed, and that, as a result of the prior abuse, the requesting spouse did not challenge the treatment of any items on the return for fear of reprisal, the actual knowledge limitation will not apply. However, if the requesting spouse involuntarily executed the return, that spouse may wish to assert duress, in which case they would not be jointly and severally liable for any deficiency in tax with respect to the return (Reg. § 1.6015-3(c)(2)(v)).

A requesting spouse may qualify for partial relief if, at the time the return was filed, he or she had no knowledge or reason to know of only a portion of erroneous item. If the requesting spouse did not know, and had no reason to know, of the extent of the understatement, he or she may be relieved of the liability attributable to that portion of the understatement.

Facts and circumstances applied. In order for a taxpayer to qualify for general innocent spouse relief, the IRS must also determine that, taking into account all the facts and circumstances, it would be inequitable to hold the requesting spouse jointly and severally liable for an understatement of tax.

The IRS considers all of the fact and circumstances in making this determination. One relevant factor is whether the requesting spouse significantly benefited directly or indirectly from the omitted item of community income. A *significant benefit* is any benefit in excess of normal support. Evidence of a benefit may consist of transfers of property or rights to property, including transfers received several years after the filing of the return. Other factors may include desertion, divorce, or separation, and the factors used for determining whether to grant equitable innocent spouse relief. Those are discussed in greater detail below.

STUDY QUESTIONS

1. Injured spouse relief applies to:

- **a.** The injured spouse's share of a joint overpayment
- **b.** The injured spouse's portion of estimated tax for the remaining quarters of the tax year
- **c.** Overpayments made by a married individual filing a separate return
- **d.** Taxes on separate property and not community property

2. A spouse may have actual knowledge of an erroneous item and still qualify for relief if he or she:

- **a.** Would have to pay any assessment from jointly held assets
- **b.** Signed the return under duress
- **c.** Does not know the source of the income or omission
- **d.** Knew about only a portion of the item

Separate Liability Relief

In addition to the general innocent spouse rule, the tax code includes a special relief provision for spouses who are divorced, separated, or widowed, or treated as no longer married because they have not been members of the same household during the last 12 months. These individuals can elect to allocate the understatement of tax, plus penalties and interest, on a joint return between the requesting and nonrequesting spouse (Code Sec. 6015(c)).

Qualifying for relief. Separate liability relief is available to an individual who, at the time the election is filed:

- Is divorced, widowed, or legally separated from the other joint filer; or
- Was not a member of the same household as the other joint filer at any time during the 12-month period ending on the date the election is filed.

Spouses are not members of the same household if they are living apart and are estranged. However, spouses are considered members of the same household if:

- They reside in the same dwelling;
- They reside in separate dwellings but are not estranged, and one of the spouses is temporarily absent from the other's household;
- Either spouse is temporarily absent from the household and it is reasonable to assume that the absent spouse will return to the household or a substantially equivalent household (Code Sec. 6015(c)(3)(A)).

Relief under this provision is available only for unpaid liabilities resulting from understatements of liability. Refunds are not authorized.

The requirements for separate liability relief are similar to those for general innocent spouse relief. To qualify for separate liability relief, the following conditions must be met:

- The liability arises from a joint tax return;
- There is an understatement of tax caused by erroneous items (i.e., omissions of income and/or improper deductions) of the nonrequesting spouse;
- The requesting spouse did not have actual knowledge of any erroneous item giving rise to an understatement when signing the return (Code Sec. 6015(c)(3)(C); and
- The requesting spouse makes an election for relief no later than two years after the date on which the IRS first attempts to collect the tax liability from him or her (Code Sec. 6015(c)(3)(B); Proposed Reg. § 1.6015-5(b)(1)).

To qualify for separate liability relief, the requesting spouse must not have had actual knowledge of the understatement at the time the return was signed (Code Sec. 6015(c)(3)(C)). In most cases, having this knowledge will preclude separate liability relief. However, this provision does not apply if the electing spouse establishes that he or she signed the return under duress (Code Sec. 6015(c)(3)(C). A return signed under duress is not considered to be that spouse's return, and so the spouse is not jointly and severally liable for the tax assessed on that return (Reg. § 1.6013-4(d)).

Additionally, if a requesting spouse establishes that he or she was the victim of domestic abuse during a time before the return was signed, and that, as a result of the prior abuse, the requesting spouse did not challenge the treatment of any items on the return for fear of reprisal, the actual knowledge limitation will not apply. However, if the requesting spouse involuntarily executed the return, that spouse may wish to assert duress, in which case they would not be jointly and severally liable for any deficiency in tax with respect to the return (Reg. § 1.6015-3(c)(2)(v)).

Transfers of assets. A separate liability election is invalid, and joint and several liability continues to apply to the entire return, if the IRS demonstrates that the taxpayers filing the joint return transferred assets between themselves as part of a fraudulent scheme (Code Sec. 6015(c)(3)(A)(ii)).

Generally, the taxpayer electing separate liability bears the burden of proof in showing that he or she is qualified to make the election, and in establishing the proper allocation of the erroneous items. The IRS bears the burden of proving that an electing spouse had actual knowledge of an incorrect item that would invalidate the election (Code Sec. 6015(c)(2)).

Equitable Innocent Spouse Relief

If a taxpayer does not qualify for general innocent spouse relief or separate liability relief, the taxpayer may still be relieved of responsibility for the liability through equitable innocent spouse relief (Code Sec. 6015(f)). Equitable relief is available for requesting spouses who do not satisfy the requirements for general innocent spouse relief or separate liability relief. For example, relief for innocent spouses or separated or divorced spouses is limited to relief from liability for proposed or assessed deficiencies. They do not authorize relief from liabilities that are properly reported on a joint return, but not paid. Equitable relief, however, can provide relief for such liabilities (Reg. § 1.6015-1(a)(2)). Equitable relief also offers relief from liabilities arising from underpayments, whereas general innocent spouse relief and separate liability relief are limited to deficiencies arising from understatements.

The IRS recently issued updated guidance regarding requests for equitable innocent spouse relief. The current rules regarding requests for equitable innocent spouse relief and the IRS's evaluation of such requests are found in Rev. Proc. 2013-34, which is effective for requests for relief filed on or after September 16, 2013, and requests for equitable relief pending on that date.

The new guidance generally reflects the procedures proposed in Notice 2012-8, which the IRS issued on January 5, 2012, and generally applied pending the issuance of the final revenue procedure. Rev. Proc. 2013-34 supersedes Rev. Proc. 2003-61, which generally applied to requests and determinations made prior to January 5, 2012.

The following discussion reflects the current rules contained in Rev. Proc. 2013-34. However, differences between the current rules and the prior rules under Rev. Proc 2003-61 are noted within the discussion.

Threshold requirements (Rev. Proc. 2013-34). To qualify for equitable relief, the following threshold requirements must be met (Rev. Proc. 2013-34):

- The requesting spouse must have filed a joint return for the tax year for which relief is sought;
- The requesting spouse must not qualify for general innocent spouse relief or separate liability relief;
- No assets were transferred between the spouses as part of a fraudulent scheme;
- The requesting spouse must establish that, taking into account all the facts and circumstances, it would be unfair to hold him or her liable for the underpaid or understated tax;
- The nonrequesting spouse did not transfer disqualified assets (i.e., property or rights to property transferred with the principal purpose of avoiding tax) to the requesting spouse. If the nonrequesting spouse transferred disqualified assets to the requesting spouse, relief is available only to the extent that the tax liability exceeds the value of the disqualified. However, a requesting spouse to whom disqualified assets were transferred may still be eligible for relief if he or she did not have actual knowledge that the disqualified assets were transferred, or if the nonrequesting spouse abused the requesting spouse or maintained control over the household finances by restricting the requesting spouse's access to financial information;
- The requesting spouse did not knowingly participate in filing a fraudulent joint return;
- The income tax liability from which the requesting spouse seeks relief is attributable to an item of the nonrequesting spouse or an underpayment resulting from the nonrequesting spouse's income. If the liability is partially attributable to the requesting spouse, then relief can only be considered for the portion of the liability attributable to the nonrequesting spouse. However, relief may be granted if the item is attributable or partially attributable to the requesting spouse solely due to:
- The operation of community property law;

- The requesting spouse's nominal ownership;
- The nonrequesting spouse's misappropriation of funds;
- The nonrequesting spouse's abuse of the requesting spouse; or
- Fraud committed by the nonrequesting spouse (Rev. Proc. 2013-34).

COMMENT

The exception to the general rule that the liability must be attributable to an item of the nonrequesting spouse when the nonrequesting spouse's fraud gave rise to the understatement or deficiency was added by Rev. Proc. 2013-34. Rev. Proc. 2003-61 did not contain such an exception.

Additionally, the claim for relief must be timely filed. If the request for relief relates to a liability that remains unpaid, the request must be made before the expiration of the statutory period of limitation on collection of the liability under Code Sec. 6402. If the request involves a claim for credit or refund of amounts paid, the request must be made before the expiration of the period of limitation on credit or refund under Code Sec. 6511 (Notice 2011-70; Rev. Proc. 2013-34; Proposed Reg. § 1.6015-5(b)(2)).

COMMENT

Prior to the issuance of Notice 2011-70, the regulations and Rev. Proc. 2003-61 required that the requesting spouse apply for equitable relief no later than two years after the IRS's first collection activity against him or her (Reg. § 1.6015-5(b)). Notice 2011-70, which became effective on July 25, 2011, provides that, until the regulations have been modified to formally remove the two-year deadline, the following transitional rules will apply:

- The two-year limitation will not be applied to new equitable relief requests or requests currently being considered by the IRS;
- If an equitable relief request was previously denied due solely to the two-year limitation and the collection statute of limitations for the tax years involved has not expired, a taxpayer may reapply for relief;
- The two-year limitation will not apply to cases currently in suspense and taxpayers having such cases are not required to reapply; and
- The two-year limit will not apply in any pending litigation involving equitable relief. If the litigation is final, collection actions will, under certain circumstances, be suspended. Taxpayers may rely upon the transitional rules until the IRS issues final regulations modifying the two-year rule or publishes other guidance that alters the applicability of this new rule.

In August 2013 the IRS issued proposed regulations that would formalize the guidance set forth in Notice 2011-70. (Proposed Reg. § 1.6015-5(b)(2)). If finalized, Proposed Reg. § 1.6015-5(b)(2) will be retroactively effective to July 25, 2011, the date Notice 2011-70 was issued (Proposed Reg. § 1.6015-9(b)).

Streamlined determinations. If the required threshold conditions are met, the IRS will consider whether the requesting spouse is entitled to a streamlined determination granting equitable relief. The IRS will make streamlined determinations granting equitable relief if the requesting spouse establishes the following:

- On the date of the request for relief, the requesting spouse is no longer married to, or is legally separated from, the nonrequesting spouse, or has not been a member of the same household as the nonrequesting spouse at any time during the 12-month period ending on the date of the request for relief;
- The requesting spouse will suffer economic hardship if the relief is not granted. In making economic hardship determinations, the IRS applies rules similar to those used for deciding whether to release a tax levy. Economic hardship generally exists when payment of the tax will cause an individual to be unable to pay his or her reasonable basic living expenses; and
- The requesting spouse did not know or have reason to know that there was an understatement or deficiency on a joint return, or that the nonrequesting spouse would not or could not pay the underpayment of tax reported of the joint return. This factor will be considered satisfied even if the requesting spouse had knowledge or reason to know of the items giving rise to the liability or that the nonrequesting spouse would not pay the liability if, because of abuse or financial control by the nonrequesting spouse, the requesting spouse was not able to challenge the treatment of any items on the joint return, or to question the payment of the taxes reported as due for fear of the nonrequesting spouse's retaliation.

COMMENT

These factors for determining eligibility for streamlined relief were identified under the prior equitable relief guidance as conditions under which relief would ordinarily be granted (Rev. Proc. 2003-61)

Factors for equitable relief. If a requesting spouse satisfies the threshold conditions for equitable relief, but does not qualify for a streamlined determination granting relief, the IRS will decide whether it is inequitable to hold the requesting spouse liable for all or part of an unpaid income tax liability or deficiency by considering several additional factors, described here.

Marital status. A requesting spouse is treated as being no longer married to the nonrequesting spouse if they are divorced, separated, or treated as no longer married because they have not been members of the same household during the last 12 months, or if the requesting spouse is a widow or widower and is not an heir to the nonrequesting spouse's estate that would have sufficient assets to pay the tax liability. If the requesting spouse is still married to the nonrequesting spouse, this factor is neutral. If the requesting spouse is no longer married to the nonrequesting spouse, this factor weighs in favor of relief.

COMMENT

The prior guidance on equitable relief contained in Rev. Proc. 2003-61 did not specify how this factor was weighed.

Economic hardship. This factor looks at whether the requesting spouse would suffer economic hardship if the IRS does not grant equitable innocent spouse relief. For purposes of this factor, an economic hardship exists if satisfaction of the tax liability in whole or in part would cause the requesting spouse to be unable to pay reasonable basic living expenses. In making this determination, the IRS considers a requesting spouse's current income, expenses and assets. In determining the requesting spouse's reasonable basic living expenses, the IRS considers whether the requesting spouse shares expenses or has expenses paid by another individual (such as a spouse).

If the requesting spouse's income is below 250 percent of the applicable federal poverty guideline, or if the requesting spouse's monthly income exceeds the requesting spouse's reasonable basic monthly living expenses by $300 or less, this factor weighs in favor of relief unless the requesting spouse has assets available for making tax payments while still paying reasonable basic living expenses. If the requesting spouse's income exceeds these standards, the IRS considers all facts and circumstances in determining whether the requesting spouse would suffer economic hardship if relief is not granted. If denying relief would not cause the requesting spouse to suffer economic hardship, this factor is neutral. If the requesting spouse is deceased, this factor is neutral (Rev. Proc. 2013-34).

COMMENT

The economic hardship equitable factor was revised by Rev. Proc. 2013-34 to provide minimum standards or determining whether the requesting spouse would suffer economic hardship if relief is not granted. The guidelines were also revised to provide that the lack of a finding of economic hardship does not weigh against relief, and instead will be neutral.

Knowledge or reason to know of the deficiency or underpayment. The third equitable factor examines whether the requesting spouse knew or had reason to know of the nonrequesting spouse's tax errors or improprieties. The rules for determining and evaluating this factor depend on whether the joint return included an understatement or deficiency, or an underpayment.

In cases involving an understatement (when tax liability is understated on the return) or a deficiency (when the couple's tax liability exceeds the amount shown on their return), the IRS looks at whether the requesting spouse did not know or have reason to know of the item giving rise to the deficiency. This factor weighs in favor of relief if the requesting spouse did not know and had no reason to know of the item giving rise to the understatement. If the requesting spouse knew or had reason to know of the item giving rise to the understatement, this factor weighs against relief. However, actual knowledge of the item giving rise to the understatement or deficiency is not weighed more heavily than any other factor.

Depending on the facts and circumstances, if the requesting spouse was abused by the nonrequesting spouse, or the nonrequesting spouse maintained control of the household finances by restricting the requesting spouse's access to financial information and, therefore, the requesting spouse was not able to challenge the treatment of any items on the joint return for fear of the nonrequesting spouse's retaliation, this factor weighs in favor of relief even if the requesting spouse had knowledge or reason to know of the items giving rise to the understatement or deficiency.

COMMENT

Under the prior guidance contained in Rev. Proc. 2003-61, reason to know of the item giving rise to the deficiency was not weighed more heavily than other factors, but actual knowledge of the item giving rise to the deficiency was a strong factor weighing against relief.

In cases involving an underpayment (when the couple's income tax liability was properly reported but was not fully paid), the IRS looks at whether the requesting spouse did not know and had no reason to know that the nonrequesting spouse would not pay the income tax liability when, or within a reasonable time after, the joint return was filed. This factor weighs in favor of relief if the requesting spouse reasonably expected the nonrequesting spouse to pay the tax liability reported on the joint return. A reasonable expectation of payment will be presumed if the spouses submitted a request for an installment agreement to pay the tax due, provided that the request was made within the latter of 90 days after the tax was due or 90 days after the return was filed.

This factor generally weighs against relief if, based on the facts and circumstances of the case, it was not reasonable for the requesting spouse to believe that the nonrequesting spouse would or could pay the tax liability shown on the joint return—as, for example, when the requesting spouse knows of the nonrequesting spouse's prior bankruptcies, financial difficulties, or other issues with the IRS or other creditors, or is otherwise aware of difficulties in timely paying bills. However, even if the requesting spouse had knowledge or reason to know that the nonrequesting spouse could not or would not pay the taxes due, this factor weighs in favor of relief if the requesting spouse was abused by the nonrequesting spouse, or the nonrequesting spouse maintained control of the household finances by restricting the requesting spouse's access to financial information and, therefore, the requesting spouse was not able to question the payment of the taxes reported as due on the joint return or challenge the nonrequesting spouse's assurance regarding payment of the taxes for fear of the nonrequesting spouse's retaliation.

COMMENT

The prior guidance on equitable relief contained in Rev. Proc. 2003-61 did not specify that this factor would weigh in favor of relief if the requesting spouse reasonably expected the nonrequesting spouse to pay the liability on the return.

The nonrequesting spouse's legal obligation to pay the liability. This factor looks at whether the nonrequesting spouse has a legal obligation to pay the outstanding income tax liability under a divorce decree or other legally binding agreement. Generally, this factor weighs in favor of relief if the nonrequesting spouse has the sole legal obligation to pay the outstanding income tax liability; however, it is neutral if the requesting spouse knew or had reason to know, when entering into the divorce decree or agreement, that the nonrequesting spouse would not pay the income tax liability. This factor weighs against relief if the requesting spouse has the sole legal obligation. This factor is neutral if the legal agreement is silent as to who must pay the tax liability or makes both spouses responsible for paying the tax, or if the spouses are not separated or divorced.

COMMENT

Under the prior guidance in Rev. Proc. 2003-61, this factor did not weigh in favor of relief if the requesting spouse knew or had reason to know, when entering into the divorce decree or agreement, that the nonrequesting spouse would not pay the income tax liability.

Significant benefit from the deficiency or underpayment. This factor looks at whether the requesting spouse received significant benefit, beyond normal support, from the unpaid income tax liability or the item giving rise to the deficiency. Evidence of direct or indirect benefit may consist of transfers of property or rights to property, including transfers that may be received several years after the year of the understatement.

EXAMPLE

Emily Nicols, a requesting spouse, receives a significant benefit from a tax item if she receives property, including life insurance proceeds, from Geoffrey, her nonrequesting spouse, because the property's value is beyond normal support and is traceable to items omitted from gross income that are attributable to Geoffrey.

This factor generally weighs against granting relief if the requesting spouse enjoyed the benefits of a lavish lifestyle, such as owning luxury assets and taking expensive vacations. However, this factor is neutral if the nonrequesting spouse controlled the household and business finances or there was abuse such that the nonrequesting spouse made the decision on spending funds for a lavish lifestyle. This fa ctor is also neutral if the amount of unpaid tax or understated tax was small such that neither spouse received a significant benefit. This factor weighs in favor of relief only if:

- The nonrequesting spouse significantly benefitted from the unpaid tax or item giving rise to an understatement or deficiency and the requesting spouse had little or no benefit; or
- The nonrequesting spouse enjoyed the benefit to the requesting spouse's detriment.

COMMENT

The prior guidance on equitable relief contained in Rev. Proc. 2003-61 did not specify how this factor was weighed.

Compliance with income tax laws. This factor looks at whether the requesting spouse makes a good-faith effort to comply with income tax laws in the tax years following the tax year for which relief is requested. If the requesting spouse is divorced from the nonrequesting spouse, this factor weighs in favor of relief if the requesting spouse is compliant. It weighs against relief if the requesting spouse is not compliant. It is neutral if the requesting spouse makes a good-faith effort to comply with the tax laws but is unable to fully do so—as, for instance, when the requesting spouse files timely and correct returns but cannot fully pay the tax liability shown because of his or her poor financial or economic situation after the divorce.

If the requesting spouse and nonrequesting spouse remain married and file joint returns (even if the spouses are legally separated or living apart), this factor is neutral if the joint returns are compliant with the tax laws. This factor weighs against relief if the returns are not compliant.

If the requesting spouse and nonrequesting spouse remain married and file separate returns, this factor weighs in favor of relief if the requesting spouse is compliant with the tax laws. This factor weighs against relief if the requesting spouse is not compliant with the tax laws. This factor is neutral if the requesting spouse makes a good-faith effort to comply with the tax laws but is unable to fully comply.

COMMENT

The prior guidance on equitable relief contained in Rev. Proc. 2003-61 did not specify that this factor may weigh in favor of relief.

Mental or physical health. This factor looks at the requesting spouse's mental and physical health at the time the return was signed or innocent spouse relief was requested. In evaluating this factor, the IRS considers the nature, extent, and duration of the condition. This factor weighs in favor of relief if the spouse was in poor physical health or mental health. It is neutral if the requesting spouse was in neither poor physical nor poor mental health.

These factors are guides, and they are not the only relevant considerations. In determining whether to grant equitable innocent spouse relief, the IRS considers all of the facts and circumstances of the case. In addition, the degree of importance of each factor varies depending on the requesting spouse's facts and circumstances. No one factor or a majority of factors necessarily determines the outcome.

The weight the IRS gives to many of these equitable factors varies if the requesting spouse establishes that he or she was the victim of abuse not amounting to duress. Depending on the facts and circumstances of the requesting spouse's situation, abuse may result in certain factors weighing in favor of relief when otherwise the factor may have weighed against relief. Abuse comes in many forms, such as physical, psychological, sexual, and emotional abuse, including efforts to control, isolate, humiliate, and intimidate the requesting spouse, or to undermine the requesting spouse's ability to reason independently and be able to do what is required under the tax laws. All the facts and circumstances are considered in determining whether a requesting spouse was abused. The impact of a nonrequesting spouse's alcohol or drug abuse is also considered in determining whether a requesting spouse was abused (Rev. Proc. 2013-34).

COMMENT

Under the prior guidance on equitable relief contained in Rev. Proc. 2003-61, abuse weighed in favor of relief if it was present, and was neutral if it was not. In addition, a history of abuse could mitigate a requesting spouse's knowledge or reason to know. Abuse was not defined in the guidance.

STUDY QUESTIONS

3. All types of innocent spouse relief do ***not*** apply to:

a. Penalties
b. Interest on deficiencies
c. Liabilities resulting from erroneous items of which the requesting spouse was actually aware
d. Underpayments

4. A requesting spouse's financial condition will weigh in favor of granting equitable relief when:

a. The requesting spouse and nonrequesting spouse are both responsible for paying the tax under the terms of their divorce decree
b. The requesting spouse has no other assets for making tax payments and covering basic living expenses
c. The nonrequesting spouse has adequate assets to pay the liability and basic living expenses
d. The requesting spouse and nonrequesting spouse are still married

COMMUNITY PROPERTY LAWS

Community property generally includes all property acquired by a husband and wife during marriage while domiciled in a community property jurisdiction, other than separate property. In community property states, income earned by either spouse is generally considered community income by operation of law, with each spouse owning one-half of the income regardless of who earned it. In contrast, separate income is taxed only to the spouse who is responsible for it.

For federal tax purposes, the concept of community income is relevant when a married couple elects to file separate income tax returns. Joint filers do not need to distinguish between community income and other income, because all income earned by either spouse is reported on a single combined return. Separate filers generally must divide their community income in equal shares, with each reporting half of the income on his or her return (Reg. § 1.66-1(a)). Thus, separate returns do not relieve the spouses of their obligation to report their equal shares of community income. As a result, a married taxpayer domiciled in a community property state may be liable for tax on a portion of a spouse's income.

COMMENT

The community property states are Arizona, California, Idaho, Louisiana, Nevada, New Mexico, Texas, Washington, and Wisconsin (IRS Publication 555, "Community Property").

Despite the general rule that rule that community income is to be reported and taxed in equal shares, in some instances community income is recharacterized as separate income for federal income tax purposes. Community property laws may be disregarded, and community income may be treated as separate income taxable only to the spouse who earns it, when:

- The spouses live apart at all times during the calendar year, file separate returns, and do not transfer income between themselves during the year (Code Sec. 66(a));

- One spouse acts solely entitled to community income and does not inform the other of its nature and amount (Code Sec. 66(b));
- A spouse who satisfies the four specific requirements for traditional innocent spouse-type relief under Code Sec. 66(c) requests such relief from the IRS; or
- A spouse who does not satisfy the traditional-relief requirements requests relief from the IRS because it would be inequitable to hold the spouse liable (Code Sec. 66(c)).

Community property laws are disregarded for separated spouses if these conditions are met:

- The individuals must have been married to each other at some time during the calendar year (not necessarily the whole year);
- They must have lived apart at all times during the calendar year;
- They must not have filed a joint return together for a tax year beginning or ending in the calendar year (although they may file a joint return with a new spouse);
- One spouse (or both) must have earned income that is community income for the calendar year; and
- Neither spouse can have transferred any portion of the earned community income to the other spouse during the calendar year (Code Sec. 66(a); Reg. § 1.66-2(a)).

Taxpayers in community property states who file separate returns may be able to avoid liability for deficiencies attributable to community income under the innocent spouse provisions of Code Sec. 66(c). There are two distinct relief provisions under Code Sec. 66(c). The first provides relief from deficiencies arising from understatements on the taxpayer's separate return if the taxpayer meets the statutory requirements ("traditional relief"). The second category of relief is equitable relief similar to the equitable innocent spouse relief available under Code Sec. 6015(f). This more general type of equitable relief applies in situations that do not fit the parameters of any other relief provision, including deficiencies that arise from underpayments.

Traditional Relief

Under the rules for traditional relief, a spouse may be relieved of tax liability attributable to the income of the other spouse if the following requirements are met:

- The spouse seeking relief cannot file a joint return for the tax year;
- The omitted income item must be an item that would be treated as the other spouse's income under the separate reporting rules of Code Sec. 879(a);
- The spouse seeking relief must establish that he or she did not know or have reason to know of the unreported community income; and

- Under the facts and circumstances, it must be inequitable to include the community income item in the gross income of the spouse seeking relief (Code Sec. 66(c); Reg. § 1.66-4(a)(1)).

A spouse has knowledge of an item of community income if he or she actually knows about it, or if a reasonable person in a similar situation would know about it. This standard is not met if the would-be innocent spouse is aware of the activity that produced the income, but is unaware of the particular amount involved; not knowing the specific dollar amount of community income is not a basis for relief (Reg. § 1.66-4(a)(2)). The IRS considers all relevant factors in determining whether a taxpayer knows or has reason to know of an item, including:

- The amount of the item;
- The couple's financial situation;
- The taxpayer's educational background and business experience; and
- Whether the item was reflected on returns for prior years.

These standards are borrowed from Reg. § 1.6015-2(c), which provides innocent spouse relief for spouses who file joint returns.

As with the "knowledge of income" question, the IRS considers all of the facts and circumstances in determining whether it is inequitable to hold the requesting spouse liable for tax on the community income (Reg. §1.66-4(a)(3)). One relevant factor is whether the requesting spouse benefitted, directly or indirectly, from the omitted item of community income. Other factors include desertion, divorce or separation, and the factors that are relevant to requests for equitable relief.

Equitable Relief

The IRS can provide equitable relief to an individual who does not qualify for traditional relief from community property laws if, taking into account all of the facts and circumstances, failure to provide relief would be inequitable (Code Sec. 66(c) (flush language)).

COMMENT

The rules for requesting and granting equitable relief from the operation of community property law are largely the same as those that apply to requests for equitable relief from joint liabilities discussed above.

COMMENT

As with requests for equitable relief from joint liabilities, requests for equitable relief from the operation of community property law made on or after September 16, 2013, and requests for equitable relief pending on that date, are governed by Rev. Proc. 2013-34.

Threshold conditions. A spouse seeking equitable relief from the operation of community property laws must meet the following threshold conditions:

- The spouses must not have transferred assets between themselves as part of a fraudulent scheme;
- The nonrequesting spouse must not have transferred disqualified assets to the requesting spouse (subject to the exceptions discussed above);
- The requesting spouse must not have knowingly participated in the filing of a fraudulent joint return;
- The income tax liability from which the requesting spouse seeks relief must be attributable, in full or in part, to an item of the nonrequesting spouse or an underpayment resulting from the nonrequesting spouse's income; and
- The request for relief must be timely.

If the threshold conditions are met, the IRS will determine whether the requesting spouse is entitled to a streamlined decision granting equitable relief, based on the same based on the same standards as those that apply to requests for equitable relief from joint liabilities.

If a requesting spouse satisfies the threshold conditions for innocent spouse relief but does not satisfy the conditions for streamlined relief, the IRS considers the additional factors that are used in evaluating requests for equitable relief from joint liabilities.

REQUESTING INNOCENT SPOUSE RELIEF

Requests for innocent spouse relief and relief from liabilities resulting from the application of community property law are made using Form 8857, *Request for Innocent Spouse Relief.*

For innocent spouse relief under Code Sec. 6015, a spouse must request relief under the general innocent spouse provision or the separation of liability provision within two years of the first IRS collection activity with respect to the individual (Code Sec. 6015). Collection activities for this purpose include:

- Issuance of a collection due process notice;
- An offset of an overpayment of the requesting spouse against the liability;
- Filing of a suit for collection; or
- Filing a claim by the United States in a court proceeding in which the requesting spouse is a part or that involves the requesting spouse's property.

They do not include:

- A notice of deficiency;
- Filing of a notice of federal tax lien; or
- A demand for payment of tax.

As discussed above, the regulations also apply this two-year requirement to requests for equitable relief (Reg. § 1.6015-5(b)(1)). However, the IRS has issued proposed regulations and interim guidance upon which taxpayers may rely so that individuals who request equitable relief under Code Sec. 6015(f) will no longer be required to submit the request within two years of the first collection activity with respect to the individual. Instead, the IRS will consider requests for equitable relief filed within the period for collection of taxes under Code Sec. 6502 or, if the relief sought involves a refund of tax, within the period of limitation on credits or refunds under Code Sec. 6511 (Notice 2011-70; Proposed Reg. § 6015-5(b)(2)).

A request can also be made before commencement of collection activity, for example, in connection with an audit or examination, or in a collection due process hearing in connection with the filing of a notice of federal tax lien (Reg. § 1.6015-5(b)(3)). However, no request can be made before the receipt of a notification of an audit or letter or notice from the IRS indicating that there may be an outstanding liability with regard to the year for which relief is requested (Reg. § 1.6015-5(b)(5)).

For requests for relief from the application of community property law, the rules are slightly different. The earliest time to request traditional innocent spouse relief is the date that the IRS notifies the spouse that there may be an outstanding liability with respect to a particular year (Reg. § 1.66-4(j)(2)). A request submitted before this date is premature, and the IRS will not consider it. The latest date for requesting traditional relief is six months before the statute of limitations on assessment expires for the nonrequesting spouse; or, if the IRS begins its examination of the return within that six-month period, within 30 days of the IRS's initial contact. However, the deadline for requesting equitable relief from the application of community property law is the same as the deadline for requesting equitable relief under Code Sec. 6015(f). Therefore, requests for equitable relief must be made within the period for collection of taxes under Code Sec. 6502 or, if the relief sought involves a refund of tax, within the period of limitation on credits or refunds under Code Sec. 6511 (Rev. Proc. 2013-34; Proposed Reg. § 1.66-4(j)(2)(ii)).

RIGHTS OF NONREQUESTING SPOUSES

When a taxpayer elects to seek innocent spouse relief from joint liabilities, the IRS must send a notice to the nonrequesting spouse's last known address that informs the nonrequesting spouse of the claim for relief. The notice must provide the nonrequesting spouse with an opportunity to submit any information that should be considered in determining whether the requesting spouse is entitled to innocent spouse relief.

The IRS considers all of the relevant information that the nonrequesting spouse submits, including information relating to:

- The legal status of the requesting and nonrequesting spouses' marriage;
- The extent of the requesting spouse's knowledge of the erroneous items or underpayment;
- The extent of the requesting spouse's knowledge or participation in the family business or financial affairs;
- The requesting spouse's education level;
- The extent to which the requesting spouse benefited from the erroneous tax items;
- Any asset transfers between the spouses;
- Any indication of fraud on the part of either spouse;
- Whether it would be inequitable to hold the requesting spouse jointly and severally liable for the outstanding liability;
- The allocation or ownership of items giving rise to the; and
- Anything else that may be relevant to the determination of whether relief from joint and several liability should be granted (Reg. § 1.6015-6(c)).

STUDY QUESTIONS

5. Separately filing spouses in a community property state:

a. May not hold community property equally
b. Must divide their community income equally
c. Must recharacterize community income as separate income
d. Must file federal returns jointly

6. A spouse requesting traditional relief from a liability arising from community property laws:

a. Cannot file a joint return for the tax year for which he or she is seeking relief
b. Must have had knowledge of the erroneous item that year
c. Must have benefitted by the omission
d. May know of the activity that produced the income if he or she is unaware of the amount of income

CONCLUSION

For married taxpayers, joint and several liability is the obligation that accompanies the privilege of filing a joint return. Thus, one spouse may be subject to joint liability for the omissions from income or erroneous deductions of the other spouse. The question then becomes whether the innocent spouse, who merely signed a joint return, should be held liable for errors on the return attributable to the actions of the other spouse. The answer is especially critical if the couple has divorced and the innocent spouse is the only source of collection for the unpaid tax. The innocent spouse provisions of Code Secs. 6015 and 66 may offer relief for taxpayers who are liable for taxes that are attributable to the income, deductions, or credits of a spouse.

MODULE 3: INDIVIDUALS: RELATIONSHIPS AND THE TAX LAW — CHAPTER 6

Identity Theft: Due Diligence and Remedies

Identity theft is a significant problem that is becoming ever more serious as criminals, who realize how lucrative it can be, become more sophisticated, more organized, and more cunning at perpetrating the crime. For several years government agencies including the Internal Revenue Service have made the fight against identity theft a priority. Nevertheless, taxpayers continue to fall prey to the crime, even when they have been especially careful to protect their personal identification information.

This chapter explains what identity theft is; how it is perpetrated; and what steps to take with the IRS to rectify any resulting tax liability. This chapter also explains what individuals, practitioners, and businesses can do to protect themselves or their clients. Finally, the chapter describes what the federal government and the states are doing to ameliorate this dangerous problem.

LEARNING OBJECTIVES

Upon completion of this chapter, you will be able to:

- Understand the severity of taxpayer identity theft;
- Identify common schemes used by thieves to obtain personal information;
- List best practices for avoiding theft of personal information that could lead to identity theft;
- Describe how to address theft once it has occurred; and
- Understand what the government is doing to prevent identity theft in the future.

INTRODUCTION

Identity theft is a crime that occurs when a perpetrator uses someone else's personal information, without that person's permission, to commit fraud or other illegal acts. Identity theft related to tax return filing has topped the IRS's "Dirty Dozen" annual list of tax scams for both 2012 and 2013, and also appeared on the list in 2011. Essentially the increased attention means the IRS has consistently placed identity theft among the "worst of the worst" tax scams. Nor is the IRS alone. According to the National Taxpayer Advocate Service (TAS), identity theft grew by more than 650 percent between fiscal years 2008 and 2012. For the past 13 years, identity theft has been the top consumer complaint reported to the Federal Trade Commission (FTC). The FTC listed government document identity theft—which includes identity theft that results in tax refund fraud—as the most common form of identity theft suffered.

Taxpayer identity theft is costly to nearly everyone affected: the victimized taxpayer; the banks, credit unions, and businesses that cannot recover money fraudulently transferred out of their accounts; and ultimately the state and federal governments that issue billions in fraudulent tax refunds every year. An audit report released in August 2012 by the Treasury Inspector General for Tax Administration (TIGTA) estimated that during the next five years, the IRS could lose a projected $21 billion to fraudulently claimed tax refunds related to identity theft. And this figure, according to TIGTA, takes into account the new fraud controls the IRS has put in place.

The IRS has consistently touted its efforts to combat identity theft among its successes. For example, the IRS reported that for the 2012 returns, it had prevented the issuance of $20 billion of fraudulent refunds, including those related to identity theft. At the same time, the IRS continues to place the fight against identity theft among its top priorities and reminds both lawmakers and the public at large of how much remains to be accomplished in this area. TIGTA reported that for 2012, nearly 1.8 million incidents of taxpayer identity theft were reported, a figure representing an 80 percent increase from the year before. However, TIGTA stated, an equal or greater number of identity theft incidents are likely to remain undetected each year.

The growing popularity of identity theft among criminals is readily explained: it is easy to perpetrate, quick to yield large results, and often very difficult to detect. Many victims, who include both individuals and businesses, do not realize they have been victimized for months or even years.

The IRS, U.S. Department of Justice (DOJ), FTC, and other organizations have focused a vast array of resources on combating this growing problem. And rightly so. The consequences of identity theft include significantly delayed tax refunds, erroneously applied tax assessments and penalties, not to mention the millions of dollars lost for individual taxpayers, businesses, banks, and the government in the blink of an eye.

HOW IDENTITY THEFT AFFECTS INDIVIDUALS AND BUSINESSES

Identity theft occurs when someone usurps personal information, such as names, Social Security numbers (SSNs), or other identifying information, without permission, to commit fraud or other crimes. Government document identity theft is the most common form of identity theft. Generally, as encountered by the IRS, a taxpayer's SSN is stolen and used to file a tax return and claim a fraudulent refund. When the legitimate taxpayer then files his or her return, the IRS rejects it. The taxpayer must correct the situation in order to obtain his or her refund and repair the records, which in many cases can consume a considerable amount of time and effort by the taxpayer. In fact, in the best case scenario the individual taxpayer must wait a minimum of six months to obtain his or her tax refund.

The crime plays out differently when a business taxpayer's identity is stolen. Similar to return filings for individuals, the theft can occur in the form of a fraudulently claimed tax refund, but often involves a more subtle subterfuge that remains undetected until the business receives a notice from a government agency related to unpaid employment taxes, erroneously claimed tax credits, unreported merchant payment card income, and more.

EXAMPLE

Jessica and Aidan Matthews, a married couple with income below an amount that would require them to file a tax return, do not file one. Months later they receive a letter from the IRS notifying them of a tax assessment against Aidan. Further investigation yields proof that an identity thief stole Aidan's SSN and address, and used them to file a fraudulent Form 1040 claiming credits against fabricated income to generate a tax refund.

EXAMPLE

Joshua Reynolds, a retiree with taxable income under the filing threshold, does not file a tax return. Later he receives an IRS notice of a tax assessment against him. Further investigation yields proof that an identity thief stole the Joshua's SSN and used it to obtain employment. The employer reported the thief's income on a Form W-2, but the thief did not file his tax returns or pay the tax owed, leaving Joshua to answer to the IRS.

EXAMPLE

An identity thief obtains a corporate document listing the personal identification information of 32 clients of Best Life, a local insurance company, and uses the data to file tax returns claiming more than $175,000 in fraudulent tax refunds.

EXAMPLE

Two individuals break into the office of Elliot Clark, a tax return preparer, stealing the files of more than 300 of his clients. The thieves file returns under these clients' names and, after receiving the tax refunds, deposit the amounts on debit cards and bank accounts opened with the fraudulent information.

EXAMPLE

Georgio and Chiara Domenico, married joint filers, receive an IRS notice informing them that they cannot claim their 10-year-old son Paolo as a dependent due to his income from full-time employment. Upon further investigation, the two learn that their Paolo's SSN has been stolen by a person wanted for failure to pay child support, forgery, and a host of other charges.

HOW ARE IDENTITIES STOLEN?

Tax information scammers employ a variety of techniques, described here, to glean information to defraud the IRS and unknowing taxpayers.

Pilfering Through Trash

Many small-time identity thieves are able to obtain taxpayers' personal information by looking through victims' trash for unshredded financial papers, bills, invoices, expired credit cards, bank statements, tax returns, Forms W-2, and other official documents.

Internet Hacking

Sophisticated, computer savvy criminals can infiltrate computer systems to collect thousands of records containing personal information. Targets can include individuals, retail businesses, investment companies, and even governments.

EXAMPLE

In September through October 2012 hackers accessed the computer records of the South Carolina Department of Revenue, which later reported that more than 3.9 million South Carolina taxpayer files and 387,000 credit and debit card numbers had been exposed during the attack. Some taxpayers were immediately victimized, such as a married South Carolina couple who lost more than $4,000 from their catering business's bank account in the first week of November 2012. Other South Carolina taxpayers reported becoming victims of taxpayer identity theft after learning their 2012 tax returns were under review before the victims had even filed.

Phishing Scams

Phishing is a scam typically involving an unsolicited e-mail, letter, or phone call sent or made to an unsuspecting taxpayer. The communication lures him or her into providing personal information that can then be used by the criminal to commit identity theft or financial theft. Potential victims reveal valuable personal and financial information such as SSNs, bank account information, passwords, personal identification numbers (PINs), credit card numbers, credit card validation codes, and card verification values (CVVs).

Examples of phishing schemes vary in terms of the amount of guile the perpetrators employ. One common scam involves an unsolicited e-mail from someone claiming to be the trustee of a large estate of which the recipient is a beneficiary. Another might pose as being from a legitimate site such as ebay or PayPal and state that a user's account will expire if he or she does not verify his or her identity.

Phishing scams also commonly take advantage of the panicked reactions inspired by communiques from the IRS.

EXAMPLE

A scheme by a phisher posing as an IRS agent involved the Electronic Federal Tax Payment System (EFTPS) used by employers to deposit their payroll taxes. The scammer sent an e-mail to an EFTPS user claiming that its tax payment was rejected and directing the user to a website for additional information. That website contained *malware,* computer programs that infiltrate computers without the users' consent. The criminal used the computer data to steal passwords, credit card account information, and other personal information necessary to commit identity theft.

COMMENT

The IRS has repeatedly emphasized that it will not, under any circumstances, initiate contact with taxpayers via e-mail, text messaging, or social media. Neither will the IRS request detailed personal information through e-mail.

NOTE

Taxpayers suspecting identity fraud can contact the IRS Identity Protection Specialized Unit at 800–908–4490.

Other recent phishing schemes seek to capitalize on human sympathy by posing as charities to help victims of natural disasters. Anytime a natural disaster or other tragedy occurs, charities begin to open and solicit donations to help the victims. The speed with which this occurs, however, might indicate that the charity is fraudulent.

EXAMPLE

One "charity" opened itself to donations two hours after the tsunami hit Japan in 2010. Recent phishing scams have fraudulently solicited funds for the victims of the Texas fertilizer plant explosion, the Boston Marathon bombing, and the Oklahoma tornadoes.

COMMENT

The IRS suggested that rather than halt their charitable giving, would-be donors perform research on a charity ahead of time. Potential donors can access the Exempt Organizations Select Check tool at irs.gov to find out whether the organization soliciting money is on the IRS's list of qualified charities. There is also a list of legitimate charities on the Federal Emergency Management Agency (FEMA) Web site at fema.gov.

The IRS also cautioned against donating to charities with names that are similar to, but not identical with, names of legitimate organizations. The IRS also cautioned donors against providing personal financial information such as their SSNs, credit card and bank account numbers, or passwords to anyone who solicits a contribution.

COMMENT

Taxpayers who suspect they have been targeted by a phishing scam should report it to the IRS. If solicited via e-mail, they may forward the e-mail message as-is immediately to phishing@irs.gov.

The Devil You Know

Sometimes identity theft is perpetrated by people known to the taxpayer, such as an ex-spouse, boyfriend or girlfriend, a child, or a business associate. Any of these people can sell a taxpayer's personal information or use it themselves for personal gain. Such events may happen, for instance, when a family member needs to obtain credit that he or she could not otherwise access under his or her own name.

EXAMPLE

Melissa Padrone checked her credit report online, only to discover that her ex-boyfriend Jonathan had taken out a loan for an automobile by using her SSN. He had subsequently defaulted, which ruined Melissa's credit score.

EXAMPLE

Federal authorities charged a notary public with selling SSNs of individuals who had disclosed them during mortgage refinancing transactions. The notary sold them to her friend for $20 each, ostensibly enabling that friend to steal the individuals' identities.

STUDY QUESTION

1. How are individuals most likely to learn that their taxpayer identities have been stolen?

a. The individuals are contacted by their return preparers
b. The IRS rejects their returns or assesses nonfilers having phony returns
c. The individuals' banks and credit card companies notify them
d. The IRS system for SSN tracking matches tax liabilities against the SSNs taxpayers submit

BEST PRACTICES FOR INDIVIDUALS

Individual taxpayer identity theft is most often discovered after legitimate taxpayers file their tax returns, only to have them rejected because an identity thief filed under their names first. But if an individual does have taxable income below a filing limit, the fraud could remain undetected for months, years, or perhaps permanently. That means that a clever identity thief will often intentionally target senior citizens, children, or those who have no income. But the truth is that everyone is at risk, and everyone must take measures to prevent taxpayer identity theft. Here are some of the precautions individuals should take to minimize the risk that they will be victimized.

File Tax Returns Early

Identity thieves generally file early in the season to ensure that the IRS will process their fraudulent returns and distribute the refunds before the legitimate taxpayer has the chance to file. The earlier taxpayers file in the season, the less likely it will be that an identity thief can assume their identities and file first.

Protect Social Security Numbers

Individuals should not carry Social Security cards outside of the house in a purse or wallet that could be stolen. Individuals should not give out SSNs unless absolutely necessary, and if one is required, challenge the requirement. Of course, individuals should never enter the SSNs into a data form located on an unsecured website.

COMMENT

A website that is secured will indicate this in its web address, which would begin with: "https://"

Internet Passwords

Bank accounts, student loan accounts, e-mail accounts, and practically all other important accounts require Internet passwords. Individuals should devise complicated passwords, containing random numbers and characters, and change them frequently. Users should not use something that would be easy to guess, such as a birth date, pet name, or favorite sports team.

Install Firewalls and Antivirus Protection

Good antivirus protection software can protect computers against malware and other spy software designed to steal personal information.

COMMENT

Individuals can inadvertently install malware by clicking on seemingly legitimate programs. One such program involves messages telling a computer user that there is a virus on his or her machine, necessitating the installation of security software. Computer users can visit http://security.getnetwise.org/tools/search to find a list of security tools from legitimate security vendors.

Safeguard Mail

Identity thieves can obtain personal information by sorting through someone's mail. Individuals should only deposit outgoing mail containing personal information in an official collection box maintained by the U.S. Postal Service. Individuals leaving on vacation should have the post office hold their mail or have someone trustworthy pick it up and place it inside a secure area.

Shred Important Documents

Before throwing documents, expired credit cards, or other important items into the trash, individuals should make sure to shred them. Documents could contain SSNs, account numbers, or other important features of personal identification, such as birthdates, former addresses, and family information that can be used by thieves to "verify" a false identity.

Check Credit Reports Regularly

Taxpayers can check their credit reports with the major credit reporting companies (Equifax, Experian, and TransUnion) once a year for free. If someone has stolen a person's identity to obtain false credit with current or future fraudulent tax records, the individual should report that to the IRS using Form 14039, *Identity Theft Affidavit,* even if no tax problem has yet occurred. Individuals that have experienced problems with identity theft in the past should check their credit reports more than once a year.

STUDY QUESTION

2. Which of the following is a best practice for individuals safeguarding their Internet passwords?

a. Consistent use of the same password over time
b. Using familiar sources such as pet names or birth dates
c. Using digits and random characters
d. Using their SSN as their password

BUSINESS TAXPAYER IDENTITY THEFT

Businesses generally deal with larger transactions, have larger account balances and credit lines than do individual taxpayers, and may set up and accept merchant credit card payments with numerous banks. Business information regarding tax identification numbers (TINs), profit margins and revenues, officers, and even officer salaries are often public and easily accessed. At the same time remedies and enforcement tend to focus more on individual identity theft. Thus, business identity theft can be more lucrative and arguably less dangerous to engage in than individual taxpayer identity theft. Despite the enormity of the problem, business taxpayer identity theft receives less attention from Congress and the media than instances of individual taxpayer identity theft. This is possibly because identity theft for individuals shows up at the IRS in a much more immediate way than business identity theft. Most notably, individual identity theft appears when somebody files a tax return and it is rejected because there is already one on file. Business identity theft, on the other hand, is much more subtle than individual identity theft.

Stealing and Using Victims' Identification Numbers

Only some of the many business identity theft schemes relate to tax. Nevertheless, such schemes can be devastating for businesses, resulting in massive employment tax liabilities for fictitious wages or huge deficiencies in reported income. Identity thieves can use a business's employer identification number (EIN) to initiate merchant card payment schemes, file false tax returns, and even generate hundreds of fake Form W-2s in furtherance of more individual taxpayer identity theft.

Business identity theft can require less effort than individual identity theft because less information is required to establish a business or open a line of credit than is required of individuals. In general, the thief needs to obtain the business's EIN, which is easy to acquire. Common sources for an EIN include:

- Filings made to the Securities and Exchange Commission (SEC), such as the Form 10-K, which includes the EIN on its first page;
- Public databases that enable users to search for business entities sometimes also display the employer's EIN;
- Guidestar.org, which enables searchers to obtain almost any registered nonprofit organization's EIN, address, and revenue information;
- Websites specifically designed to search for EINs, such as EIN-Finder.com;
- Business websites that sometimes openly display the EIN; and
- Forms W-2, W-9, and 1099.

The problem presented by issuing paper copies of W-2s or 1099s is that employers must distribute them to their employees—sometimes they can number into the thousands—and those employees may not safeguard the identifying information that is on those forms.

Thieves targeting return preparer businesses can obtain *electronic filing identification numbers* (EFINs) just as easily. They, like EINs, are found on the taxpayer's copy of a tax return and on filing confirmations of tax returns filed by the return preparer. Thus, return preparers are also at risk of having their identities stolen and used in furtherance of fraudulent tax refund schemes. Worse yet, if an identity thief also steals the SSNs of the return preparer's clients, he or she can file fraudulent tax returns in their names as well. This can have serious consequences for a return preparer's business.

EXAMPLE

In January 2013 a Texas grand jury indicted two people with mail fraud and wire fraud. They had obtained a registered return preparer's EFIN and used it to file tax returns that resulted in more than $2.6 million in fraudulent tax refunds.

EXAMPLE

Audrey McAllison, a tax return preparer, maintained a database of her clients and their tax return information on her office computer. Thieves broke into her office in December, stealing the laptop and using the SSNs stored on its hard drive to file fraudulent tax returns. When Audrey began to file tax returns on behalf of her clients in February, they were all rejected because the thieves had already filed tax returns under her clients' SSNs.

If a business taxpayer does not safeguard its identification information, it could wind up in the hands of an identity thief. Once a thief has an organization's EIN, he or she may file reports with various state Secretaries of State to change registered business addresses, registered agents' names, or even appoint new officers. In some cases the thief will apply for a line of credit using this invented information. Because the official Secretary of State records display the changed information, potential creditors will not be alerted to the fraud.

EXAMPLE

In one case criminals changed the names of a business's officers by filing with the Secretary of State's office and then sold the whole business to a third party.

In the end, however, once an identity thief has established a business name, EIN, and address information, he or she has all the basic tools necessary to perpetrate business identity theft.

EXAMPLE

Harry and Iris Montgomery, the owners of a small aviation business, dissolved it early in 2012. Subsequently identity thieves reinstated the business and filed a 2012 tax return in its name, on which they claimed a $140,000 fuel aviation tax credit for which they obtained a tax refund. The Montgomerys discovered the scheme after the IRS sought the return of the refund.

EXAMPLE

Criminals stole a restaurant franchise's EIN and used it to create 100 fake Form W-2s, reporting to the IRS approximately $4 million paid in salaries. Ostensibly the thieves planned to use the fake Form W-2s to file individual tax returns and claim fraudulent refunds. Meanwhile, after the IRS agent saw the W-2s, the agent assessed a deficiency against the restaurant franchise for $800,000 in unpaid payroll taxes.

Payment Settlement Entities and Form 1099-K

Misused identities associated with *payment settlement entities* (PSEs) occur when a business opens and wishes to accept credit card payments from its clients or purchasers. The business opens a business bank account linked to credit card payments. When a client pays the business using a credit card, the business's bank deposits that payment in the business bank account, generally after charging a small processing fee.

EXAMPLE

Criminals set up more than 100 fake businesses with names similar to legitimate businesses and mailing addresses located within the same vicinity to avert suspicion. After establishing merchant payment accounts with local banks, they began making thousands of small charges using stolen credit cards. When it came time for the local banks to prepare their Forms 1099-K, *Payment Card and Third Party Network Transactions*, the thieves produced the legitimate businesses' names, addresses, and EINs. Because the actual businesses had no knowledge of what turned into more than $9.5 million in total credit card income generated over a four-year period, none of the legitimate businesses could account for the amounts appearing on the Form 1099-K.

When identity thieves steal a business's identity, they can also set up a business account with a PSE, which would be responsible for reporting all income from credit card transactions to the IRS. The clever identity thief provides a PSE with the information from the real business, so that the business cannot understand how to account for the income after receiving a Form 1099-K.

COMMENT

Form 1099-K is a relatively new type of information return that was introduced by the IRS for use by PSEs, such as local banks or payment companies like PayPal, to report payment card and third-party network transactions made between third parties and businesses that hold accounts with those PSEs.

In addition, many business taxpayers victimized by this kind of identity theft scheme can run afoul of the IRS if the IRS subsequently matches the income reported for a particular business on a Form 1099-K to the business's tax return, on which it the income item does not match.

COMMENT

Because the Form 1099-K was so recently introduced (in 2011), the IRS only announced that it would match the form against the income reported by small businesses on their tax returns (i.e., Forms 1120, 1120S and 1065) in late 2012. The IRS stated that legitimate income from such payments should already be included in a business's reported gross receipts. However, the IRS stated that if it found an unexpected discrepancy between a small business's reported income and what the IRS expected based on a Form 1099-K, the IRS would issue a notice to the business taxpayer.

STUDY QUESTION

3. All of the following are reasons identity theft is easier to perpetrate against a business than individuals ***except:***

   a. Businesses file tax returns less frequently
   b. Business tax information is more readily available than that of individuals
   c. Businesses open credit accounts using less information than individuals
   d. Business employer identification numbers are easily accessed

BEST PRACTICES FOR BUSINESSES

Businesses can also take precautions to lower their risk of becoming victims of identity thieves. Some of these best practices are noted here.

Account Monitoring

Businesses should monitor their accounts on a daily basis and follow up immediately on any suspicious activity. They should enroll in e-mail alerts to immediately be apprised of any change in account name, address, or other information. A manager should monitor the information on the business's registration frequently, whether the business is active or inactive.

Safeguarding a Dissolved Business

Businesses that have closed are particularly susceptible to business identity theft. This is especially the case where a business has closed shop without undergoing the formal dissolution process, which terminates all of the corporate authority. Businesses that fail to do this often wait until their business charter is forfeited by the state Secretary of State. Identity thieves can easily reinstate forfeited charters and then use that former business's entity to conduct tax fraud and other identity theft schemes.

Bank Protections

Businesses should also review their banks' policies and recommendations regarding fraud protection. The entities should know what security measures are being offered and, if commercially reasonable, take them.

COMMENT

A U.S. District Court in Missouri recently found that a bank was not liable for a fraudulent $440,000 wire transfer because it had offered the business a commercially reasonable security procedure, and the business had rejected it. The decision cited Uniform Commercial Code Article 4A-202(b), as adopted by the Missouri Code. Many other states have also adopted the UCC, meaning victimized businesses might find themselves without recourse against their banks in the event of a large fraudulent wire transfer.

COMMENT

One recommended security procedure is the use of two-factor or multifactor authentication. This requires authentication by more than one party to complete a wire transfer. In some cases authentication requires use of multiple methods, such as e-mail, fax, telephone, or physical token (i.e., a USB device or card).

Safeguarding Documents and Identification Information

Businesses should also try to protect their EINs by giving them out only when required. Moreover, they should take pains to ensure that documents bearing their EINs are either locked in a safe place or, if they are no longer necessary, destroyed before being thrown in the trash.

Changing Passwords

Practitioners should also be careful to change the default passwords on their computer software and to secure all portable devices, such as thumb drives, portable hard drives, or laptops that contain any TINs.

Return Preparers

Return preparers in particular should take pains to safeguard their business files, for both their sakes and those of their clients. Recommendations cited by the American Institute of Certified Public Accountants in a written statement issued to the IRS Oversight Board listed several easy tasks that tax practitioners can perform to protect their clients' sensitive information. These include:

- Locking desk drawers and file cabinets;
- Using encrypted flash drives;
- Using other encrypted procedures in electronically transferring a client's information to a third party;
- Redacting or truncating SSNs, EINs, EFINs, and other personal information;
- Using couriers and certified mail to ensure that the correct person receives his or her correspondence;
- Training staff and notifying clients about the proper handling of client information and how to avoid Internet schemes; and
- Installing and requiring antivirus and other security software on all firm computers.

STUDY QUESTION

4. Which of the following is a means by which tax return preparers can safeguard their business client files?

a. Saving computer files in only one location.
b. Redacting or truncating SSNs on all forms and correspondence.
c. Waiting until the end of the tax season to file a client's tax return.
d. Calling the IRS to obtain a client's former tax returns to verify current information.

WHEN ID THEFT HAS OCCURRED

Individuals who have been victimized by taxpayer identity theft have a number of resources at hand to help them rectify the situation.

Closing Accounts

Taxpayers should immediately identify any of their accounts that have been subject to identity theft-related fraud. They should then close any accounts that have been tampered with or opened fraudulently.

Contacting Equifax, Experian, and TransUnion

Taxpayers should contact the three major credit reporting agencies to have the agencies place a fraud alert on their reports that remains active for 90 days. Fraud alerts can be renewed.

Taxpayers should also obtain copies of their credit reports. The three credit reporting companies can be contacted at:

- Equifax: 800–525–6285, www.equifax.com;
- Experian: 888–397–3742, www.experian.com; and
- TransUnion: 800–680–7289, www.transunion.com.

Following Up on Fraudulent Credit Report Information

Taxpayers should review their reports and identify any open fraudulent home addresses, fraudulent accounts, and inquiries from companies that have received fraudulent applications. Taxpayers should then notify any credit card companies, banks, or other creditors that may have extended credit to the identity thief. Wherever possible, the taxpayer should attempt to obtain account numbers and other pertinent information, and should keep all documents and records of conversations associated with those accounts. This information could be used later when compiling the Form 14039, *Identity Theft Affidavit,* and police report.

Fraud Alerts

Taxpayers should notify their banks, other institutions, and all creditors that they have been a victim of identity theft and ask the organizations to place a fraud alert on these accounts.

Social Security Administration

Taxpayers should also report any misuse of their SSNs to the Social Security Administration (SSA).

Identity Theft Affidavit

Taxpayers should also place a fraud alert on their accounts with the IRS as soon as they suspect they have been victimized by identity theft, such as when they have received a notice from the IRS that their tax return has been rejected because one has already been filed with their SSN. To do this, taxpayers should fill out IRS Form 14039.

Taxpayers may do this even if no tax problem has yet occurred. When the IRS receives the affidavit, it will flag the taxpayer's account with a marker indicating that a tax return filed under his or her name could be fraudulent. In some cases the IRS will issue that taxpayer an *identity protection personal identification number* (IP PIN). This IP PIN must be included on the tax return for the tax year for which it was issued, or the tax return will be automatically rejected.

Federal Trade Commission

Individuals that have been victimized should also visit the website of the Federal Trade Commission (FTC) (www.ftc.gov/idtheft) or call the FTC Identity Theft hotline at 877–438–4338 or TTY 866–653–4261. The website contains a link to the online FTC Identity Theft Report, which taxpayers can fill out. Once the complete form is submitted, they will be able to obtain an Identity Theft Affidavit from the FTC, which can be helpful to local law enforcement officials trying to complete a police report.

Notifying Local Law Enforcement

Victims of identity theft should notify their local law enforcement authorities. Furthermore, they should obtain a detailed police report, which is of critical importance when the taxpayer tries to explain its situation to creditors.

Some local law enforcement agencies may be slow to pursue identity theft crimes. This delay may be because the taxpayer has not yet suffered a long-term economic loss.

COMMENT

Local law enforcement agencies are now able to obtain tax records from the IRS, with the taxpayer's permission, which could facilitate an investigation into the perpetrator of the particular identity theft.

IRS Identity Protection Specialized Unit

Finally, a taxpayer that has previously been in contact with the IRS regarding tax-related identity theft and has not achieved a resolution may contact the IRS Identity Protection Specialized Unit at 800–908–4490. The IRS established an Identity Protection Specialized Unit (IPSU) in 2008 as a means to provide centralized assistance to victims of identity theft.

Taxpayer Advocate Service

Taxpayers may also contact the Taxpayer Advocate Service (TAS) through the state/territory links at http://www.irs.gov/uac/Contact-Your-Advocate!, which has helped thousands of taxpayers attempting to resolve identity theft related issues. TAS itself handled nearly 55,000 identity theft cases in fiscal year 2012.

Businesses that have been victims of taxpayer identity theft (or identity theft in general), however, have fewer resources available to them. This is because most of the resources made available by government agencies have been designed for individuals.

Despite this, businesses could try to approach the crime in the same way as individuals, by checking their credit reports and placing a fraud alert on them, closing accounts that have been tampered with, and contacting the Federal Trade Commission to use its resources.

Businesses might also try to avail themselves of the Form 14039. But before submitting it to the IRS, they should indicate at the top of the form that the crime concerned theft of a business entity's information.

Changing the Employer Identification Number

A victimized business might also consider changing its EIN. This, however, must be done at the end of the fiscal year.

Business Victims of Merchant Payment Account Schemes

If a business discovers from a Form 1099-K that it has an unusually large and unexpected amount of credit card payment income, that could be an indication that the business has become a victim of identity theft. If the IRS has sent such a business a notice relating to potentially unreported or underreported Form 1099-K income, the IRS instructed the business to:

- Read the notice thoroughly and complete any attached worksheets;
- Gather all tax records, including any Form 1099-Ks, received for the tax year in question;
- Determine whether there has been a legitimate underreporting of gross receipts;
- Direct any questions to the contact information provided on the notice; and
- Consider consulting a tax professional.

STUDY QUESTION

5. Once taxpayers notify the IRS of fraudulent activities on the accounts, filers receive IP PINs in order to:

   a. Prepare Form 14039, *Identity Theft Affidavit*
   b. Share the fraud alerts with the FTC and SSA
   c. Prompt the IRS to automatically resolve the fraudulent issues
   d. Have an alternate identification number from their SSN, enabling them to file their returns electronically for the tax year

WHAT THE GOVERNMENT IS DOING

Treasury and the IRS are aware of the problem posed by identity theft and have taken measures to prevent it and also to protect its past or potential victims. Such measures include new filters placed on submitted tax returns during processing, issuance of unique identification numbers to potential identity theft victims, closer control of the Social Security Death Master File, and more. The IRS is also using intrafunctional and intragovernmental coordination to make identity theft detection more efficient and successful.

COMMENT

Government watchdogs such as TIGTA or the Government Accountability Office (GAO) have made additional suggestions for how the IRS could improve its effectiveness against identity theft. Some of them included:

- Using the National Directory of New Hires (NDNH) to verify wage information on tax returns (assuming, of course, that Congress first granted the IRS the requisite authority to do this). The NDNH is a database maintained by the Department of Health and Human Services that contains information on nearly all recently hired employees such as Form W-4 information, quarterly wage data reports, and unemployment compensation claims;
- Cross-verify Social Security benefit income reported on tax returns with the information provided to the SSA on Form SSA-1099, *Social Security Benefit Statement*; and
- Work with banks and relevant government agencies to develop processes that would ensure tax refund deposits were made only into an account held in the taxpayer's name.

Filters

The IRS uses "filters" that detect potential indicators of fraud prior to issuance of a tax refund. Filters are important for stopping fraudulent tax refunds from ever leaving the IRS's coffers. They are also relatively easy to update and administer and do much to halt significant losses of tax revenues. For example, during the 2011 filing season, the IRS added 13 new filters to detect and flag potentially fraudulent tax returns during processing. In November 2012, the IRS reported that for the 2011 filing season it had stopped approximately 480,000 tax returns, connected to $1.5 billion in fraudulently claimed tax refunds.

The IRS has continued to update its filters. During the 2013 filing season the IRS reported that it had "dozens" now in place. The filters can be updated based on, for example, an increase of fraudulent returns filed from a specific geographic area or address.

Third-Party Document Matching

Business identity theft often does not take the same form as individual identity theft. One common scheme is to steal a business's identity and use it to set up a merchant payment account with a PSE, as described earlier. Using stolen credit card information, which can easily be purchased from black market Internet websites, identity thieves can charge millions of dollars in small, incremental credit card charges that go largely undetected by the legitimate users of those credit cards.

Now that such merchant credit card income is reportable, businesses may realize they have been victimized by identity thieves when they receive a Form 1099-K from a PSE with which they do not hold an account or a notice from the IRS stating it has detected a potential underreporting of income.

The IRS has slowly introduced the new information reporting Form 1099-K (discussed earlier), which would be required of certain PSEs, which generally include banks or other organizations responsible for reporting the total dollar amount of payments made to payees participating in their organization. Apart from a local bank, PayPal is a common payee. Amazon.com, which facilitates the sale of goods by third parties through its system, is another.

The IRS has already begun to use Form 1099-K to detect suspicious discrepancies between merchant payment card income reported by PSEs and the gross receipts reported by small businesses on their tax returns. If the IRS detects a potential underreporting, it will notify the taxpayer by letter. However, the IRS does not have the ability to match the reported income on Form 1099-K to a specific line item on a business tax return, meaning that the letters will not propose specific adjustments to income.

Each letter instead will carry instructions. The required response by the taxpayer will vary and may sometimes require only a small amount of effort on the business's part and at other times a full review and accounting of a business's books preceding an audit.

COMMENT

In its July 19 audit report, TIGTA also noted that part of the hindrance to the IRS's ability to detect fraudulently filed tax returns during the initial processing stage was that tax filing season begins in January, but many third-party information documents, such as the Form W-2, *Wage and Tax Statement,* do not become available until later.

COMMENT

Some policy and lawmakers have suggested moving the filing season due date for individual tax returns from April 15 until later in the year to provide the IRS with more time to verify return information and process refunds. Others have suggested moving the due date for Forms W-2 to an earlier date. Thus far none of these suggestions have met with much support. Moving the filing season back would delay issuance of refunds. Moving the due date for the Form W-2 forward would arguably pose difficulties for payroll specialists.

Identity Theft Affidavits

Form 14039 is somewhat related to the IRS's filters. Upon receipt of a Form 14039, the IRS will immediately enter the information into its screening filters and place an identity theft marker on the taxpayer's account.

Form 14039 is designed for individual taxpayers whose financial information has been compromised. IRS officials have stated that such taxpayers should immediately submit a Form 14039 to the IRS, even if they do not yet have a tax problem. In other words, if taxpayers have encountered instances of credit card fraud or other type of identity theft committed against them—even if they have only had their purse or wallet stolen—those taxpayers can list these problems on Form 14039, even if the taxpayers are unsure whether this fraud will result in a tax problem.

Identity Protection Personal Identification Numbers

Another measure of protection includes issuance to certain taxpayers of a number that replaces their compromised SSN, the identity protection personal identification number (IP PIN). The IRS issues IP PINs to certain taxpayers whose accounts have been flagged with an identity theft indicator. The six-digit IP PIN must be used on the taxpayer's tax return or the return will be rejected. For every tax year that the identity theft indicator remains on the account, the taxpayer will receive a new IP PIN. A taxpayer may not use the IP PIN issued for previous tax years.

A taxpayer who has been assigned an IP PIN will receive two notices in the mail from the IRS. The first will arrive in early to mid-November and tells the taxpayer to expect receipt of his or her IP PIN number in the mail in December. The second notice contains the IP PIN itself. A taxpayer cannot file electronically without this IP PIN, nor can the taxpayer receive this particular IP PIN from any other source if it is lost.

COMMENT

The IRS first launched the IP PIN program in 2011. For filing season 2012, the IRS issued approximately 250,000 IP PINS to taxpayers with identity theft indicators on their tax accounts. If a return for a taxpayer who had received an IP PIN was filed without the IP PIN, the IRS automatically rejected it. For the 2013 filing season, the IRS expanded the IP PIN program to more than 600,000 taxpayers.

Locking SSNs for Deceased Individuals

The IRS stated that it has been making efforts to reduce the ability of identity thieves to use the personal identification information of deceased persons to commit taxpayer identity theft. During testimony delivered in late November 2012 before the House Committee on Oversight and Government Reform Subcommittee on Government Organization, Efficiency, and Financial Management, the IRS reported that during the first nine months of calendar year 2012, it had stopped processing of 130,000 returns using information belonging to deceased persons.

The IRS stated that it then placed locks on those accounts to prevent further misuse. IRS official Beth Tucker, Deputy Commissioner for Operations Support, reported that as of November 29, 2012, "We have locked over 97,000 accounts." She also stated that the IRS was collaborating with the SSA on promoting legislative changes to the practice of routine release of the Social Security Death Master File.

COMMENT

When a U.S. citizen dies, his or her SSN is entered the Death Master File, which also contains the names, dates of birth, and dates of death for more than 85 million people who died between 1936 and the present. Although the list was created in the 1980s in part as a means of preventing identity theft by enabling credit reporting agencies, banks, insurance companies, and state and local governments to cross-verify a person's identity against the SSNs on the list, this is not always done. In fact, the SSNs on the file, which are available for $10 at the website of the National Technical Information Service, a U.S. Department of Commerce affiliate, are frequently used to perpetrate identity theft schemes.

Collaboration with Local Law Enforcement

Although federal law generally imposes restrictions on what taxpayer information can be shared with others (including state and local law enforcement), in April 2012 the IRS established the Law Enforcement Assistance Pilot Program on Identity Theft Activity in Florida, through which identity theft victims could authorize the IRS to share information with local law enforcement. The IRS has since expanded the program nationwide in March 2013.

The program allows taxpayers to authorize the IRS to disclose their taxpayer information, including the fraudulent returns submitted using their SSNs, to state and local law enforcement officials, specifically to aid assist them in building a case against identity theft perpetrators.

The process specifies that law enforcement officials must contact the identity theft victims in order to request and secure the victims' consent for disclosure of the taxpayer records. In certain instances, the IRS assists law enforcement in locating taxpayers and soliciting their consent.

Law enforcement officials then submit a disclosure authorization form, created by the IRS solely for use by victims of identity theft for this pilot program, to the IRS Criminal Investigation (CI) Division. Officials should also enclose a copy of the police report and the IRS Form 14039, if one is available. The IRS processes the disclosure forms and forward the documentation to the law enforcement officer who made the request. The documents are not sent directly to the taxpayer.

COMMENT

Ostensibly the IRS chose Florida for its pilot program because in 2011 the state carried the unfortunate distinction of having the highest rate of identity theft in the United States. Of all cities in Florida, Miami's ratio of identity theft complaints to total residents is the worst. In 2011 it was 324.1 complaints per 100,000 residents. A TIGTA report from September 2012 stated that it had identified 74,496 potentially fraudulent returns filed in Miami alone. These returns resulted in more than $280 million in fraudulent refunds. Placed into a wider context, Miami's per capita number of false returns based on identity theft was 46 times the national average.

Truncated SSNs or Barcodes

The IRS is also working to reduce the number of times a SSN appears on official notices and forms, which would reduce the risk of an identity thief obtaining personal identification information from discarded or mislaid official government documents. This action is part of a federal government-wide initiative requiring all agencies to examine their systems, forms, and processes to determine where they could eliminate any unnecessary appearance of SSNs in correspondence.

Many of the IRS notices have already replaced a taxpayer's SSN with a two-dimensional barcode. In other instances, such as the Notice of Federal Tax Lien, the IRS simply truncated the SSN so that all that appears are the last four digits. However, for documents such as a statutory notice of deficiency or a Collection Due Process notice, the appearance of the SSN is required by law and can only be removed by an act of Congress.

Additional Staff Training and Hires

In 2012, the IRS assigned more than 3,000 IRS employees to work on identity theft-related issues such as preventing refund fraud, investigating identity theft-related crimes, and assisting victims of taxpayer identity theft. The IRS also trained 35,000 employees who work with taxpayers to recognize identity theft indicators and provide aid to victims.

Sweep of Check-Cashing Businesses

During 2012, IRS auditors and investigators visited 197 check-cashing businesses located in 17 cities to verify that they are not assisting identity theft or refund fraud when they cash checks. Check-cashing businesses are frequently used by identity thieves to cash fraudulently obtained tax refund checks. This is likely because check-cashing businesses are less likely to scrutinize the transaction.

Federal Law Enforcement

Enforcement of the laws against identity theft is the last resort in the IRS's efforts to prevent the crime. In recent years the IRS CI Division announced that it was collaborating with the Department of Justice (DOJ) officials and other agencies, such as the Department of Homeland Security, in a coordinated approach to combating identity theft.

In early February 2013, the IRS reported that these efforts were paying off. For example, the combined work of several federal agencies along with state and local law enforcement resulted in a large nationwide sweep targeting identity theft suspects in 32 states and Puerto Rico, involving a total of 215 cities. The sweep also involved 389 individuals and lead to hundreds of enforcement actions in January 2013, the IRS stated.

The DOJ stated that it had placed a point of contact for stolen identity refund fraud in each U.S. Attorney's Office. It was also setting up multi-jurisdictional working groups nationwide to combat identity theft.

Meanwhile, the IRS CI Division recently announced that it had opened approximately 900 identity theft investigations in fiscal year 2012. In the first four months of fiscal year 2013 the CI Division reported that it had opened more than 500 criminal investigations.

STUDY QUESTION

6. IRS auditors perform sweeps of check-cashing businesses for all of the following reasons ***except:***

   a. The businesses may assist in cashing fraudulent refund checks
   b. Such businesses are frequently used by identity thieves
   c. Refund checks cashed by such businesses are for larger sums than average refunds
   d. Such businesses are not as scrupulous as taxpayers' banks in verifying the checks are nonfraudulent

CONCLUSION

Identity theft can strike anyone, anywhere, and it may or may not be committed in a form that affects a taxpayer's tax records. Nevertheless, if it the theft does result in tax return fraud, the result can be significant losses of time and money for the taxpayer, the taxpayer's financial institution, and the government. Moreover, tax return fraud perpetrated against a return preparer can cripple his or her business in addition to harming the clients. There are precautions that taxpayers, both individual and business, can take to try to minimize the risk of having their identities stolen in furtherance of tax return fraud. Tax return preparers can also take careful precautions to safeguard their clients and their businesses. Even these preventative measures can fail, however. When they do, the victims of tax return fraud must act quickly to record the evidence of the crime, reporting the fraud to their creditors, credit reporting agencies, and the IRS.

The IRS, Treasury, SSA, and FTC are aware of the growing problem of identity theft and have made resources available to victims. Taxpayers and businesses that have experienced taxpayer identity theft, or even those who suspect they might be victimized but have not yet been harmed, are encouraged to come forth and report incidents to the government. Doing so can aid the government in preventing the processing of fraudulent tax returns. Detailed reports can also aid the government in investigating and prosecuting identity theft criminals and preventing them from committing more crimes against other individuals or businesses in the future.

MODULE 3: INDIVIDUALS: RELATIONSHIPS AND THE TAX LAW — CHAPTER 7

Boomer Retirement Strategies

This chapter explores some of the important tax planning considerations facing individuals who fall within the category "baby boomer," generally considered to be those individuals born after World War II between 1946 and 1964. Individuals age 65 and older currently number approximately 40 million according to the federal government's Administration on Aging; they make up around 13 percent of the U.S. population. The number of individuals age 65 and older is projected to increase to almost 70 million by 2030.

LEARNING OBJECTIVES

Upon completion of this chapter, you will be able to:

- Understand key considerations in rebalancing assets with an eye toward retirement, including strategies for capital gains within investment portfolios as well as the sale of a residence;
- Describe some of the special rules for retirement savings vehicles applicable to boomers;
- Identify medical deduction opportunities and strategies;
- Understand the taxation of Social Security benefits;
- Describe considerations in winding down participation in a business;
- Describe gift planning techniques for boomers; and
- Identify some estate planning strategies for boomers.

INTRODUCTION

As the first wave of baby boomers begins to retire, these shifts in income and employment have many potential tax consequences. Today, retirement for many individuals is not necessarily a time to sit back and relax. One of the key differences between retiring today and one or two generations ago is mobility of job skills and locations. Technology opens countless employment opportunities. Many individuals are starting second or third careers, relocating to new places for business or leisure, or winding down or starting a business. Tax professionals play a key role in advising baby boomers of the myriad options available to them.

REBALANCING INVESTMENTS

Most boomers have seen economic fortunes rise and fall during their lifetime. Many have assisted, or are currently assisting, their parents in their old age, some parents doing quite well and others having lived long enough to deplete their assets. Still other boomers have had the good fortune to inherit assets. Unlike previous generations, many boomers cannot rely on a monthly pension check in their retirement; others have found that financial demands over the years have compromised what they could put away on their own in retirement savings.

No matter what their situation, boomers sooner or later generally ask the question: Will I outlive my money? Part of the solution to avoiding depletion of funds may involve reexamining financial assets for risk and growth, both within individual retirement accounts (IRAs) or qualified retirement savings plans, and investment savings outside of these plans. Another part of the solution may include downsizing a residence, especially selling a principal residence and/or vacation home that has increased significantly in value over the years. Most solutions require a good mix of tax planning and sound financial advice.

COMMENT

As a person reaches retirement age, a reexamination of assets for both risk and growth is usually in order. "Risk" is relevant because the ability to add to a portfolio through wage or self-employment income is usually limited, thereby making future portfolio losses particularly painful. "Growth" is considered because the interest rate paid on secured/insured investments typically will not keep up with inflation. This chapter does not advise the correct mix of investments for any particular client. Instead, it focuses on a review of the tax impact of typical transactions that form a part of most strategies: selling securities (stocks and bonds), buying into an annuity, buying government bonds, and selling a residence.

Selling Securities

A boomer with a diverse portfolio may want to retain a portion of his or her investments in the stock and bond markets in order to better protect a portion of his or her future income stream from inflation. Some boomers may have more than enough money to live on and want to increase the size of their estates for the eventual benefit of their children and grandchildren.

Strategies that involve staying invested in equities generally require a rebalancing of assets. That rebalancing should also coordinate what assets may be rebalanced within a qualified retirement plan or IRA. While the sale of securities in a regular investment account will produce immediate taxable gains and losses, a rebalancing within a qualified plan or IRA produces no taxable gain or loss, with income tax imposed only when funds are withdrawn.

COMMENT

Strategies also may also involve being more reliant on mutual funds rather than individual stocks and bonds. Owning individual stocks and bonds often results in less diversification and more of a need to monitor performance, which becomes more difficult for many individuals as they age.

Capital gains. *Capital gain net income* is the excess of an individual's capital gains, long-term and short-term, over capital losses, long-term and short-term. Capital gain net income is included in gross income. Capital assets—including stocks and bonds—yield short-term gains or losses if the holding period is one year or less, and long-term gains or losses if the holding period exceeds one year. The excess of net long-term gains over net short-term losses is *net capital gain.* Although short-term capital gains are taxed at ordinary rates, net capital gain of noncorporate taxpayers, as adjusted for certain types of long-term gain (adjusted net capital gain), is eligible for lower maximum tax rates than ordinary income. That rate is usually 15 percent, except to the extent income falls within an individual's:

- 10 or 15 percent income tax rate bracket, whereupon it is taxed at zero percent; or
- 39.6 percent income tax rate, when it is taxed at 20 percent.

Further, *net investment income,* including long- or short-term capital gains, or otherwise, is taxed at an additional 3.8 percent to the extent certain adjusted gross income (AGI) threshold amounts are exceeded ($250,000 for joint filers, $150,000 for married filing separately, and $200,000 for all others (including unmarried single individuals)).

Basis. Gain is determined by subtracting an asset's basis from its selling price. *Selling price* in the case of securities is generally the trade price less commissions. *Basis* in an asset is generally the cost of acquiring the securities (its purchase price plus commissions). Inherited securities have a basis keyed to their date-of-death value for estate tax purposes. The basis for securities received by gift, however, is the donor's basis. Brokers are generally now required to report basis to the IRS in addition to account holders at the end of each year.

Distributions from mutual funds to shareholders may be ordinary income, capital gain, tax-exempt income, or return of capital. The cost or other basis of mutual fund shares is adjusted for reinvestments, load charges, and return of capital. The basis of shares actually sold, exchanged, or redeemed is determined by how a taxpayer accounts for shares in the same mutual fund. Exchanges within the same family of funds is a taxable event. Special rules may affect whether capital gain on sale, exchange or redemption of shares is short or long-term.

Home Sale Exclusion

For many boomers, their home is their most valuable asset. Planning for the income produced from the sale of the home should be taken into account, if possible, before a sale is entered into either voluntarily or when circumstances, such as a change in health or death of a spouse, may necessitate the sale. One of the most potentially valuable tax benefits and planning tools for boomers is the *home sale exclusion,* which allows a taxpayer to exclude gain from the sale of his or her principal residence if certain criteria are met. In some cases, taxpayers may be eligible for a reduced home sale exclusion if they do not qualify for the maximum amount.

A taxpayer may exclude from income gain from the sale of his or her principal residence if:

- At any time during the five years preceding the sale, he or she owned the property for at least two years;
- At any time during the five years preceding the sale, he or she used the property as his or her principal residence for two years; and
- The taxpayer did not use the exclusion during the prior two years.

Single individuals who satisfy all of the requirements may exclude up to $250,000 of gain from income in the year of sale. Married couples who satisfy all of the requirements may exclude up to $500,000 of gain if they file a joint income tax return. Married couples filing separately can each exclude up to $250,000 of gain. There are special rules for surviving spouses (discussed below).

COMMENT

Many boomers, particularly married couples who purchased a home when newly married and who are now downsizing after many years of residing in the home will easily satisfy the ownership and use requirements. However, there are exceptions to the general rule (discussed below), which could help boomers in the event they do not satisfy the ownership and use criteria.

The home sale exclusion is applicable only to the sale of a taxpayer's principal residence. The determination of whether a property is a taxpayer's principal residence is determined based on all the facts and circumstances. Among the factors (not an exhaustive list) are:

- The address listed on the taxpayer's federal and state tax returns, driver's license, automobile registration, and voter registration card;
- The taxpayer's mailing address for bills and correspondence;
- The taxpayer's place of employment; and
- Location of the taxpayer's place of worship, recreational clubs, or other organizations with which he or she is affiliated.

EXAMPLE

Steven Tomason purchased a home in Minneapolis in 1999 and a home in Miami in 2005. Steven, age 58, is an architect. Currently, Steven lives in the house in Minneapolis eight months and the house in Miami four months each year. Absent any facts and circumstances that would indicate otherwise, Steven's principal residence is the house in Minneapolis.

For taxpayers who own a home, the requisite two years of ownership and use during the five-year period ending on the date of sale does not need to be continuous. A taxpayer needs to have owned and lived in the home as his or her principal residence for 24 full months—or 730 days—during the five-year period ending on the date of sale.

COMMENT

A taxpayer's short, temporary absence from his or her principal residence generally does not take away from the time counted as use.

There are a number of exceptions to the ownership and use tests. The exception for taxpayers with a disability may be of value to boomers who experience physical or mental disabilities. The use exception for taxpayers with a disability applies if the taxpayer becomes physically or mentally unable to care for him- or herself and the taxpayer lived in the home as his or her principal residence for a total of at least one year during the five-year period before the sale of the home. The taxpayer must also satisfy the two-year ownership test.

Special rules apply when a spouse has died and the survivor did not remarry before the date of sale. The surviving spouse is considered to have owned and lived in the property as his or her principal residence during any period of time when the spouse owned and lived in it as a main home. There are additional requirements:

- The survivor must not have remarried;
- The sale or exchange must have taken place no more than two years after the date of death of the spouse;
- The survivor and the decedent must have met the use test at the time of the spouse's death;
- The survivor and the decedent met the ownership test at the time of the spouse's death;
- Neither the survivor nor the spouse may have excluded gain from the sale of another home during the last two years before the date of death; and
- The sale or exchange must have taken place after 2008.

EXAMPLE

Claire Jameson owned and used a home in Dallas as her principal residence beginning on May 31, 2010. Claire married Jonah Stamford on June 1, 2013. Claire and Jonah thereafter used the Dallas home as their principal residence. Claire died suddenly and unexpectedly on August 30, 2013. Jonah sold the house on October 1, 2013, at which time Jonah had not remarried. Although Jonah owned and used the home for less than two years, Jonah is treated as having met the ownership and use tests because his period of ownership includes the period of ownership and use by Claire.

Taxpayers who fail to meet the ownership and use criteria for the full home sale exclusion may qualify for a reduced exclusion. Taxpayers may also qualify for a reduced exclusion if they have used part of the exclusion within two years of selling their current home. The sale of the taxpayer's principal residence must be on account of a change in place of employment, a change in health, or unforeseen circumstances. For boomers, a change in their health or the health of a parent or other relative may satisfy the criteria for claiming the reduced exclusion.

To satisfy the criteria for health, the sale of a taxpayer's principal residence must be to obtain, provide, or facilitate the diagnosis, cure, mitigation, or treatment of disease, illness, or injury of a qualified individual, or to obtain or provide medical or personal care for a qualified individual suffering from a disease, illness, or injury.

EXAMPLE

Heather and Justin McCall were married and in January 2012 purchased a home in Seattle. Twelve months later, Justin's father, Karl, who is 93 and resides in Denver, is diagnosed with advanced lung cancer and cannot care for himself. Heather and Justin sell their home in Seattle in May 2013 and move into Karl's home to care for him. Heather and Justin may take advantage of the reduced home sale exclusion.

Vacation homes offer owners many of the tax breaks similar to those for primary residences. For example, real estate taxes are deductible, as is mortgage interest up to a combined mortgage balance of $1 million for both a primary residence and a second home. Whereas gain on the sale of a principal residence can be excludable up to the $250,000/$500,000 exemption amount, gain on the sale of a vacation home is not so excludable. Homeowners can consider converting a vacation home to their primary residence in order to qualify for the exclusion. However, the amount of the exclusion is reduced to account for the periods in which the seller owned the home but did not use it as a primary residence.

COMMENT

Under Code Sec. 121, gain is allocated to periods of nonqualified use based on the ratio that the aggregate periods of nonqualified use during the period such property was owned by the taxpayer, bears to the period such property was owned by the taxpayer. However, the partial home sale exclusion that results after applying the apportionment rule may still be sufficient to offset the gain, depending upon the circumstances.

STUDY QUESTION

1. Why do individuals approaching retirement rebalance their investment portfolios?

- **a.** To remove holdings of equities
- **b.** To protect nest eggs from risk while allowing for growth of funds to exceed inflation
- **c.** To take short-term gains as ordinary income before retirement rather than hold equities until proceeds are long-term gains in retirement
- **d.** To make tax-free exchanges of mutual funds in the same fund family

ANNUITIES

Assuming a major concern of most boomers is whether their retirement savings are adequate to last their lifetime, the purchase of an annuity that provides a lifetime of payments may form a useful component within an overall plan.

COMMENT

Financial planning aspects over and above the tax ramifications usually involve, among other considerations, the fees charged, inflation clauses, and any residual value that may be passed on to heirs.

Taxable Amounts

Annuity payments in excess of return of capital are taxable income to recipient. Other amounts received under an annuity, endowment, or life insurance contract are not received as annuity benefits and are taxable to extent cash value exceeds investment.

In contrast to a life insurance policy, which pays a beneficiary an amount of money on the death of the insured, the typical annuity pays a specified amount of money until the death of the annuitant or the expiration of a fixed term. Payments made under annuity contracts are taxed differently, depending on whether the payment qualifies as an amount received as an annuity.

Amounts Received as an Annuity

Generally, amounts received as an annuity are amounts payable under an annuity contract at regular intervals. Amounts received as an annuity are included in gross income to the extent that they exceed the "exclusion ratio." The *exclusion ratio* is determined by taking the original investment in the contract, deducting the value of any refund features, and dividing the result by the expected yield on the contract as of the annuity starting date.

Payments made under a life insurance, endowment, or annuity contract that do not satisfy the statutory definition of amounts received as annuities are amounts not received as annuities. Amounts not received as an annuity include dividends, refunds of consideration paid, death benefits, cash withdrawals, and amounts received on the surrender, redemption, or maturity of the contract. Dividends or cash withdrawals received after the annuity's benefit starting date are included in gross income.

RETIREMENT SAVINGS

There are many retirement savings vehicles. Traditional individual retirement accounts (IRAs) for which taxpayers make tax-deductible contributions are among the most popular type of retirement savings vehicle. Boomers with traditional IRAs, especially IRA holders who are married, may be able to maximize their savings with spousal IRA rules and special catch-up contributions. Additionally, the tax treatment of their IRA funds after their death is an important tax-planning consideration. The tax treatment of a traditional IRA after the owner's death differs if the beneficiary is the owner's spouse or another individual.

Types of Qualified Retirement Savings

The *Small Business Job Protection Act of 1996* created spousal IRAs (now known as Kay Bailey Hutchison IRAs after the senator who advocated for their creation in the 1996 law). Spouses who are nonwage earners may make equal, fully deductible contributions to IRAs. For 2013, in the case of a taxpayer who is married, files a joint return, and has taxable compensation less than that of his or her spouse, the maximum that can be contributed to an IRA is the smaller of:

- $5,500 ($6,500 if age 50 or older), or
- The total compensation included in the gross income of both the taxpayer and his or her spouse for the year, reduced by the following two amounts:
  - The spouse's IRA contribution for the year to a traditional IRA, and
  - Any contributions for the year to a Roth IRA on behalf of the spouse.

COMMENT

A taxpayer's deduction for an IRA contribution may be limited if one or both spouses are covered by an employer retirement plan. The thresholds for 2013 are more than $95,000 but less than $115,000 for a married couple filing a joint return (or a qualifying widow(er)); more than $59,000 but less than $69,000 for a single taxpayer or head of household; and less than $10,000 for a married individual filing separately.

Individuals who are age 50 and older (almost all individuals who fall within the boomer category) can make additional contributions to an IRA. The amount of the *catch-up contribution* differs depending on the type of retirement savings vehicle. For 2013, the catch-up amounts are:

- $1,000 for IRAs (traditional IRA and Roth IRA);
- $5,500 for 401(k) plans (but not SIMPLE 401(k) plans), 403(b) plans, and governmental 457(b) plans; and
- $2,500 for SIMPLE IRA or SIMPLE 401(k) plans.

Funds in a traditional IRA cannot be rolled over to the spouse's IRA while both the owner and his or her spouse are living. After the owner of a traditional IRA dies, the surviving spouse can:

- Treat it as his or her own IRA by designating him- or herself as the account owner;
- Treat it as his or her own by rolling it over into a traditional IRA, or to the extent it is taxable, into a qualified employer plan, qualified employee annuity plan (Code Sec. 403(a) plan), tax-sheltered annuity plan (Code Sec. 403(b) plan), or deferred compensation plan of a state or local government (Code Sec. 457(b) plan); or
- Treat himself or herself as the beneficiary rather than treating the IRA as his or her own IRA.

COMMENT

Because of the Supreme Court's decision in ***Windsor,*** 2013-2 USTC ¶50,500 (2013) to strike down Section 3 of the Defense of Marriage Act (DOMA), surviving spouses in a same-sex marriage will presumably be treated the same as surviving spouses in opposite-sex marriages. The IRS is expected to issue guidance.

COMMENT

The rules for surviving spouses for other retirement savings plans, such as Code Sec. 401(k) plans, are different from the rules for traditional IRAs and are not addressed in this chapter.

If a surviving spouse receives a distribution from his or her deceased spouse's IRA, it can be rolled over into an IRA of the surviving spouse within the 60-day time limit, as long as the distribution is not a required minimum distribution (RMD). If the decedent's IRA passes through a third party before being distributed to the surviving spouse, generally the spouse is treated as having acquired the IRA from the third party and not the decedent. In this case, the IRA is an "inherited IRA" (discussed below).

If the beneficiary of an IRA is not the owner's surviving spouse, the IRS is treated as an inherited IRA. The rules governing inherited IRAs differ from those that govern IRAs held by a surviving spouse beneficiary. In the case of an inherited IRA, the beneficiary cannot treat it as his or her own.

COMMENT

The beneficiary of an inherited IRA cannot make any contributions to the IRA or roll over any amounts into or out of the IRA. However, the beneficiary can make a trustee-to-trustee transfer as long as the IRA into which amounts are being moved is set up and maintained in the name of the deceased IRA owner for the benefit of the beneficiary.

Early Retirement

Some boomers are retiring early (that is, before their full retirement age for Social Security benefits), either because they have determined they have adequate resources to do so or because they have been effectively forced out of the job market. When a retirement plan or IRA participant or owner receives a distribution, the amounts are generally taxed at ordinary rates. (Roth IRA distributions are not subject to income tax, because Roth IRA contributions are not deductible.) An early withdrawal penalty of 10 percent may be imposed if distributions are made contrary to certain early-retirement rules and the retiree is less than 59½ years old.

A qualified plan may provide for commencement of payments at a normal retirement age or an earlier retirement age upon satisfaction of a minimum service requirement. However, the plan must include two important provisions with respect to an employee who satisfies the service requirements for the plan's early retirement benefit but separates from service before the specified early retirement age with a nonforfeitable right to an accrued benefit from the plan:

- The plan must specify that the participant who retires before the specified early retirement age will only be entitled to receive payments upon reaching the specified early retirement age; and
- The plan must provide that payments to such a retiree may not exceed the normal retirement benefit, reduced in accordance with reasonable actuarial assumptions.

COMMENT

An employee who is covered by a defined contribution plan and retires after satisfaction of the service criterion for the early retirement benefit but before satisfaction of the age requirement is likewise entitled to the early retirement benefit upon attainment of the required age. The benefit from the defined contribution plan would constitute the amounts maintained in the participant's accounts under the plan.

The 10 percent penalty on early distributions does not apply to distributions from a traditional IRA that are part of a series of substantially equal periodic payments made no less frequently than annually over the life expectancy of the owner or the joint life expectancies of the owner and the designated beneficiary. Once an owner begins receiving substantially equal periodic payments, any changes to the method of distribution prior to age 59½, other than by reason of the owner's death or disability, result in a retroactive imposition of the 10 percent penalty, with interest, on all previously taxed distributions. Changes in the method of distribution occurring after age 59½ are subject to the 10 percent penalty only if the IRA owner has received less than five years of substantially equal periodic payments.

Normal Retirement

Participants in retirement plans generally must start receiving their retirement savings when they retire or when they reach a certain age. Distributions from a qualified plan generally must take place after a specified time, but before a given end date. The plan must provide for distributions to begin no later than 60 days after the close of the plan year in which the latest of these events occurs:

- The participant turns 65 or, if earlier, reaches the normal retirement age specified in the plan;
- The participant marks the tenth anniversary of enrollment in the plan; or
- The participant terminates service with the employer.

Most qualified plans must also make RMDs of amounts that a plan participant must withdraw each year after the participant retires or reaches age 70, depending on the type of plan. RMDs can be made through annuity or nonannuity distributions. The RMD rules generally limit the time period that funds may remain tax-deferred in qualified retirement plans.

A participant who receives a lump-sum distribution of the balance in the account is taxed on the amount of the lump-sum distribution, less the investment (if any), unless it is properly rolled over into an IRA. A participant who does not receive a lump-sum distribution may receive an annuity, which is an amount payable at regular intervals over a period of more than one full year. The total amount payable can be determined as of the annuity starting date, either from the terms of the annuity contract or from actuarial tables.

COMMENT

Retirement savings may be affected by an earlier divorce or family law issue. For instance, a *qualified domestic relations order* (QDRO) is a judgment, decree, or order made under a state's domestic relations or community property law, that requires a plan to make distributions to someone other than the plan participant. Distributions to an alternate payee under a QDRO are taxable to the alternate payee, not to the participant. QDROs must relate to the provision of child support, alimony, or marital property rights to a spouse, former spouse, child, or other dependent of a plan participant.

The owner of a traditional IRA must receive the entire balance in periodic distributions starting no later than April 1 of the year following the year in which the owner reaches age 70½. In the case of an inherited IRA, the applicable required distribution rules depend on whether the IRA owner died before or after his or her required beginning date of distributions. Distributions from inherited IRAs are taxable to the recipient as ordinary income.

Charitable Contributions from IRAs

Individuals age 70½ or older may make qualified charitable distributions (QCDs or gifts) of funds from their IRAs to a qualified charity. The advantages of doing so are:

- The contribution is excluded from the donor's taxable income; and
- The donation may be used to satisfy the donor's RMD requirements.

The maximum amount of the gift is $100,000. As of this writing, this special treatment is scheduled to expire after 2013.

STUDY QUESTION

2. Which of the following is ***not*** permitted for the spouse when the owner of a traditional IRA dies?

a. Treating him- or herself as the beneficiary of the deceased's account
b. Rolling over the account balance of the traditional IRA tax-free into a Roth IRA under his or her own name
c. Treating the IRA as his or her own and rolling it over into a traditional IRA or qualified plan
d. Treating the IRA as his or her own by redesignating him- or herself as the account holder

MEDICAL COSTS

As individuals age, it is natural that they start to have more medical expenses. They also start contemplating the likelihood of needing more care. Considerations can include not only medical care but also basic custodial care, such as nursing care, home healthcare, rest home care, or even adult daycare.

Aging individuals not only want to maintain their health insurance but may want to purchase long-term care insurance. Like ordinary medical insurance, the cost of long-term care insurance can be deducted on the tax return, but only up to specified limits and only if certain requirements in the tax code are satisfied. Premiums paid for Medicare are also deductible as medical expenses.

Medical Expense Deduction

The basic rule is that medical expenses can be deducted as an itemized deduction, but only to the extent that they exceed a specified threshold. Historically, this threshold has been 7.5 percent of AGI. Beginning in 2013, the threshold was raised to 10 percent of AGI. However, if the taxpayer (or spouse on a joint return) is 65 at the close of the tax year, the threshold remains at 7.5 percent.

The cost of lodging may be deducted as a medical expense if the lodging is primarily for medical care provided by a doctor in a hospital or similar facility. However, the tax code limits this deduction to $50 per night for the person obtaining the medical care. The cost of meals in the hospital is deductible for the patient but not for others; meal costs outside a hospital are not deductible.

Transportation expenses related to medical care such as train or plane fares, gasoline costs, and parking fees, can also be deducted. Actual car expenses can be deducted or claimed at a standard mileage rate set by the IRS. The rate is 24 cents for 2013.

Medical insurance premiums are treated as medical expenses. Insurance premiums are deductible only if they are for medical care and are separately identified. If the insurance provides coverage for other, nonmedical items, such as indemnity insurance, the expense of those items cannot be deducted.

Long-Term Care

Most medical insurance plans, including Medicare, do not provide for long-term care. Plans may explicitly exclude custodial care and be limited to skilled acute health care. Thus, to ensure that they have necessary coverage, individuals should consider purchasing a separate long-term care policy. Policies may cover nursing home care, home healthcare, or a combination of the two.

The tax code defines *long-term care* as diagnostic, preventive, therapeutic, curing, treating, mitigating, rehabilitative, and maintenance or personal-care services. Insurance premiums are deductible if the policy satisfies the following requirements:

- The insurance provides protection only for long-term care;
- The contract is guaranteed to be renewable;
- The contract does not have a cash surrender value;
- Any premium refunds or dividends must reduce future premiums or increase benefits; and
- The contract meets certain consumer protection laws.

The tax code limits the deductible amount per year as follows. The amounts are indexed for inflation, as shown in the table.

Table 1. Maximum Deduction for Long-Term Care Premiums

Individual's Age	Inflation-Adjusted Limit (for 2013)
Ages 40 or younger	$360
Ages 41,–50	$680
Ages 51–60	$1,360
Ages 61–70	$3,640
Ages 71 and older	$4,550

Medicare

Individuals become eligible for Medicare at age 65 or upon disability, as determined by the Social Security Administration (SSA). The program comprises four parts:

- All eligible individuals receive Medicare Part A (hospitalization) automatically and at no premium cost;
- Medicare Part B covers doctor and outpatient services;
- Medicare Part C provides supplemental health insurance through privately sold policies; and
- Medicare Part D covers outpatient prescription drugs.

Premiums paid for Parts B–D are deductible like other medical insurance premiums.

STUDY QUESTION

3. Which of the following is ***not*** eligible to deduct as a medical expense?

a. Car mileage and other transportation expenses for medical visits
b. Lodging of up to $50 per person per night for medical care
c. Medical insurance premiums
d. Meal costs at the family's lodging

SOCIAL SECURITY BENEFITS

Social Security benefits include monthly retirement, survivor, and disability benefits. The amount of Social Security benefits that must be in…d on a taxpayer's income tax return and used to calculate his or her i… tax liability depends on the total amount of income and benefits f… tax year, as well as the taxpayer's age.

Working and Taking Benefits

Some boomers may be taking Social Security benefits and also w… Between age 62 and a taxpayer's full retirement age, his or her Social … benefits may be reduced if wages exceed a threshold amount. The S… deduct $1 for every $2 earned by the taxpayer. In the year that the t… reaches full retirement age, the SSA deducts $1 for every $3 earne… the month before the taxpayer reaches full retirement age. After a ta… reaches full retirement age, the SSA does not deduct any amount fr… taxpayer's benefits.

COMMENT

Full retirement age is the age at which a person may first become entitled to full o… unreduced retirement benefits. For individuals born between 1943 and 1954, full retirement age is age 66.

COMMENT

For 2013, the threshold amount for deducting benefits on an individual's wages is $15,120.

Taxation of Social Security Benefits

To determine whether a taxpayer's Social Security benefits are taxable, the base amount of the taxpayer's filing status must be compared with the total of one-half of the Social Security benefits and all of the taxpayer's other income. The base amounts are:

- $25,000 for a single taxpayer, head of household, or qualifying widow(er);
- $25,000 if married, filing separately and living apart from the spouse for the entire year;
- $32,000 if married filing jointly; and
- $0 if married, filing separately, and living with the spouse at any time during the tax year.

If the ...l is more than the taxpayer's base amount, some of the taxpayer's Soci...curity benefits may be taxable.

...MMENT

...plemental security income (SSI) payments for disabled adults and children are not ...able.

...DY QUESTION

4. Which of the following types of Social Security benefits are never taxable, even if the taxpayer earns more than the base amount?
   - **a.** Retirement benefits taken by a taxpayer after full retirement age
   - **b.** Survivor benefits for widow(er)s
   - **c.** Supplemental security income payments
   - **d.** Each type of benefit is taxable if the recipient's income exceeds the base amount

SELLING OR TRANSFERING A BUSINESS

Many boomers have found success in developing a business, either from the ground up over the years or only lately in a recent career move. A business owner can usually begin to sense when his or her "time has come" when active involvement in the business, whether full- or part-time, is no longer appealing, necessary, or even possible. A business owner may also begin to need those assets tied up in the business to fund his or her retirement. All or some of these situations may persuade the boomer that it is time to sell the business or pass it on to younger family members, who may or may not already be involved in the business.

Sale of a Business Outside of the Family

Generally, if a business owner is voluntarily ending or disposing of a business outside of the family setting, tax alternatives within the sale of the business should be considered. Depending in part on the owner's preference and in part on the business entity's form, the owner can either accomplish the sale of a business through the sale of business assets or through the sale of the owner's entire ownership interest. When an owner sells assets of a business, each asset is treated as being sold separately for the purpose of determining the treatment of gain or loss.

Sole proprietor. Selling the assets of the sole proprietorship almost always constitutes a taxable transaction. This is because the sole proprietorship does not involve a legal entity that is separate and distinct from its owner. Gain or loss is calculated based on the amount allocated as consideration for the assets that is in excess of (or is less than) the amount of the proprietor's basis in those assets. Sometimes, use of an installment sale can help by smoothing out the amount of income otherwise realized all in one year. A sale of a business that is not a sole proprietorship may also involve planning with respect to the tax entity in which it has operated.

C corporation. A corporation can sell its business by selling its business assets. It must recognize gain or loss on the sale and, if it makes distributions, the shareholder must recognize gain or loss on them. In other words, proceeds from the sale of corporate assets are generally taxed twice, once at the corporate level and next on the shareholder level.

A taxpayer with an ownership interest in a corporation can also sell all of his or her stock in the corporation. Such sales of stock are subject to the rules on taxation of capital gains and losses. Sellers generally prefer to sell their ownership interest in a stock sale because that involves only one level of tax at capital gains rates. Buyers engaged in a stock purchase can elect under Code Sec. 338 to treat certain stock purchases as an acquisition of assets. The buyers would receive a stepped-up basis in the corporate assets; the result would be higher deductions for depreciation and amortization.

S corporation. Sales of S corporations, however, are generally taxed like other passthrough entities, meaning they are subject to only one level of tax after the S corp income is passed through to the owners. One exception to this rule is when a C corporation recently converted to an S corporation and then began to sell its assets and stock. In such cases, the rules on recognition of built-in gains would prevent tax-free treatment of gains from S corp asset sales at the corporate level.

Partnership interests. The sale of an entire partnership generally takes one of two forms:

- The partners sell all of their partnership interests; or
- The partnership sells some or all of its assets, and the partnership distributes the cash and any remaining property to the partners.

In general, when a partnership sells all of its assets and then liquidates, the sale results in one level of tax on the asset sale. This tax would pass through to the partners. Gain or loss may be recognized by the partners by comparing the liquidating distributions against the partner's basis in his or her partnership interest.

Transfers to Family Members

As the owner of a business gets older and considers retirement, he or she may want to transfer the business to children or other family members. An owner should consider a current transfer of part or all of the business as part of an estate plan. In addition to keeping the business in the family, the owner's goals may include the following:

- Providing for a spouse, children, grandchildren, or others before and after death;
- Retaining some control over the business; and
- Minimizing estate and gift taxes on the transfer.

However, the business owner cannot cast a blind eye and must pay attention to practical considerations:

- Whether the younger generation is interested in the business;
- Whether family members can work together; and
- The nature of the business.

The owner should consider forming a family limited partnership (FLP) or a family limited liability company (FLLC) and transferring business assets to this entity. Using an FLP, for example, the existing owner can transfer a business in exchange for a small general partnership interest (perhaps as low as 1 or 2 percent) and a large limited partnership interest. By holding the general partnership interest, the owner retains control over the operation of the business and other assets transferred to the entity.

The owner can then transfer limited partnership interests to younger family members, particularly children and grandchildren. The owner can avoid gift tax by transferring interests whose value is below the gift tax exclusion ($14,000 per recipient for 2013) or the combined exclusion for a husband and wife ($28,000 per recipient).

CAUTION

An FLP or FLLC is not a guaranteed solution in all cases, however. The IRS may challenge it as a sham if it is established shortly before the owner's death or may collapse it for tax purposes if the holders of limited interests do not have bona fide capital interests in the entity. Furthermore, the entity may be included in the owner's estate if the owner retains too much control over the interests or the underlying assets.

An interest in a business transferred to family members may be valued at a discount, based on the interest's lack of marketability and lack of control exercisable over the partnership (a minority interest). The value of the interest depends on the nature of the interest transferred, an appraisal of the interest, and an appraisal of the underlying assets. Thus, cash and marketable securities held by an entity would not be discounted as much as business assets. It may be useful to obtain an appraisal when an interest is transferred.

To protect the business from outsiders, an owner of a closely held business may want to restrict the ownership, to prevent its transfer to a third party outside the family. A closely held corporation, partnership, or LLC can accomplish this through a buy-sell agreement. In a buy-sell agreement, the interest holders agree to sell their interests to the entity or to the other interest holders. The agreement will set the price, terms, and conditions for the sale.

A buy-sell agreement is useful because it can prevent a sale or other transfer to a third party without the consent of the interest holders. The agreement can also create a market for the owner's interests upon the owner's disability, retirement or death. Furthermore, the buy-sell agreement can create a pricing mechanism that will prevent disagreements over value and establish a value for estate and gift tax purposes. The agreement should provide for an appraisal process, rather than attempt to fix the price or provide a formula, because value may change over time.

STUDY QUESTION

5. When partners liquidate a partnership:

a. The proceeds are taxed at the partnership and partner levels
b. Only the partnership interests are taxed
c. The sale of assets is taxed and the tax liability paid by the partners
d. Liquidating distributions are taxed equally, regardless of varying partnership interests

ESTATE PLANNING

For many years, estate planning was in a state of flux because many important and far-reaching estate tax rules were temporary and not permanent. In January 2013, Congress passed and President Obama signed the *American Taxpayer Relief Act of 2012* (ATRA), which, among other provisions, made permanent many of the previously temporary provisions. As a result, boomers should revisit their estate plans to take into account the changes in ATRA, highlights of which are described here.

Gifts

Gifts can significantly reduce a taxpayer's taxable estate if made within the parameters of the various exclusions and rules. Special rules apply to married couples who want to make gifts. These rules can be very valuable in estate planning and are frequently overlooked. Married couples (unless one spouse is not a U.S. citizen) can make unlimited gifts between themselves.

Additionally, married couples are allowed to "split" gifts to take advantage of a doubled gift tax exclusion: $14,000 each for 2013, for a total tax-free gift per recipient of $28,000. A taxpayer can currently also contribute up to $70,000 per recipient in a single year to a qualified tuition plan ("529 plan") and treat the gift as made over five years, so that gift tax does not apply. All taxpayers, regardless of marital status, can make tax-free gifts to pay qualified tuition or medical expenses paid directly to an educational or medical institution for someone else.

EXAMPLE

The Silvermans—Aaron, age 73, and Samantha, age 71, both U.S. citizens—are married. Samantha purchases a new automobile valued at $34,000 for Aaron and gives it to him as a birthday gift. There are no gift tax consequences for this gift because it is exchanged between legally married spouses who both are U.S. citizens. Aaron and Samantha also give $28,000 to their daughter Victoria, age 44, on November 30, 2013. Because Aaron and Samantha are married, they can "split" their gift to Samantha to take advantage of a doubled gift tax exclusion of $28,000 available for gifts made in 2013.

COMMENT

The gift tax rules are different when one spouse is not a U.S. citizen. In that case, the annual exclusion from gift taxes for gifts made to the noncitizen spouse is $143,000 for 2013.

Estate Taxes

Before ATRA became law, the maximum estate tax rate was scheduled to revert to 55 percent with a $1 million exclusion amount for estates of decedents dying after December 31, 2012. ATRA set the maximum estate tax rate at 35 percent for estates of decedents dying after December 31, 2012, and also set the exclusion amount at $5 million. ATRA also permanently abolished the 5 percent surtax that had previously applied to decedent's estates larger than $10 million and up to $17.184 million before 2002.

COMMENT

Adjusted for inflation, the $5 million maximum exclusion is $5.25 million for 2013.

ATRA introduced the concept of portability to the estate tax rules with respect to the unused portion of the estate tax exclusion of a predeceased spouse. In order for a decedent's estate to take advantage of the unused exclusion amount of the decedent's predeceased spouse, the executor of the predeceased spouse's estate must have filed an estate tax return on which the amount of the deceased unused exclusion was computed and made an election on the return that such amount may be taken into account by the surviving spouse's estate. Once the above election is made, it is irrevocable.

Before ATRA, there was a state death tax credit allowed for qualified estate, inheritance, legacy, or succession taxes paid to any state or the District of Columbia. The state death tax credit was subject to gradual repeal starting in 2002 and was repealed for 2005 through 2012. ATRA permanently repeals the state death tax credit and replaces it with a deduction. The deduction allows state death taxes paid to a state or the District of Columbia to be deducted from the decedent's estate.

Trusts

Trusts are popular estate planning tools. There are various trusts that may shelter funds from both the beneficiary and creditors, such as the spendthrift trust, the support trust, and the discretionary trust.

A *spendthrift trust* gives the trustee the discretion to decide how much income or principal, if any, should be used for the beneficiary's benefit. Trust terms expressly prohibit the beneficiary from voluntarily or involuntarily alienating his or her interest in the trust. The beneficiary's creditors are not able to attach the beneficiary's interest in the trust. Thus, a spendthrift trust prevents an irresponsible, indebted, or incapacitated individual from divesting him- or herself of the trust assets.

COMMENT

The IRS has determined that spendthrift provisions cannot defeat a federal tax lien (CCA 200614006).

A *support trust* directs that the trustee pay income, principal, or both to the beneficiary for his or her support and education. A support trust gives the trustee the discretion to decide how much, if any, income or principal should be used for the beneficiary's support. Thus, the beneficiary cannot divest his or her interest in the trust.

A *discretionary trust* gives the trustee complete discretion in deciding how much, if any, income, principal, or both should be distributed for the beneficiary's benefit. Neither the beneficiary nor the beneficiary's creditors may demand distributions from the trust.

STUDY QUESTION

6. How can unmarried individuals exceed the annual gift limit of $14,000 per recipient without incurring gift tax?

a. Paying qualified tuition or medical expenses incurred by the recipient directly to the institution

b. Gifting up to $4,000 in quarterly installments or $1,300 in monthly payments to the recipient

c. Gifting an unlimited amount to the recipient shortly before the donor's expected death

d. Single donors may never exceed the $14,000 limit of gifting funds tax-free to benefit one recipient

CONCLUSION

Most boomers must face the prospects of funding a long retirement. Life expectancy for the average retiree is now well into his or her 80s. Being the first generation not only living considerably longer but also living through those additional years largely without the safety-net of a fixed payout from an employer's retirement plan, boomers are required to be more proactive in managing their financial affairs to guarantee that they do not outlive their assets and, hopefully, can pass on some wealth down to the next generation. Taking inventory of their assets and then managing them in a tax-efficient way will be essential to many, if not the majority of boomers, concerned about reaching those goals.

CPE NOTE: When you have completed your study and review of chapters 5–7, which comprise Module 3, you may wish to take the Quizzer for this Module.

Go to **CCHGroup.com/PrintCPE** to take this Quizzer online.

MODULE 4: COMPLIANCE ISSUES FOR FOREIGN ACCOUNTS AND EXEMPT ORGANIZATIONS — CHAPTER 8

FATCA: New Rules for International Disclosure and Account Reporting

As part of what seems an ever-expanding effort to close the "tax gap," or the taxable amounts underreported on tax returns, Congress and the Internal Revenue Service continue to extend the information reporting requirements for taxpayers and financial institutions, both at home and abroad. With an estimated $395 billion falling into the gap every year, it is easy to understand the rationale for these requirements. By being able to locate and collect excess monies already owed, Congress can, in effect, increase revenues without having to deal with the messy politics of tax hikes. Information reporting is useful to the IRS, meanwhile, because collecting such data provides the agency the ability to match what is reported by one taxpayer with that provided by another and pounce upon discrepancies. As a result, these matching efforts are likely to expand even further. In keeping with this trend, this chapter examines the far-reaching requirements imposed by the *Foreign Account Tax Compliance Act (*FATCA) and its complement, Foreign Bank Account Reports (FBAR).

LEARNING OBJECTIVES

Upon completion of this chapter, you will be able to:

- Understand the rationale behind Congress and the IRS' ongoing efforts to expand information reporting, both at home and abroad;
- Articulate the connection between the FBAR and FATCA requirements;
- Discuss Intergovernmental Agreements and understand their significance;
- Identify foreign financial and other institutions affected by FATCA;
- Articulate the obligations placed upon domestic and foreign withholding agents by the new rules;
- Understand the requirements, and significance, of foreign financial institution agreements, as well as the consequences of both entering into such an agreement and failing to do so;
- Relate key provisions of the due diligence, verification, reporting, and withholding requirements required of participating foreign financial institutions going forward;
- Articulate what membership in an expanded affiliated group means with respect to the new requirements;
- Identify the categories qualifying for deemed-compliant status; and
- Discuss the implementation timeline for the new provisions.

INTRODUCTION

With its recently delegated authority to enforce a host of stringent rules against U.S. taxpayers that fail to disclose foreign financial assets, the IRS appears ready to compel compliance by those failing to report offshore holdings. Thus, although the *Bank Secrecy Act of 1970* (BSA) provides that the Secretary of the Treasury "shall require a resident or citizen of the United States, or a person in, and doing business in, the United States, to…keep records and file reports, when the…person makes a transaction or maintains a relation for any person with a foreign financial agency," prosecution of those failing to comply with the Foreign Bank Account Reports (FBAR) reporting requirements have hitherto been rare. Regulations promulgated in 2011, however, promise to change that situation.

REPORTING BY U.S. PERSONS OF THEIR FOREIGN FINANCIAL ASSETS

FBAR Requirements

By the terms of the FBAR requirements, a U.S. person must disclose any financial interests in, signature authority over, or other authority over foreign financial accounts if the aggregate value of the accounts exceeds $10,000 at any time during the calendar year. The information is acknowledged on a taxpayer's tax return but reported on Form TD F 90-22.1, *Report of Foreign Bank and Financial Accounts* (commonly referred to as FBAR). Thus, for example, whereas persons must indicate on their Form 1040, Schedule B, whether they have an interest in a foreign financial account by checking the appropriate box, the Schedule B then directs the taxpayer to the FBAR.

FBARs must be received (not just filed) by the Department of Treasury for each calendar year on or before June 30 of the succeeding year. The June 30 deadline may not be extended. Relief has been provided, however, to certain individuals with signature authority over, but no financial interest in, foreign financial accounts. Under this relief, the deadline for filing FBARs held during the 2011 and 2012 calendar year has been extended until June 30, 2014, for the applicable individuals.

Those subject to FBAR reporting are U.S. citizens, resident aliens, and entities created, organized, or formed under U.S. laws, including, but not limited to, domestic corporations, partnerships, limited liability companies (LLCs), trusts, and estates. The federal tax treatment of a person or entity does not determine whether an FBAR filing is required.

CAUTION

An entity disregarded for federal tax purposes must still file an FBAR if filing is otherwise required.

EXAMPLE

FBARs are required under Title 31 and not under any provisions of the Internal Revenue Code. Thus, a single-member LLC, which is a disregarded entity for U.S. tax purposes, must file an FBAR if otherwise required.

CAUTION

The penalties for failing to meet one's FBAR obligations are steep. A person who is required to file an FBAR and fails to properly file may be subject to a civil penalty not to exceed $10,000 per violation. , Criminal penalties are even more harsh. A person who willfully fails to report an account or account identifying information may be subject to a civil monetary penalty equal to the greater of $100,000 or 50 percent of the balance in the account at the time of the violation.

Specified Foreign Financial Assets

Although the FBAR requirements may seem onerous enough, the *Foreign Account Tax Compliance Act* (FATCA) mandates that a second, completely separate report of foreign financial assets be made. Accordingly, under FATCA, any individual who holds an interest in a "specified foreign financial asset" during the tax year must attach to his or her tax return a Form 8938, *Statement of Specified Foreign Financial Assets,* to report certain information for each asset if the total value of all such assets exceeds an *applicable reporting threshold* amount.

COMMENT

The requirement applies to any U.S. citizen and any individual who is resident alien for any part of the tax year. A nonresident alien who makes the election to be treated as a resident alien for purposes of filing a joint return for the tax year must also file Form 8938, as must a nonresident alien who is a bona fide resident of American Samoa or Puerto Rico.

Form 8938 must also be filed by any domestic entity formed or availed for purposes of holding, directly or indirectly, specified foreign financial assets, in the same manner as if the entity were an individual.

COMMENT

Proposed regulations have designated specified domestic entities subject to the reporting requirement. They include certain closely held domestic corporations or partnerships, as well as certain domestic trusts. Reporting by specified domestic entities, however, will not be required before the date provided in final regulations.

A *specified foreign financial asset* includes:

- A depository, custodial, or other financial account maintained by a foreign financial institution;
- A stock or security issued by a person other than a U.S. person;
- A financial instrument or contract held for investment that has an issuer or counterparty other than a U.S. person; or
- An interest in an entity that is not a U.S. person.

The filing of Form 8938 does not relieve an individual of the requirement to file the FBAR for disclosing foreign financial accounts. Similarly, the filing of the FBAR does not relieve an individual of the requirement to file Form 8938. An individual may be required to file both Form 8938 and FBAR to report the same information on certain foreign accounts. The FBAR, however, is not filed with the individual's federal income tax return.

The applicable threshold amount that determines whether a taxpayer must file Form 8938 depends on the taxpayer's filing status and where individual lives. The total value of specified foreign financial assets for this purpose is the asset's fair market value as determined in U.S. dollars using the Treasury's currency exchange rate on the last day of the tax year. The applicable threshold amounts are summarized in the table.

Table 1. Applicable Reporting Thresholds for U.S. Taxpayers for Filing Form 8938

Taxpayer Type	Threshold Reached for Total Value of Foreign Assets
Unmarried taxpayers living in the United States	Financial assets exceeding $50,000 on the last day of the tax year or exceeding $75,000 at any time during the tax year
Jointly filing married taxpayers living in the United States	Financial assets exceeding $100,000 on the last day of the tax year or exceeding $150,000 at any time during the tax year
Separately filing married taxpayers living in the United States	Financial assets exceeding $50,000 on the last day of the tax year or exceeding $75,000 at any time during the tax year
Jointly filing married taxpayers living abroad and filing a joint return	Specified foreign assets exceeding $400,000 on the last day of the tax year or exceeding $600,000 at any time during the year
Other taxpayers living abroad	Specified foreign assets exceeding $200,000 on the last day of the tax year or exceeding $300,000 at any time during the year

The individual must disclose the asset's maximum value during the tax year and provide specific information based on the asset type.

CAUTION

The penalties for failure to report under FATCA are also severe:

- A $10,000 civil penalty applies to any failure to properly furnish the required information; and
- If the failure is not corrected within 90 days after the IRS mails notice of it to the taxpayer, an additional $10,000 penalty applies for each 30-day period (or portion thereof) in which the failure continues after that 90-day period expires. This additional penalty with respect to any failure is limited to $50,000 for a total penalty of $60,000.

Criminal penalties may also apply.

STUDY QUESTIONS

1. On December 31, 2014, Deirdre Malone, an unmarried U.S. taxpayer, owns a bank account in Ireland with a balance of $52,000. In 2015, Deirdre must file:

a. Only an FBAR, Form 90-22-1, by June 30, 2015
b. Only Form 8938, *Statement of Specified Foreign Financial Assets,* attached to her regular tax return by April 15, 2015
c. Both the FBAR and Form 8938 by their respective due dates
d. Neither Form 90-22-1 nor Form 8938 because her balance in the account is less than the reporting threshold

2. The maximum annual penalty for failure to submit Form 8938 during the 2014 calendar year under FATCA rules is:

a. $10,000
b. $50,000
c. $60,000
d. 10 percent of the year's unreported balance in all foreign holdings

FOREIGN FINANCIAL INSTITUTIONS SUBJECT TO THE FOREIGN ACCOUNT TAX COMPLIANCE ACT

In addition to obligating U.S persons to report foreign financial accounts, FATCA, enacted in 2010 as part of the *Hiring Incentives to Restore Employment Act* (HIRE Act), adds a new Chapter 4 to the tax code that, among other things, imposes far-reaching withholding and reporting requirements on "foreign financial institutions," (FFIs) as well as certain "nonfinancial foreign entities" (NFFEs). The overarching goal of these new requirements is to ensure compliance with the new reporting requirements imposed upon U.S. persons with respect to their ownership interests in most foreign accounts. In other words, FATCA is intended to ensure amounts reported by FFIs match the total of holdings reported by individual taxpayers.

FATCA was, accordingly, specifically designed to prevent tax evasion by U.S. citizens and residents via the use of offshore accounts. In a significant extension of long-arm jurisdiction, FATCA takes direct aim at FFIs and other financial intermediaries by:

- Extending the scope of the U.S. information-reporting regime to reach FFIs that maintain U.S. accounts;
- Imposing increased disclosure obligations on certain NFFEs deemed to present a high risk of U.S. tax avoidance; and
- Providing for withholding tax on those FFIs and NFFEs that fail to comply with the requirements of Chapter 4.

COMMENT

This withholding may generally be credited against the U.S. income tax liability of the beneficial owner of the payment and generally may be refunded to the extent the withholding exceeds such liability. An FFI that does not comply with the requirements of Code Sec. 1471(b), however, and that beneficially owns the payment from which tax is withheld under Chapter 4, may not receive a credit or refund except to the extent required by a U.S. treaty obligation.

EXAMPLE

The "big stick" of FATCA is the inclusion of gross proceeds in the definition of amounts subject to U.S. 30 percent tax withholding. Banque Extraordinaire, a St. Martin investment bank, fails to enter into an agreement with the IRS and report the required information but still wants to invest in U.S. securities. FATCA withholding on any U.S. source FDAP payments made to the bank will be required beginning on July 1, 2014. This withholding requirement will be extended to any **gross proceeds** from the sale or other disposition of any property owned by the bank that can produce interest or dividends that are U.S. source FDAP income after December 31, 2016.

FATCA FRAMEWORK

FATCA obligates any "withholding agent," as defined below, to withhold 30 percent of any "withholdable payment" made to an FFI unless the FFI meets certain requirements. These requirements will be met if the FFI:

- Enters into an FFI agreement with the United States with respect to its U.S. accounts (and the accounts of each FFI that is a member of the same affiliated group);
- Meets requirements to be deemed to comply with the requirements of Code Sec. 1471(b); or

- Is resident in a country that executes a Model 1 or Model 2 Intergovernmental Agreement (Model 1 or Model 2 IGA) with the United States.

COMMENT

FFIs that enter into an FFI agreement are deemed *participating FFIs*, whereas those that do not are referred to as *nonparticipating FFIs*. FFIs meeting the prescribed requirements to be deemed in compliance are considered *deemed-compliant FFIs*.

CAUTION

FATCA's mandates are stringent, requiring any person that, in any capacity, has control, receipt, disposal, or payment of any withholdable payment to apply the 30 percent withholding.

COMMENT

Participating FFIs and grantor trusts are specifically included within the definition of withholding agent, whereas individuals making payments not in the ordinary course of business are specifically excluded.

Intergovernmental Agreements

In many cases, foreign law would prevent an FFI from reporting directly to the IRS the information required under FATCA and, thus, potentially expose it to withholding. Treasury collaborated with foreign governments to develop two alternative model intergovernmental agreements that facilitate implementation of FATCA in a manner that removes domestic legal impediments to compliance, fulfills FATCA's policy objectives, and further reduces burdens on FFIs located in partner jurisdictions. These efforts resulted in a *reciprocal model intergovernmental agreement* (Model 1 IGA) and a *nonreciprocal model intergovernmental agreement* (Model 2 IGA).

A jurisdiction signing an agreement based on the Model 1 IGA agrees to adopt rules to identify and report information about U.S. accounts that meet the standards set out in the Model 1 IGA. FFIs covered by a Model 1 IGA not otherwise excepted or exempt pursuant to the agreement must identify U.S. accounts pursuant to due diligence rules adopted by the partner jurisdiction and report specified information about the U.S. accounts to the partner jurisdiction. This information will be reported directly to the tax authorities of the partner jurisdiction, which will, then exchange the information with the IRS automatically. The United States, in turn, will provide information regarding certain account holders who are nationals of the partner jurisdiction to the tax authorities of that partner jurisdiction on a reciprocal basis.

A jurisdiction signing an agreement based on the Model 2 IGA agrees to direct and enable all FFIs that are located in the jurisdiction, not otherwise excepted or exempt pursuant to the Model 2 IGA, to register with the IRS and report specified information about U.S. accounts directly to the agency in a manner consistent with Chapter 4, except as expressly modified by the Model 2 IGA. In the case of certain recalcitrant account holders, the information reported by FFIs covered by a Model 2 IGA is supplemented by government-to-government exchange of information. In contrast to Model 1 IGAs, a Model 2, or nonreciprocal, IGA does not require the provision of information to the partner jurisdiction by the United States.

The IRS will publish a list of all countries having in effect a Model 1 or Model 2 IGA.

Both models contemplate that the partner jurisdiction will require all financial institutions that are located in the jurisdiction, and that are not otherwise excepted or exempt pursuant to the agreement, to identify and report information about U.S. accounts. In consideration of the full cooperation of the partner jurisdiction, the model agreements contemplate a number of simplifications and burden reductions associated with the application of FATCA in the partner jurisdiction.

COMMENT

Though FFIs resident in Model 1 jurisdictions will only be subject to the requirements of the IGA, those in Model 2 countries will also be subjected to requirements akin to those of FFI agreements. Accordingly, with the latter's more onerous mandates, FFIs may find it desirable to be resident in jurisdictions entering Model 1 IGAs.

FFIs that are covered by a Model 1 IGA and that are in compliance with local laws implemented to identify and report U.S. accounts in accord with the terms of the Model 1 IGA will be treated as satisfying the due diligence and reporting requirements of Chapter 4. FFIs covered by a Model 2 IGA will be required to implement FATCA in the manner prescribed, except to the extent expressly modified by the Model 2 IGA.

COMMENT

As of August 2013, countries that have signed FATCA Model 1 IGAs include: Denmark (11–19–2012), Germany (5–31–2013), Ireland (1–23–2013), Mexico (11–19–2012), Norway (4–15–2013), Spain (5–14–2013) and the United Kingdom (9–12–2012). Model 2 IGA countries include Japan (6–11–2013) and Switzerland (2–14–2013).

COMMENT

Financial institutions operating within jurisdictions that have signed an IGA covering their financial institutions' compliance with FATCA will be deemed to have an effective IGA.

For FFIs not resident in a country having in effect an IGA, the following statutory definition is determinative.

Foreign Financial Institution

FATCA's broad definition of *foreign financial institution* includes virtually any foreign institution, other than a financial institution organized under the laws of a possession of the United States, engaged in financial activity of any sort, including:

- Any deposit-accepting entity ordinarily engaged in the business of banking;
- Any entity that, as a substantial portion of its business, holds financial assets on account for others;
- An investment entity;
- An insurance or holding company that is part of an expanded affiliated group; or
- Certain holding companies or treasury centers.

An entity is considered engaged in a banking or similar business if, in the ordinary course of its business with customers, it accepts deposits or other similar investments of funds and regularly:

- Makes personal, mortgage, industrial, or other loans or provides other extensions of credit;
- Purchases, sells, discounts, or negotiates accounts receivable, installment obligations, notes, drafts, checks, bills of exchange, acceptances, or other evidences of indebtedness;
- Issues letters of credit and negotiates drafts drawn thereunder;
- Provides trust or fiduciary services;
- Finances foreign exchange transactions; or
- Enters into, purchases, or disposes of finance leases or leased assets.

NOTE

An entity is *not* engaged in a banking or similar business if it solely accepts deposits from persons as collateral or security pursuant to a sale or lease of property, or in connection with a similar financing arrangement between the entity and the person holding the deposit.

CAUTION

Entities considered engaged in a banking or similar business include, but are not limited to, entities that would qualify as banks under Code Sec. 585(a)(2), including banks as defined in Code Sec. 581, and any corporations to which Code Sec. 581 would apply but for the fact that they are foreign corporations.

An entity holds financial assets for the account of others as a *substantial portion of its business* if the entity's gross income attributable to holding financial assets and related financial services equals or exceeds 20 percent of the entity's gross income during the shorter of:

- The three-year period ending on December 31 of the year preceding the year in which the determination is made; or
- The period during which the entity has been in existence before the determination is made.

COMMENT

A startup entity with no operating history on the determination date is considered to hold financial assets for the account of others as a substantial portion of its business if it expects to meet the gross income threshold described above, based on its anticipated functions, assets, and employees, with due consideration given to any purpose or functions for which the entity is licensed or regulated, including those of any predecessor.

Finally, an *investment entity* is any entity that:

- Primarily conducts, as a business for its customers, one or more of the following activities:
  - Trading in money market instruments, foreign currency or exchange, interest rate and index instruments, transferable securities or commodity futures;
  - Portfolio management; or
  - Otherwise investing, administering, or managing funds, money or financial assets on behalf of others;
- Primarily attributes its gross income to investing, reinvesting or trading in financial assets, and the entity is managed by another entity; or
- Functions, or holds itself out, as a collective investment vehicle, mutual fund, exchange traded fund, private equity fund, hedge fund, venture capital fund, leveraged buyout fund, or any similar investment vehicle established with an investment strategy of investing, reinvesting, or trading in financial assets.

COMMENT

Financial asset means a security, defined by reference to Code Sec. 475(c)(2), including Code Sec. 1256 contracts, partnership interest, commodity, as defined in Code Sec. 475(e)(2), notional principal contract, as defined in Reg. § 1.446-3(c), insurance contract or annuity contract or any interest in a security, partnership interest, commodity, notional principal contract, insurance contract or annuity contract.

Nonfinancial Foreign Entities

FATCA defines a *nonfinancial foreign entity* as any foreign entity that is not a financial institution, as delineated above. These entities will also be subject to the 30 percent withholding requirement unless the entity (or another nonfinancial foreign entity that is the beneficial owner of the payment) provides the withholding agent with a certification that the beneficial owner does not have any "substantial United States owners" or, if it does, each owner's name, address, and tax identification number (TIN).

COMMENT

In general, a *substantial United States owner* is a U.S. person who owns, directly or indirectly:

- More than 10 percent of the stock of a corporation, by vote or value;
- More than 10 percent of the capital or profits interest of a partnership; or
- More than 10 percent of the beneficial interests of certain trusts.

CAUTION

In the case of a financial institution that is engaged primarily in the business of investing, reinvesting, or trading in securities, or the like—including, notably, hedge or equity funds—any United States person with *any* interest is a substantial United States person.

COMMENT

A specified U.S. person is not treated as a substantial U.S. owner if the fair market value of the currency or other property distributed by the trust during the previous calendar year to such specified U.S. person is $5,000 or less, and in the case of a specified U.S. person that is entitled to receive mandatory distributions, the value of such person's interest in the trust is $50,000 or less. Furthermore, a grantor trust owned only by a U.S. person is not required to treat any of its beneficiaries as substantial U.S. owners.

Withholdable Payments

To trigger the FATCA requirements, the payment must be a *withholdable payment,* defined to mean, subject to certain exceptions:

- Any U.S. source payment of interest, dividends, rents, salaries, wages, premiums, annuities, compensations, remunerations, emoluments and other fixed or determinable annual or periodical (FDAP) gains, profits, and income; and
- For sales or other dispositions after December, 31, 2016, any gross proceeds from the sale or other disposition of any property that can produce interest or dividends from sources within the United States, as long as the income is not effectively connected to the conduct of a U.S. trade or business.

CAUTION

Though *FDAP income* is given the same meaning as in Chapter 3, an exclusion from withholding under Chapter 3 or from taxation under Code Sec. 881 does not exclude the amount from the definition of U.S. source FDAP income for purposes of determining whether a payment is withholdable under FATCA.

Certain payments are excluded from inclusion in withholdable payments, including:

- Certain short-term original issue discounts;
- Income effectively connected to the conduct of a U.S. trade or business;
- Certain nonfinancial payments;
- Gross proceeds from sales of excluded property;
- Certain broker transactions involving the sale of fractional shares; and
- Under a transitional rule prior to 2017, offshore payments of U.S. source FDAP income.

COMMENT

Code Sec. 103-exempt payments with respect to state and local bonds are also not withholdable payments.

In addition, with some exceptions, payments to the following are not withholdable payments, as discussed below:

- A participating FFI;
- A deemed-compliant FFI;
- An exempt beneficial owner; and
- A territory financial institution.

Withholding Agents

A *withholding agent* is any person having control, receipt, custody, disposal, or payment of a withholdable payment or foreign passthrough payment, including:

- A participating FFI possessed of control, receipt, custody, disposal or payment of a passthrough payment;
- A registered deemed-compliant FFI to the extent that it is required to withhold on a passthrough payment as part of the conditions for maintaining its status as a deemed-compliant FFI as described below; and
- Certain grantor trusts.

NOTE

An individual is not a withholding agent with respect to withholdable payments he or she makes outside the course of his or her trade or business, including as an agent with respect to the payment.

COMMENT

When several persons qualify as a withholding agent with respect to a single payment, only one tax amount is required to be withheld and deposited.

Withholding Requirements

Exclusions from withholding. Under the FATCA requirements, withholding agents must withhold 30 percent of any withholdable payment made after June 30, 2014, to a payee that is an FFI unless:

- The withholding agent can reliably associate the payment with documentation upon which it is permitted to rely to treat the payment as exempt from withholding;
- The payment is made under a grandfathered obligation, as discussed below; or
- The payment constitutes gross proceeds from the disposition of a grandfathered obligation.

CAUTION

In general, and absent an exception, withholding agents must withhold tax under FATCA on any withholdable payments made after June 30, 2014, to an FFI regardless whether the FFI receives the payment as a beneficial owner or as an intermediary.

COMMENT

The Treasury Department and the IRS hope to coordinate withholding requirements under Chapters 3 and 4 by requiring withholding agents to withhold on payments of U.S. source FDAP income under Chapter 4 when the agent would be responsible for withholding under Chapter 3.

COMMENT

A transitional rule exempts from withholding certain payments made prior to July 1, 2016, with respect to a preexisting account for which a withholding agent does not have documentation indicating the payee's status as a nonparticipating FFI, unless the payee is a prima facie FFI. When the payee is a prima facie FFI, a withholding agent must treat that payee as a nonparticipating FFI beginning on January 1, 2015, and continue to do so until the agent receives documentation sufficient to establish otherwise.

FATCA also obligates participating FFIs to withhold 30 percent of any passthrough payment made after June 30, 2014, to recalcitrant account holders or to FFIs that neither enter an FFI agreement nor otherwise qualify as a deemed-compliant entity (nonparticipating FFI). A *passthrough payment* is any withholdable payment or other payment to the extent attributable to a withholdable payment.

A participating FFI may elect not to withhold on passthrough payments, instead withholding on payments it receives, to the extent those payments are allocable to recalcitrant account holders or nonparticipating FFIs. A participating FFI that does not make such an election must withhold on passthrough payments it makes to any other participating FFI that does make such an election.

Finally, participating FFIs that comply with the withholding requirements applicable to certain passthrough payments and FFI agreements will be deemed to have satisfied the withholding requirements.

COMMENT

Regarding the scope and ultimate implementation of withholding on foreign passthrough payments, which is not yet defined, the Treasury Department and IRS intend to promulgate further proposed regulations, possibly including a *de minimis* exception from foreign passthrough payment withholding.

Withholding agents must withhold 30 percent of any withholdable payment to an NFFE if the payment is beneficially owned by the NFFE, or another NFFE, unless FATCA requirements are met with respect to the beneficial owner of the payment. These requirements will be met with respect to the beneficial owner of a payment if:

- The beneficial owner of the payment is the NFFE or any other NFFE;
- The withholding agent can treat the beneficial owner of the payment as an NFFE that does not have any substantial U.S. owners or as an NFFE that has identified its substantial U.S. owners; and
- The withholding agent reports the following information with respect to any substantial U.S. owners of the beneficial owner of the payment—
  - The name of the NFFE; the name, address, and TIN of each substantial U.S. owner of the NFFE,
  - The total of all payments made to the NFFE, and
  - Any other information that may be required.

COMMENT

The withholding requirements do not apply to payments beneficially owned by certain classes of persons or to any class of payment identified as posing a low risk of tax evasion.

EXAMPLE

Exempt from withholding are payments beneficially owned by certain persons, including any foreign government, international organization, foreign central bank of issue, or any other class of persons identified as posing a low risk of tax evasion.

Grandfathered obligations. Treasury and the IRS, in an effort to ease implementation burdens incumbent upon withholding agents and FFIs, have excluded from the definition of withholdable payments and passthrough payments those made under an obligation outstanding on July 1, 2014. In addition, also excluded is any obligation that produces withholdable payments solely because the obligation is treated as giving rise to a dividend equivalent under Code Sec. 871(m) (including certain equity swaps), and that is executed on or before the date that is six months after the date on which obligations of its type are first treated as giving rise to dividend equivalents.

NOTE

If collateral, or a pool of collateral, secures both grandfathered obligations and nongrandfathered obligations, the collateral posted to secure the grandfathered obligation(s) must be determined by allocating, pro rata by value, the collateral or, in the case of a pool of collateral, each item composing the pool of collateral to all outstanding obligations it secures.

Whether an obligation is outstanding on July 1, 2014, depends on the type of instrument. For debt, the date on which the obligation is outstanding is based on the instrument's issue date. Thus, whether debt issued in a qualified reopening will be treated as a grandfathered obligation depends on the issue date of the original debt. The date on which a nondebt obligation is considered outstanding, meanwhile, is the date a legally binding agreement is executed. Thus, a line of credit or a revolving credit facility for a fixed term may qualify as an obligation, if the agreement, as of its issue date, fixes the material terms, including a stated maturity date, under which the credit will be provided.

CAUTION

In an area certain to generate much uncertainty, final regulations provide that, in the case of an obligation constituting indebtedness for U.S. tax purposes, a material modification of the instrument is any significant modification, as defined in Reg. § 1.1001-3(e). Whether a modification is material in all other cases is to be determined under all facts and circumstances.

Establishing Payee Status

In general, the FATCA rules for determining the status of a payee track those set forth in Reg. 1.1441-1(b)(2). However, FATCA does modify these rules in several significant ways. Specifically, modifications have been made to account for the requirement imposed upon withholding agents to determine an FFI's status for FATCA purposes and to determine the status of certain NFFEs.

COMMENT

Final Forms W-8 and W-9 will permit payees to establish their status both for FATCA and Chapter 3 purposes. In addition, the IRS has issued a draft Form 8966, *FATCA Report*. Early releases of draft forms and instructions are at **IRS.gov/draftforms.**

In addition, the FATCA rules provide that, in certain cases, withholding agents may reliably associate a withholdable payment with valid documentation. Specifically, a withholding agent can reliably associate a withholdable payment with valid documentation if, prior to the payment, the agent:

- Holds such documentation appropriate to the payee's FATCA status;
- Can reliably determine how much of the payment relates to the valid documentation; and
- Does not know, or have reason to know, that any of the information, certifications, or statements in, or associated with, the documentation are unreliable or *incorrect.*

A withholding agent may also rely on information and certifications contained in withholding certificates or other documentation without having to inquire into the truthfulness of the information or certifications, unless the agent knows or has reason to know that the information or certifications are untrue.

COMMENT

In an effort to minimize the burden on withholding agents to collect new documentation, in the case of withholdable payments made prior to January 1, 2017, with respect to a preexisting account, withholding agents may treat a payee as a participating FFI or a registered deemed-compliant FFI if the payee possesses a valid withholding certificate establishing the payee's foreign status and the agent has verified the payee's employer identification number (FFI-EIN).

Recalcitrant Account Holders

Generally, a *recalcitrant account holder* is any holder of an account maintained by a participating FFI if the account holder is not an FFI and the account holder fails to:

- Comply with the participating FFI's request for documentation or information to establish whether the account is a U.S. account;
- Provide a valid Form W-9 upon request;
- Provide a correct name and TIN upon request after the participating FFI receives notice from the IRS indicating a name/TIN mismatch; or
- Provide a valid and effective waiver of foreign law if foreign law prevents reporting with respect to the account holder by the participating FFI.

STUDY QUESTIONS

3. Each of the following is considered a foreign financial institution under FATCA ***except:***

a. An investment entity
b. A substantial United States indirect owner of more than 10 percent of corporate stock
c. An insurance company in an expanded affiliated group
d. Any entity in which a substantial portion of business involves holding financial assets for others

4. Which of the following does ***not*** exempt withholding agents from withholding 30 percent of withholdable payments to payees?

a. A payment of gross proceeds from a disposition of grandfathered obligations
b. Association of the payment with reliable documentation of an exemption from withholding
c. Payments made to the FFI as an intermediary
d. Payments outstanding on July 1, 2014

FFI AGREEMENTS

An FFI will be subjected to the 30 percent withholding tax unless the institution enters into an agreement with the IRS, becoming a participating FFI, in which it agrees to:

- Obtain sufficient information regarding its account holders to ascertain whether any of the accounts it holds are "United States accounts;"
- Comply with certain verification procedures;
- Comply with annual reporting requirements with respect to "specified U.S. persons;" and
- Deduct and withhold the 30 percent tax on any "passthrough payment" made to recalcitrant account holders and others.

United States Accounts

A *United States account* is any financial account held by one or more "specified U.S. persons" or, subject to certain exceptions discussed below, "United States owned foreign entities."

A financial account, meanwhile, is any depository or custodial account, as well as any debt or equity interest in an FFI, except for interests regularly traded on an established securities market.

COMMENT

Commercial, checking, savings, time, or thrift accounts all qualify as depository accounts, as do accounts evidenced by a certificate of deposit (CD) or the like, and interest-bearing amounts held by an insurance company.

COMMENT

Custodial accounts include accounts that hold for investment for the benefit of another person any financial instrument or contract.

NOTE

Treasury and the IRS have proposed excluding from the definition of financial accounts some savings accounts, including both retirement and pension accounts, as well as nonretirement savings accounts that satisfy certain requirements with respect to contribution limits and tax treatment. In addition, financial accounts held solely by one or more exempt beneficial owners, or by a nonparticipating FFI solely as an intermediary for such owners, may also be excluded.

A *specified U.S. person* is any U.S. person, subject to certain exceptions, including:

- Corporations whose stock is regularly traded on an established securities market and their affiliates;
- Organizations exempt under Code Sec. 501(a);
- Individual retirement plans;
- Real estate investment trusts (REITS);
- Regulated investment companies (RICS);
- Common trust funds;
- Dealers in securities, commodities, and notional principal contracts;
- Brokers; and
- The United States and its agencies.

Similarly, a *U.S.-owned foreign entity* is any foreign entity with one or more *substantial U.S. owners,* defined, in turn, as any specified U.S. person that owns, either directly or indirectly, more than 10 percent of the stock of a corporation or more than 10 percent of the profits or capital interests in a partnership. In the case of trusts, a substantial U.S. owner is a specified U.S. person directly or indirectly holding more than 10 percent of the beneficial interests in the trust.

COMMENT

Attribution rules are applicable in determining stock ownership for purposes of the controlled foreign corporation (CFC) rules.

Due Diligence Requirements

A foreign financial institution that enters into an FFI agreement (participating FFI) must identify its U.S. accounts and comply with certain due diligence and verification requirements. These requirements vary depending upon whether the accounts in question are individual accounts or entity accounts. In addition, preexisting accounts and new accounts are subject to different levels of diligence. FFIs that adhere to the guidelines set forth below will be treated as compliant and, thus, not held to a strict liability standard.

Preexisting individual accounts. Accounts with a value or balance not exceeding $50,000 are exempt from review, as are certain cash value insurance or annuity contracts with a value or balance of $250,000 or less. Accounts with a value in excess of $50,000 ($250,000 in the case of insurance or annuity contracts) but $1 million or less, meanwhile, are subject to a review of "electronically searchable data" only for any indicia of U.S. status.

Accounts that are offshore obligations with an aggregate balance or value that exceeds $50,000 ($250,000 for a cash value insurance or annuity contract) but does not exceed $1 million are subject only to review of electronically searchable data for indicia of U.S. status. For these purposes, U.S. indicia include:

- Identification of an account holder as a U.S. person;
- A U.S birthplace;
- A U.S address;
- A U.S. telephone number;
- Standing instructions to transfer funds to an account maintained in the United States;
- A power of attorney or signatory authority granted to a person with a U.S. address; or
- A U.S. "in-care-of" or "hold-mail" address representing the only address on file for the account holder.

An enhanced review requirement for certain high-value accounts is required. Thus, with respect to preexisting individual accounts that have a balance exceeding $1 million as of the effective date of the FFI agreement, or at the end of any subsequent calendar year, a participating FFI must apply an enhanced review, in addition to an electronic search, to identify any U.S. indicia associated with the account.

COMMENT

For purposes of determining the balance or value of an account, a participating FFI must apply certain aggregation rules.

COMMENT

If a participating FFI applied the enhanced review to an account in a previous year, the participating FFI will not be required to reapply such procedures to the account in a subsequent year.

COMMENT

The identification and documentation procedures must be completed by the deadline of two years after the effective date of the FFI agreement for other than high-value preexisting accounts and by the deadline of one year after the effective date of the FFI agreement for preexisting high-value accounts.

NOTE

For purposes of determining whether an account is exempt from review, subject only to an electronic search for indicia or subject to enhanced review, account balance or value will initially be measured as of June 30, 2014.

New individual accounts. For new individual accounts, a participating FFI must determine whether the account is a U.S. account by obtaining records of documentation to support the Chapter 4 status of the account holders. The participating FFI must also review all information collected in opening or maintaining the account and apply the standards of knowledge to determine whether a claim of foreign status is unreliable or *incorrect.* For accounts that are required to be treated as U.S. accounts, a participating FFI is generally required to collect a Form W-9 from each individual account holder.

Entity accounts. Generally, preexisting entity accounts with aggregate account balances or values of $250,000 or less are exempt from review until the account balance or value exceeds $1 million, unless the participating FFI elects otherwise. For purposes of applying this exception, the account balance must be determined as of the effective date of the FFI agreement and certain aggregation rules apply. For remaining preexisting entity accounts, FFIs can generally rely on antimoney laundering or know-your customer (AML/KYC) records and other existing account information to determine whether the entity is an FFI, a U. S. person, excepted from the requirement to document its substantial U.S. owners, or a passive investment entity (a passive NFFE).

For preexisting entity accounts, a participating FFI must perform the requisite identification and documentation procedures within six months of the effective date of the FFI agreement for any account holder that is a prima facie FFI, and within two years of the effective date of the FFI agreement for all other entity accounts, subject to certain exceptions.

For accounts other than preexisting entity accounts, a participating FFI must determine whether the account is a U.S. account or an account held by a recalcitrant account holder or nonparticipating FFI and to establish the Chapter 4 status of each account holder and each payee regardless whether the participating FFI makes a payment to the account. If an account holder receiving a payment is not the payee, the participating FFI must also establish the Chapter 4 status of the payee or payees in order to determine whether the withholding requirements apply.

COMMENT

A participating FFI must perform the requisite identification and documentation procedures by the earlier of the date a withholdable payment or a foreign passthrough payment is made or within 90 days of the date on which the participating FFI opens the account.

If the participating FFI cannot obtain the necessary documentation, or knows or has reason to know that the documentation provided for an entity account is unreliable or incorrect, the participating FFI must apply certain presumption rules to determine the Chapter 4 status of the account.

STUDY QUESTION

5. Due diligence requirements of FFI agreements stipulate all of the following for preexisting individual accounts ***except:***

a. Review of annuity contracts with a value of less than $250,000
b. Review of electronically searchable data for bank or investment accounts having a value of $50,000 to $1 million
c. An enhanced review for high-value accounts with values exceeding $1 million
d. Exemption from review of bank or investment accounts whose aggregate value is less than $50,000

Verification Procedures

In addition to adhering to due diligence requirements to identify U.S. accounts, a participating foreign financial institution must also comply with certain IRS verification requirements designed to assess the FFI's compliance with the FFI agreement. These requirements will, among other things:

- Obligate the FFI to adopt written policies and procedures governing the participating FFI's compliance;
- Conduct periodic internal reviews; and
- Call for periodic provision of information to the IRS that will allow it to determine whether the participating FFI has satisfied its obligations under the agreement.

COMMENT

Responsible officers must certify that the FFI has complied with the terms of the FFI agreement. Thus, barring extenuating circumstances, verification through third-party audits is not required.

CAUTION

Repetitive or systemic failures of the participating FFI's processes related to compliance with its FFI agreement may result in enhanced compliance verification and that certain egregious circumstances could cause the participating FFI to default on its FFI agreement.

Reporting Requirements

Participating FFIs are subject to a series of information reporting requirements for U.S. accounts, accounts held by owner-documented FFIs, and recalcitrant account holders, with special rules for accounts held with territory financial institutions and sponsoring FFIs and branches. Accordingly, participating FFIs must report, by March 31 of the year following the reporting year, certain information about each U.S. account and comply with requests for additional information pertaining to any U.S. account. The information that must be reported for each U.S. account includes:

- The name, address, and TIN of each account holder that is a specified U.S. person;
- The account number;
- The account balance or value of the account;
- The payments made with respect to the account during the calendar year; and
- Any other information that may be required.

COMMENT

Although initially considering requiring the reporting of the highest of a given account's month's-end balances, the IRS ultimately decided to require only an account's year-end balance. Additionally, this amount may be reported in the currency in which the account is maintained. Should the participating FFI elect to report balance information in U.S. dollars, the participating FFI must calculate the account balance or value of the account by applying the spot rate at the close of the year or, if the account was closed during the year, as of the date of closure.

Types of payments. Payment information required to be reported during the year by participating FFIs varies depending on the type of account:

- For depository accounts, "payments" consist of the aggregate gross amount of interest paid or credited to the account during the year;
- In the case of custodial accounts, "payments" consist of
  - The aggregate gross amount of dividends paid or credited to the account during the calendar year,
  - The aggregate gross amount of interest paid or credited to the account during the calendar year,

  - The gross proceeds from the sale or redemption of property paid or credited to the account during the calendar year for which the FFI acted as a custodian, broker, nominee, or otherwise as an agent for the account holder, and
  - The aggregate gross amount of all other income paid or credited to the account during the calendar year; and
- For all other accounts, gross amounts paid or credited to the account holder during the calendar year must be reported, including the aggregate amount of redemption payments made to the account holder during the calendar year.

COMMENT

For purposes of payment reporting, the amount and characterization of payments made for an account may be determined under the same principles that the participating FFI uses to report information on its resident account holders to the tax administration of the jurisdiction in which the FFI is located. Thus, the amount and characterization of items of income need not be determined in accordance with U.S. federal income tax principles.

COMMENT

Payments may be reported in the currency in which the payment is denominated or in U.S. dollars. In the case of payments denominated in one or more foreign currencies, a participating FFI may elect to report the payments in a currency in which payments are denominated and is required to identify the currency in which the account is reported.

Participating FFIs must report for the 2014 calendar year by March 31, 2015.

Chapter 61 election. In lieu of reporting the account balance or value, gross receipts, and gross withdrawals or payments, a participating FFI may elect to report the information required under Code Secs. 6041, 6042, 6045, and 6049 as if such institution were a U.S. person, and each holder of such U.S. account that is a specified U.S. person or U.S. owned foreign entity as if it were a natural person and U.S. citizen. If foreign law would prevent the FFI from reporting the required information absent a waiver from the account holder, and the account holder fails to provide that waiver within a reasonable period of time, the FFI is required to close the account.

NOTE

An insurance company participating FFI that is not licensed to do business in the United States may also elect to report its Chapter 4 account information with respect to its life insurance and annuity contracts in a manner similar to Code Sec. 6047(d) reporting.

For accounts held by recalcitrant account holders, reporting is to be made separately for each of three categories of accounts. The separate categories of accounts held by recalcitrant account holders subject to reporting are:

- Accounts with U.S. indicia;
- Accounts of other recalcitrant holders; and
- Dormant accounts.

COMMENT

In general, *dormant accounts* are those treated as inactive accounts under applicable laws or regulations or the normal operating procedures of the participating FFI that are consistently applied for all accounts maintained by such institution in a particular jurisdiction.

Expanded Affiliated Groups

The requirements of the FFI agreement apply to the U.S. accounts of not only the participating FFI but to the U.S. accounts of every other FFI that is a member of the same expanded affiliated group, as well.

COMMENT

An *expanded affiliated group* is an affiliated group with one or more chains of includible corporations connected through stock ownership with a common parent that is an includible corporation, provided certain requirements are met.

Subject to exceptions for certain branches, FFI affiliates, and qualified intermediaries (QIs), for any member of an expanded affiliated group to be a participating FFI or registered deemed-compliant FFI, each FFI that is a member of the group must be either a participating FFI or registered deemed-compliant FFI. An FFI may be considered a participating FFI even though all of its branches might not be able to satisfy all of the requirements set forth in the FFI agreement.

A *branch* is a unit, business, or office of the FFI that is treated as a branch under the regulatory regime of the nation in which it is located, or otherwise regulated as separate from other branches, units, or offices of the FFI, and that keeps its books and records separate from those of the FFI.

NOTE

All units, businesses, or offices of a participating FFI in a single country are treated as a single branch.

A *limited branch* is a branch that is unable to report the information required with respect to U.S. accounts or that cannot withhold on its recalcitrant account holders or nonparticipating FFIs and cannot close or transfer these accounts. To qualify for limited branch status, the FFI must meet certain requirements.

CAUTION

Under a transitional rule, a participating FFI with one or more limited branches will cease to be a participating FFI after June 30, 2016, unless otherwise provided pursuant to a Model 1 or 2 IGA. Similarly, a branch will cease to be a limited branch at the beginning of the third calendar quarter following the date on which the branch is no longer prohibited from complying with the requirements of a participating FFI. In such a case, the participating FFI will retain its status as a participating FFI, so long as it notifies the IRS by the date the branch ceases to be a limited branch that it will comply with the requirements of an FFI agreement, or as otherwise provided pursuant to a Model 1 IGA or 2 IGA.

An FFI that is a member of an expanded affiliated group may obtain status as a participating FFI even if one or more of its members cannot satisfy the requirements of the FFI agreement. Such *limited FFIs* are FFIs that cannot, under local law, report or withhold as required by the FFI agreement. Nevertheless, participating and deemed-compliant FFIs must treat limited FFIs as nonparticipating FFIs with respect to withholdable payments made to these affiliates.

COMMENT

The registration requirements for limited FFI status are similar to those for limited branches. In addition, similar transitional rules apply.

CAUTION

A special rule is also provided for QIs. Generally, a QI is a person (defined broadly to include entities as well as individuals) is a party to a withholding agreement with the IRS and is:

- A foreign financial institution or clearing operation, other than a U.S. branch or a U.S. office of the institution;
- A foreign branch or office of a U.S. financial institution or a foreign branch or office of a U.S. clearing organization;
- A foreign corporation for purposes of presenting claims of benefits under an income tax treaty on behalf of its shareholders; or
- Any other person acceptable to the IRS.

FATCA Registration Portal. FFIs registering with the IRS will be able to use a secure online web portal, the FATCA Registration Portal (Portal). The Portal has been designed to accomplish an entirely paperless registration process. The Portal is the primary way the FFI will interact with the IRS to complete and maintain Chapter 4 registrations agreements and certifications. The FATCA registration website became accessible to financial institutions on August 19, 2013. Prior to January 1, 2014, however, any information entered into the system, even if submitted as final, will not be regarded as final, but rather will be stored until the information is submitted as final on or after January 1, 2014. Thus, financial institutions may use the remainder of 2013 to familiarize themselves with the registration process, input preliminary information, and refine that information. On or after January 1, 2014, each financial institution will be able to finalize its online registration information and receive its global intermediary identification number (GIIN). The GIIN is required for financial institutions that need to demonstrate their FATCA compliance on an expedited basis. The IRS expects to electronically post the first IRS FFI List by June 2, 2014, and will update the list on a monthly basis thereafter. To ensure inclusion in the June 2014 IRS FFI List, FFIs would need to finalize their registration by April 25, 2014.

DEEMED-COMPLIANT FFIs

Certain FFIs, deemed to pose a low risk of U.S. tax evasion, are identified as "deemed-compliant FFIs." *Deemed-compliant FFIs* may avoid withholding under Chapter 4 without entering an FFI agreement. These FFIs include registered deemed-compliant FFIs, certified deemed-compliant FFIs, and, to a limited extent, owner-documented FFIs. A deemed-compliant FFI that complies with the due diligence and withholding requirements applicable to its entity type will be deemed to have satisfied its withholding obligations under Code Secs. 1471(a) and 1472(a). For this purpose, an intermediary or flow-through entity with a residual withholding obligation must fulfill that obligation to be considered a deemed-compliant FFI.

Registered Deemed-Compliant FFIs

A *registered deemed-compliant FFI* is an FFI that meets certain procedural requirements and that is either treated as a registered deemed-compliant FFI under a Model 2 IGA or qualifies under one of the following registered deemed-compliant FFI categories:

- Local FFIs meeting certain requirements;
- Certain nonreporting members of participating FFI groups;
- Qualifying qualified collective investment vehicles;
- Some restricted funds;

- Qualified credit card issuers; and
- Certain sponsored investment entities and controlled foreign corporations.

COMMENT

A registered deemed-compliant FFI also includes any FFI, or branch of an FFI, that is a reporting Model 1 FFI that complies with the registration requirements of a Model 1 IGA.

Registered deemed-compliant FFIs must satisfy a series of procedural requirements to maintain their status, and, although they may use one or more agents to perform the necessary due diligence to identify its account holders and to take any required action associated with obtaining and maintaining its deemed-compliant status, the FFIs remain responsible for ensuring that the requirements for its deemed-compliant status are met.

To qualify as a *local FFI,* each FFI in the group—or, in the case of a standalone FFI, the FFI itself—must meet certain licensing and regulation requirements. In addition, it must have no fixed place of business outside its country of organization and must not solicit account holders beyond its own borders. Finally, 98 percent of the accounts maintained by the FFI must be held by residents of the FFI's country of organization, and the FFI must be subject to withholding or reporting requirements in its country of organization with respect to resident accounts.

COMMENT

An FFI organized in a European Union (EU) member state may treat account holders that are residents of another EU member state as residents of the FFI's country of origin for this purpose.

Local FFIs must also establish procedures to ensure they do not open or maintain accounts for specified U.S. persons that are not residents of the country in which the FFIs are organized, for nonparticipating FFIs, or for entities controlled or beneficially owned by specified U.S. persons, and must perform due diligence with respect to their entity, and certain individual, accounts.

Nonreporting members of participating FFI groups that are members of an expanded affiliated group satisfy the requirements of the registered deemed-compliant category as long as they transfer any preexisting accounts that are identified under specified procedures as U.S. accounts, or accounts held by nonparticipating FFIs to an affiliate that is a participating FFI or U.S. financial institution. The nonreporting member(s) must also implement policies and procedures to ensure that if it opens or maintains and U.S.

accounts or accounts held by nonparticipating FFIs, it either transfers the accounts to an affiliate that is a participating FFI or to a U.S. financial institution, or itself becomes a participating FFI.

COMMENT

In such cases, the entity will have 90 days from the date on which the account is opened or on which it has knowledge, or reason to know, of a change in circumstance resulting in an account becoming a U.S. account or an account held by a nonparticpating FFI to make the transfer.

Generally, an FFI regulated as a qualified collective investment vehicle is eligible to become a registered deemed-compliant FFI if all holders of record of a direct interest are participating FFIs, deemed FFIs, or exempt beneficial owners.

Investment funds regulated under the laws of their country of organization are eligible to become registered deemed-compliant FFIs as restricted funds, as long as each distributor of the investment fund's interests is a participating FFI, a registered deemed-compliant FFI, a nonregistering local bank, or a restricted distributor. In addition, each agreement governing the distribution of the fund's equity or debt interests must prohibit the sale of such interests to U.S. persons, nonparticipating FFIs, or passive NFFEs with one or more substantial U.S. owners. Also, the prospectus must indicate that sales to these classes of persons are prohibited. Finally, the FFI must also establish policies and procedures to review accounts and ensure the proper treatment of new accounts.

NOTE

Each registered deemed-compliant FFI, of all categories, must certify to the IRS that it:

- Meets the requirements of the applicable category;
- Agrees to the conditions for deemed-compliant status; and
- Agrees to renew its certification every three years, or earlier in the event of a change in circumstance.

Certified deemed-compliant FFIs. A *certified deemed-compliant FFI* is an FFI that qualifies in a relevant deemed-compliant category that has certified its status by providing a withholding agent with the documentation applicable to its relevant deemed-compliant category. A certified deemed-compliant FFI is not required to register with the IRS. The relevant deemed-compliant categories in which an FFI can qualify for certified deemed-compliant FFI status include:

- Qualifying nonregistering local bank;
- Certain FFIs with only low-value accounts;

- Certain sponsored, closely held investment vehicles; and
- On a transitional basis, limited life debt investment entities.

Finally, an *owner-documented FFI,* described below, is eligible for certified deemed-compliant status if it:

- Does not accept deposits in the ordinary course of a banking or similar business, holds, as a substantial portion of its business, financial assets for the account of others, or is not an insurance company that issues or is obligated to make payments with respect to a financial account;
- Does not maintain financial accounts for nonparticipating FFIs;
- Does not issue debt constituting a financial account in excess of $50,000 to any person; and
- Provides a withholding agent with all required documentation regarding its owners and that withholding agent agrees to report to the IRS regarding any owners that are specified U.S. persons.

COMMENT

Because an owner-documented, certified deemed-compliant FFI is required to provide each withholding agent such documentation, and the agent must agree to report on behalf of the owner-documented FFI, such FFIs may have certified deemed-compliant status only with respect to a specific withholding agent(s).

Owner-documented FFIs. An FFI meets the requisite owner-documented FFI requirements only if:

- The FFI is an FFI solely because it is an investment entity;
- The FFI is not owned by or in an expanded affiliated group with any FFI that is a depository institution, custodial institution, or specified insurance company;
- The FFI does not maintain a financial account for any FFI that has failed to enter into an FFI agreement;
- The FFI provides the designated withholding agent with certain documentation and agrees to notify the withholding agent if there is a change in circumstances; and
- The designated withholding agent agrees to report to the IRS or, in the case of a reporting Model 1 FFI, to the relevant foreign government, all of the necessary information with respect to any specified U.S. persons.

An FFI may only be treated as an owner-documented FFI with respect to payments received from, and accounts held with, a designated withholding agent, or with respect to payments received from, and accounts held with, another FFI that is also treated as an owner-documented FFI by the designated withholding agent. A *designated withholding agent* is a U.S. financial institution, participating FFI, or reporting Model 1 FFI that agrees to undertake additional due diligence and reporting. An FFI meeting the requirements will only be treated as a deemed- compliant FFI with respect to a payment or account for which it does not act as an intermediary.

NOTE

A designated withholding agent is not required to report information regarding an indirect owner of the FFI that holds its interest through a participating FFI, a deemed-compliant FFI other than an owner-documented FFI, an entity that is a U.S. person, an exempt beneficial owner, or an excepted NFFE.

Final regulations make several modifications that also take into account the policy considerations presented by owner-documented FFIs.

STUDY QUESTIONS

6. Which of the following is ***not*** a requirement for a local FFI?

- **a.** Ensuring that 51 percent of accounts are held by citizens of its country of organization
- **b.** Establishing procedures to ensure it does not open or maintain accounts for specified U.S. persons that are not residents of its country
- **c.** Being subject to withholding or reporting requirements in its country of organization with respect to resident accounts
- **d.** No solicitation of customers outside of its country's borders

7. Qualified credit card issuers are categorized as:

- **a.** Registered deemed-compliant FFIs
- **b.** Certified deemed-compliant FFIs
- **c.** Individual deemed-compliant depository FFIs
- **d.** Owner-documented FFIs

RESPONSIBILITIES OF WITHHOLDING AGENTS

Liability for Tax Withheld

Under the FATCA rules, every person required to deduct and withhold any tax to enforce reporting on certain foreign accounts is liable for that tax and is indemnified against the claims and demands of anyone for the amount of the payments. A withholding agent that is unable reliably to associate a payment with documentation on the date of payment and fails to withhold, or withholds less than 30 percent, is liable for the tax, unless the withholding agent:

- Has appropriately relied on certain presumptions set forth in the regulations to treat the payment as exempt from withholding; or
- Obtained valid documentation to establish that the payment was exempt from withholding after the date of payment.

COMMENT

A withholding agent may use an agent to fulfill its withholding obligations.

Filing Responsibilities

Duty to pay tax and file tax return. A withholding agent who withholds tax pursuant to Chapter 4 must deposit the tax with an authorized financial institution or remit the tax by electronic funds transfer. In addition, the withholding agent must file Form 1042, *Annual Withholding Tax Return for U.S. Source Income of Foreign Persons*, to report Chapter 4 reportable amounts. This income tax return must indicate the aggregate amount of payments that are Chapter 4 reportable amounts and report the tax withheld by the withholding agent for the preceding calendar year.

CAUTION

Unless the IRS prescribes differently, any withheld tax that has not been deposited during the tax year is due and payable with the Form 1042 tax return.

Duty to file information return. A withholding agent must also file an information return on Form 1042-S, *Foreign Person's U.S. Source Income Subject to Withholding,* by March 15 of the calendar year following the year in which the amount was paid to report to the IRS Chapter 4 reportable amounts that were paid to a recipient during the preceding calendar year. A copy of Form 1042-S must be furnished to the recipient.

CAUTION

A withholding agent, other than a financial institution, that is required to file 250 or more Form 1042-S information returns for a tax year must file its Form 1042-S returns on magnetic media. Financial institutions must file Form 1042-S, or Form 8966, *FATCA Report,* on magnetic media regardless of how many they must file.

Chapter 4 reportable amounts include the following items subject to withholding under Chapter 4:

- U.S. source fixed or determinable annual or periodic (FDAP) income paid on or after July 1, 2014, and reportable on Form 1042-S;
- Gross proceeds;
- A foreign passthrough payment; and
- A foreign reportable amount paid by a participating FFI.

A *foreign reportable amount* is a payment of FDAP income that would be a withholdable payment if paid by a U.S. person.

A *recipient* is a person that is a recipient of a Chapter 4 reportable amount and includes, with respect to a payment of U.S. source FDAP income, for instance:

- A QI;
- A withholding foreign partnership (WP);
- A withholding foreign trust (WT);
- A participating FFI, or a registered deemed-compliant FFI that is a nonwithholding QI, NWP, or NWT and that provides its withholding agent with sufficient information to determine the portion of the payment allocable to its reporting pools of recalcitrant account holders, nonparticipating FFI payees, and participating FFIs, deemed-compliant FFIs, and certain QIs that are U.S. persons; and
- Any other person required to be reported as a recipient by Form 1042-S and its accompanying instructions, or under a FFI agreement.

CREDITS AND REFUNDS

Whether an overpayment of tax deducted and withheld on payments to FFIs and nonfinancial foreign entities (NFFEs) has occurred is determined in the same manner as if the tax had been deducted and withheld on nonresident aliens and foreign corporations. In addition, any tax deducted and withheld pursuant to an FFI agreement is treated as a tax deducted and withheld by a withholding agent on a withholdable payment made to a FFI. The term *overwithholding* means an amount actually withheld from an item of income or other payment pursuant to Chapter 4 that is in excess of the greater of:

- The amount required to be withheld with respect to such item of income or other payment under Chapter 4; and
- The actual tax liability of the beneficial owner that is attributable to the income or payment from which the amount was withheld.

In the event of overwithholding, the general rule is that the withholding agent may repay the beneficial owner or payee for an amount of overwithheld tax. The withholding agent may then reimburse itself in that same amount by reducing the amount of any deposit of tax made by the withholding agent for any subsequent payment period occurring before the end of the calendar year following the calendar year of overwithholding. In the event of underwithholding, the procedures set forth in Reg. § 1.1461-2(b) should be followed.

COMMENT

The beneficial owner of income is required to report the gross amount of income on the return required to be made by the beneficial owner. The amount of tax actually withheld is reported as a credit on the beneficial owner's return.

COMMENT

The credit and refund mechanism ensures that the withholding provisions of Chapter 4 are consistent with U.S. obligations under existing income tax treaties. A specific procedure need not be followed for achieving treaty benefits. If proof of treaty benefit entitlement is provided prior to a payment, the United States may permit reduced withholding or exemption at the time of payment. Alternatively, withholding may be required at the time of payment and treaty country residents may obtain treaty benefits through the refund.

If a beneficial owner of a payment is an FFI, the payment is a *specified financial institution payment*. Generally, credits and refunds with respect to specified financial institution payments are not allowed. However, if an FFI beneficial owner of a payment is entitled to a reduced rate of withholding tax under an income tax treaty, the beneficial owner may be eligible for a credit or refund of the excess amount withheld over the amount permitted to be withheld under the treaty.

CAUTION

No interest is payable with respect to any credit or refund of tax properly withheld on the specified financial institution payment. Furthermore, no credit or refund is allowed unless the beneficial owner provides the IRS with sufficient information regarding whether it is a U.S.-owned foreign entity and the identity of any substantial U.S. owners of the entity.

A NFFE claiming a refund must provide information regarding its substantial U.S. owners or certify that there are no such owners. This rule does not apply to refunds attributable to a reduced rate of tax under a tax treaty obligation of the United States.

The grace period during which the IRS is not required to pay interest on any overpayment is increased from 45 days to 180 days for overpayments resulting from excess amounts deducted and withheld under the nonresident alien and foreign corporation withholding rules of Code Sec. 1441 and the foreign account withholding rules of Code Secs. 1471 and 1472.

STUDY QUESTION

8. If a withholding agent overwithholds tax:

a. The withholding agent does not deposit the full amount but retains it in escrow against tax due in a subsequent period
b. The beneficial owner or payee is repaid and the withholding agent reduces the deposit of an equal amount in a subsequent period
c. The withholding agent follows the procedures in Reg. § 1.1461-2(b)
d. The withholding agent is penalized in the amount of 30 percent of the excess withheld

COORDINATION WITH OTHER WITHHOLDING PROVISIONS

Rules are provided to coordinate withholding under Chapter 4 with withholding under other provisions of the tax code, as discussed here.

Coordination with Withholding Under Code Secs. 1441 to 1443

In cases in which a payment is subject to withholding under both Chapter 4 and Reg. § 1.1441-2(a), a withholding agent may credit the withholding applied under Chapter 4 against its liability for any tax due under Code Sec. 1441, 1442, or 1443.

COMMENT

For this purpose, withholding is applied by a withholding agent under Code Sec. 1441, 1442, or 1443 when the withholding agent has withheld on the payment and designated that withholding as having been made under the applicable provision, to the extent required. For purposes of allowing an offset of withholding, and a credit to a withholding agent against its liability for tax, withholding is treated as applied once the agent has actually withheld on a payment and made no adjustment for overwithheld tax applicable to the amount withheld that might otherwise be permitted.

A special rule for certain substitute dividend payments is set forth. Thus, in the case of a dividend equivalent under Code Sec. 871(m) paid pursuant to a securities lending transaction of the type described in Code Sec. 1058 or pursuant to a sale-repurchase transaction, a withholding agent may offset its obligation to withhold under Chapter 4 for amounts withheld by another withholding agent under Chapters 3 and 4 with respect to the same underlying security, but only to the extent that there is sufficient evidence, as required under Chapter 3, that tax was actually withheld on a prior dividend equivalent paid to the withholding agent, or a prior withholding agent, with respect to the same underlying security in the transaction.

Coordination with Code Sec. 1445 Withholding

Amounts subject to withholding under Code Sec. 1445 are generally not subject to withholding under Chapter 4. Rules to coordinate withholding under Chapter 4 with those delineated in Reg. § 1.1441-3(c) for distributions by qualified investment entities and United States real property holding corporations (USRPHCs) are provided, however. Generally, to the extent withholding under Code Sec. 1441 is applicable to a distribution, or a portion of the distribution, made by a qualified investment entity or USRPHC, the coordination rules described above in connection with Code Secs. 1441–1443 withholding, apply to such amounts.

COMMENT

The intermediary reliance rule of Reg. § 1.1441-3(c)(2)(ii)(C) with respect to determinations made by a USRPHC regarding the portion of the distribution that is estimated to be a dividend has also been adopted.

Coordination with Code Sec. 1446 Withholding

A withholdable payment or a foreign passthrough payment subject to withholding under Code Sec. 1446 is generally not subject to withholding under Chapter 4. Coordination of withholding on distributions of gross proceeds subject to tax under Code Sec. 1446 has been reserved.

FATCA EFFECTIVE DATES

The FATCA regulations generally became applicable on January 28, 2013, but a number of additional effective dates apply.

Withholding

Unless otherwise provided in an applicable Model 2 Intergovernmental Agreement, the IRS withholding rules apply to U.S. source FDAP payments made on or after July 1, 2014. The withholding rules also apply to any gross proceeds from the sale of any property than can produce U.S. source interest or dividends, for sales or other dispositions after December 31, 2016. A participating FFI is not required to withhold on foreign passthrough payments until the later of January 1, 2017, or six months after the date of publication in the *Federal Register* of final regulations defining the term *foreign passthrough payments.*

Reporting for 2013 through 2015. Although initially special transitional reporting rules were to apply for accounts maintained for the 2013 through 2015 calendar years, Treasury and the IRS intend to modify these rules to require reporting on March 31, 2015, only with respect to the 2014 calendar year for U.S. accounts identified by December 31, 2014.

Due diligence. Documentation requirements for withholding agents, other than participating FFIs, are the following:

- Payees that are prima facie FFIs by January 1, 2015;
- Other FFIs by July 1, 2016;
- High-value accounts (greater than $1 million) with participating FFIs by July 1, 2015; and
- Other individual accounts with participating FFIs by July 1, 2016.

A participating FFI is required to perform the necessary identification procedures about preexisting obligations and obtain the appropriate documentation to determine whether a prima facie FFI payee is itself a participating FFI, deemed-compliant FFI, or nonparticipating FFI, within six months after the effective date of its FFI agreement. For any FFI that enters into an FFI agreement on or before June 30, 2014, the due date is June 30, 2014.

Identification Procedures

Account balance or value will be measured initially as of June 30, 2014, for purposes of determining whether an account is exempt from review, subject only to an electronic search for indicia, or subject to enhanced review. An account with a balance or value that was initially $1 million or less, and with respect to which there has been no change in circumstances, will not be subject to enhanced review unless the account balance or value exceeds $1 million as of the end of 2015 or any subsequent calendar year. Thus, the obligation to monitor the account balance or value of preexisting accounts to determine whether enhanced review is required has been deferred for one year.

Table 2 summarizes the various effective dates for FATCA.

Table 2. Effective Dates for Key FATCA Requirements

JANUARY	2013	2014	2015	2016	2017	2018
1	Effective date for FATCA.	Each financial institution will be expected to finalize its registration information by logging onto the FATCA registration website, making necessary changes, and submitting as final.	Begin FATCA withholding on undocumented individual preexisting high-value accounts.	Deadline for limited FFIs or limited branches to become participating FFIs and avoid other participating FFIs within the expanded affiliated group from losing their participating FFI status.	FATCA withholding on gross proceeds payments to nonparticipating FFIs and recalcitrant payees begins.	
1		GIINs will begin to be issued as registrations are finalized. Reporting Model 1 FFIs will be able to register and obtain GIINs beginning on January 1, 2014; they will have additional time beyond July 1, 2013, to register and obtain a GIIN to ensure inclusion in the IRS FFI list before January 1, 2015.		Begin FATCA withholding on remaining undocumented preexisting accounts.	FATCA withholding begins on foreign passthrough payments.	
MARCH	**2013**	**2014**	**2015**	**2016**	**2017**	**2018**
15			Form 1042-S reporting on withholdable income payments made in 2014 begins.	FFIs begin temporary Form 1042-S aggregate reporting on payments made to nonparticipating FFIs during calendar year 2015.	Last year for FFI temporary Form 1042-S aggregate reporting on payments made to nonparticipating FFIs (with respect to 2016 calendar year).	Begin Form 1042-S reporting on gross proceed payments for calendar year 2017.
31			USWAs begin Form 8966 U.S. owner reporting.	Form 8966 reporting on U.S. Account income by participating FFIs begins in addition to account information and balance for the 2015 calendar year.	Form 8966 reporting on U.S. account gross proceeds by participating FFIs begins in addition to account information, balance, and income for calendar year 2016.	
31			FFIs begin Form 8966 U.S. account information and balance reporting (with respect to the 2014 calendar year).		Begin full FATCA reporting on Form 8966 for calendar year 2016.	
31			Begin aggregate FATCA reporting for recalcitrant accounts on Form 8966.			
APRIL	**2013**	**2014**	**2015**	**2016**	**2017**	**2018**
25		To be included in the June 2014 IRS FFI list, FFIs must finalize their registration by this date.				

JUNE	2013	2014	2015	2016	2017	2018
2		IRS to electronically post the first IRS FFI list and to update it monthly.				
30		U.S. withholding agents, participating FFIs, and registered deemed-compliant FFIs must document preexisting entity accounts identified as pima facie FFIs. If the FFI signed an agreement after January 1, 2014, the deadline is six months from the effective date of the FFI agreement.				
30		Withholding begins on payments made after this date to payees that are FFIs and NFFEs with respect to obligations that are grandfathered obligations, unless the payments can be reliably associated with documentation on which the withholding agent can rely to treat the payments as exempt from withholding.				
30		FFI agreement of a participating FFI that registers and receives a GIIN from the IRS on or before June 30, 2014, has an effective date of June 30, 2014.				
JULY	**2013**	**2014**	**2015**	**2016**	**2017**	**2018**
1		Begin FATCA withholding on preexisting entity account holder that are undocumented prima facie FFIs.				
1		Grandfathered obligations includes obligations outstanding on July 1, 2014, and associated collateral.				
1		Withholding agent generally required to implement new account opening procedures (or for participating FFI by the later of July 1, 2014 or the effective date of its FFI agreement).				
AUGUST	**2013**	**2014**	**2015**	**2016**	**2017**	**2018**
19	IRS's Registration Portal available.					
DECEMBER	**2013**	**2014**	**2015**	**2016**	**2017**	**2018**
31		Participating FFIs to document preexisting high-value individual accounts by December 31, 2014. If the FFI signed an agreement after January 1, 2014, the deadline is one year from the effective date of the FFI agreement.	U.S. withholding agents, participating FFIs, and registered deemed-compliant FFIs must document preexisting entity accounts not identified as prima facie FFIs. If the FFI signed an agreement after January 1, 2014, the deadline is two years from the effective date of the FFI agreement.	End of first compliance certification period.		
31			Participating FFIs must document all remaining preexisting nonhigh-value individual accounts by December 31, 2015. If the FFI signed an agreement after January 1, 2014, the deadline is two years from the effective date of the FFI agreement.	Deadline for qualification as limited life debt investment entity.		

STUDY QUESTION

9. Chapter 4 withholding generally is applied in addition to amounts of withholding under:

a. Code Secs. 1441 through 1443
b. Code Sec. 1445
c. Code Sec. 1446
d. Chapter 4 withholding is not applied in addition to payments withheld under provisions of Code Secs. 1441 through 1443, 1445, and 1446

CONCLUSION

FATCA requires certain U.S. taxpayers holding foreign financial assets with an aggregate value exceeding $50,000 to report certain information about those assets on a new form (Form 8938) that must be attached to the taxpayer's annual tax return. Reporting applies for assets held in taxable years beginning after March 18, 2010. Failure to report foreign financial assets on Form 8938 will result in a penalty of $10,000 (and an additional penalty up to $50,000 for continued failure after IRS notification). Further, underpayments of tax attributable to undisclosed foreign financial assets will be subject to an additional substantial understatement penalty of up to 40 percent for certain transactions that should have been reported under Code Secs. 6038, 6038B, 6046A, 6048 or new Code Sec. 6038D.

At the same time, the FATCA requirements discussed in this chapter were designed to enlist the aid of financial institutions and governments the world over to help identify noncompliant US taxpayers. As a result, compliance, and the rules that govern compliance, are expected to increase significantly.

Together, these new far-reaching requirements demonstrate the U.S. government's continuing commitment to closing the tax gap. By all estimates, these efforts will persist in the years ahead.

MODULE 4: COMPLIANCE ISSUES FOR FOREIGN ACCOUNTS AND EXEMPT ORGANIZATIONS — CHAPTER 9

Public Charities and Private Foundations: Current Compliance Issues

Changes and modifications in the methods and requirements related to the federal government's oversight of tax-exempt organizations have increased in both scope and frequency lately, with that trend promising to continue into the near future. This chapter provides updates on the recent government oversight of exempt organizations, including private foundations, with particular focus on several areas in which the IRS has been especially active.

LEARNING OBJECTIVES

Upon completion of this chapter you will be able to:

- Explain the class of practitioners on which private foundations may rely when determining foreign charitable status;
- Determine whether an organization improperly intervened in a political campaign;
- Describe how to start a charitable organization for disaster relief;
- Illustrate the important requirements in the new regulations for Type III supporting organizations; and
- Describe the new rules for charitable hospital compliance.

INTRODUCTION

The nonprofit sector continues to grow rapidly despite facing a number of substantial issues, including funding concerns in a weak economy, increasingly complex governance requirements from funding sources, and shifting reporting requirements—all of which increase the difficulty in managing tax-exempt organizations. Concern has continued to grow over the appropriateness of exempt status for some types of organizations, even as Congress has created new types of organizations to help deal with some of society's ills.

Tax-exempt organizations complain about the difficulty of completing Form 990, *Return of Organization Exempt From Income Tax*. Moreover, the need for greater transparency comes with these increasing complexities. The IRS believes that greater transparency on the exempt organization's annual information return leads to correct reporting.

EXPANDED CLASS OF PRACTITIONERS ON WHICH PRIVATE FOUNDATIONS RELY TO DETERMINE FOREIGN CHARITABLE STATUS

The IRS has issued proposed regulations on the standards applicable to a private foundation that makes a good faith determination that a foreign organization is a qualified charitable organization (NPRM REG-134974-12). The IRS has expanded the class of practitioners on whose written advice a private foundation may base a good faith determination.

COMMENT

The IRS reported that it might limit the length of time on which a private foundation may rely on written advice. One possible timeframe, according to the preamble to the regulations, would be 12 months.

COMMENT

Every organization that qualifies for tax exemption as a Code Sec. 501(c)(3) organization is a private foundation unless it falls into one of the categories specifically excluded from the definition of that term. Organizations that fall into the excluded categories are institutions such as hospitals or universities and those that generally have broad public support or actively function in a supporting relationship to such organizations.

Background

Code Sec. 4942 provides that private foundations (other than a private operating foundation) are required to make "qualifying distributions" equal to or exceeding a minimum "distributable amount" for each tax year. In general, a private operating foundation is a private foundation that devotes most of its resources to the active conduct of its exempt activities.

A *qualifying distribution* is a grant or expenditure paid to accomplish a charitable purpose. However, grants to organizations controlled, directly or indirectly, by the foundation or one or more disqualified persons are generally not qualifying distributions. Grants to other private foundations similarly are not qualifying distributions.

A private foundation's *distributable amount* for any tax year is the *minimum investment return* of a private foundation reduced by the sum of any income taxes and the *tax on investment income*, and increased by:

- Amounts received or accrued as repayments of amounts taken into account as qualifying distributions for any tax year;
- Amounts received or accrued from the sale or other disposition of property to the extent that the acquisition of the property was considered a qualifying distribution for any tax year; and
- Any amount set aside for a specific project to the extent the amount was not necessary for the purposes for which it was set aside.

EXAMPLE

Expenditures to accomplish a charitable purpose include amounts paid to:

- Provide goods, shelter, or clothing to disaster victims if the foundation maintains some significant involvement in the activity rather than merely making grants to the recipients;
- Conduct educational conferences; and
- Operate a facility for physically challenged individuals.

Taxable expenditures. Under Code Sec. 4945, private foundations and their managers may be liable for excise taxes on expenditures that fall within the definition of "taxable expenditures." These are amounts paid or incurred by private foundations:

- To influence legislation;
- To influence the outcome of any specific public election;
- To grant to an individual for travel, study, or other similar purposes, unless the grant meets certain requirements;
- As a grant to an organization unless the organization is a public charity or unless the grantor private foundation exercises "expenditure responsibility" over the grant; or
- For any purpose other than one under Code Sec. 170(c)(2)(B) (such as charitable, scientific, literary, or educational purposes).

Expenditure responsibility means that the foundation exerts all reasonable efforts and establishes adequate procedures:

- To see that the grant is spent only for the purpose for which it is made,
- To obtain full and complete reports from the grantee organization on how the funds are spent, and
- To make full and detailed reports on the expenditures to the IRS.

For purposes of Code Sec. 4942, a grant for charitable purposes to a foreign organization that does not have a determination letter from the IRS may nevertheless be treated as a qualifying distribution. To qualify, the grantor private foundation must make a good faith determination that the foreign organization is a private operating foundation or a public charity that is not a disqualified supporting organization, provided that the foreign organization is not controlled by the foundation or its disqualified persons (Reg. § 53.4942(a)-3(a)(6)).

Good faith determination. A private foundation will ordinarily be considered to have made a good faith determination if the determination is based on an affidavit of the grantee or on an opinion of counsel of either the grantor or the grantee. The affidavit or opinion must show sufficient facts concerning the operations and support of the grantee for the IRS to determine that the grantee would be likely to qualify as a public charity or a private operating foundation.

Proposed Regulations

Current regulations provide that a grant to a foreign organization that does not have a determination letter from the IRS be treated as a grant to a public charity, for which the grantor is not required to exercise expenditure responsibility, if the grantor has made a good faith determination that the grantee is a public charity.

The proposed regulations modify the current regulations to identify a broader class of tax practitioners upon whose written advice a private foundation may base a good faith determination. Under the proposed regulations, a private foundation's good faith determination ordinarily may be based on written advice given by a "qualified tax practitioner" who is subject to the requirements in Circular 230. A *qualified tax practitioner* under the proposed regulations includes a certified public accountant, enrolled agent (EA), or attorney. The expanded class of practitioners, however, would not include foreign counsel unless the foreign counsel is a CPA, EA, or attorney licensed in the United States.

COMMENT

The IRS explained that it selected these types of practitioners because they generally provide advice to clients about tax positions on returns and are authorized to represent taxpayers before the agency.

The proposed regulations also provide that a taxpayer would not be considered to have reasonably relied in good faith on written advice unless Reg. § 1.6664-4(c)(1) is satisfied. That regulation states that all facts and circumstances must be taken into account, including the taxpayer's education, sophistication, and business experience in determining whether a taxpayer has reasonably relied in good faith on advice.

EXAMPLE

A private foundation's reliance on written advice is not reasonable and in good faith if the private foundation knows, or reasonably should have known, that a professional tax advisor lacks knowledge of the relevant aspects of federal tax law or that the professional tax advisor is otherwise not qualified or competent to render the written advice.

EXAMPLE

A private foundation may not rely on written advice if it knows, or has reason to know, that relevant facts were not disclosed to the professional tax advisor or the written advice is based on a representation or assumption that the private foundation knows, or has reason to know, is unlikely to be true.

The Treasury Department and the IRS believe that expanding the class of practitioners on whose written advice a private foundation may base a good faith determination will decrease the cost of seeking professional advice regarding these determinations, enabling foundations to engage in international philanthropy in a more cost-effective manner. At the same time, expressly allowing reliance on a broader spectrum of professional tax advisors may encourage more private foundations to obtain written tax advice, thus promoting the quality of the determinations being made.

Although the proposed regulations generally expand the class of practitioners on whose written advice a private foundation may ordinarily base a good faith determination, unlike the current rule the expanded class would not include foreign counsel unless the foreign counsel is a qualified tax practitioner (as defined in the proposed regulations). The proposed rule is consistent with the general requirements of Circular 230 that an attorney or CPA be licensed in a state, territory, or possession of the United States, and an enrolled agent be enrolled by the IRS, in order to practice before the IRS.

Foreign Affidavits

The IRS is contemplating removal of the current provision that allows private foundations to base a good faith determination on an affidavit of a foreign grantee. Future guidance could prohibit the use of foreign affidavits for grants exceeding a certain dollar threshold, or could require supporting factual information that might serve to corroborate the content of foreign affidavits.

Effective Date

The proposed regulations would apply to grants made after the date the regulations are finalized. However, private foundations may rely on the proposed regulations for grants made on or after September 24, 2012.

STUDY QUESTIONS

1. Excise taxes may be imposed on private foundation expenditures for all of the following ***except:***

a. Travel and study grants that do not meet certain requirements
b. Making qualifying distribution grant
c. Influencing the outcome of a specific public election
d. Influencing legislation

2. The IRS believes that under the proposed regulations a broader class of practitioners should be enabled to provide written advice about good faith determinations to private foundations because:

a. Costs of seeking professional advice will be lower and international philanthropy will be more cost effective
b. International philanthropic private foundations will be encouraged to locate in the United States
c. Proper information filings by private foundations will increase
d. Foreign practitioners other than accountants, enrolled agents, and attorneys will be qualified to advise the organizations

CODE SEC. 501(C)(3) ORGANIZATIONS PROHIBITED FROM POLITICAL CAMPAIGN INTERVENTION

When any election year cycle kicks into high gear, and even in nonelection years, Code Sec. 501(c)(3) organizations must tread carefully. Code Sec. 501(c)(3) organizations are absolutely prohibited from engaging in any political campaign intervention. In addition, the role of the IRS and Code Sec. 501(c)(4) social welfare organizations in elections has come under scrutiny in Congress.

COMMENT

In 2008, the IRS launched a Political Activities Compliance Initiative for the election cycle. The initiative, the IRS explained, was intended to:

- Educate the public and the relevant community;
- Provide guidance on the prohibition on political campaign intervention by Code Sec. 501(c)(3) organizations; and
- Maintain a meaningful enforcement presence in this area.

In its fiscal year (FY) 2013 work plan, IRS Exempt Organizations (EO) Division reported that it would continue its work to enforce the rules relating to political activities. "In FY 2012, EO combined what it had learned from past projects on political activities with new information gleaned from the redesigned Form 990. Using the Form 990 data, EO developed indicators to potential noncompliance that allows us to better focus our research," the IRS stated.

Absolute Prohibition on Campaign Activities

Under the Internal Revenue Code, all Code Sec. 501(c)(3) organizations are absolutely prohibited from directly or indirectly participating in, or intervening in, any political campaign on behalf of (or in opposition to) any candidate for elective public office. The prohibition applies to all campaigns, including campaigns at the federal, state, and local level. Violation of this prohibition may result in denial or revocation of tax-exempt status and the imposition of certain excise taxes.

COMMENT

Public office includes any elective office: federal, state, or local.

Political campaign intervention, the IRS has explained on its website and in Rev. Rul. 2007-41, includes all activities that favor or oppose one or more candidates for public office. The prohibition extends beyond candidate endorsements. Violations include:

- Contributions to political campaign funds or public statements of position (verbal or written) made by or on behalf of an organization in favor of or in opposition to any candidate for public;
- Distributing statements prepared by others that favor or oppose any candidate for public office; and Allowing a candidate to use an organization's assets or facilities (if other candidates are not given an equivalent opportunity).

COMMENT

The determination of whether an organization has engaged in political campaign intervention is facts and circumstances sensitive.

Websites

A website, the IRS has explained, is a form of communication. If an organization posts something on its website that favors or opposes a candidate for public office, the organization will be treated the same as if it distributed printed material, oral statements, or broadcasts that favored or opposed a candidate.

COMMENT

Use of social media, such as Facebook and LinkedIn, present new challenges. In addition, the Federal Election Commission has addressed some aspects of fundraising and other political activities on the Internet (www.fec.gov/pages/brochures/internetcomm.shtml).

When an organization links to another website, the organization is responsible for the consequences of establishing and maintaining that link, even if the organization does not have control over the content of the linked site, the IRS has cautioned. Because the linked content may change over time, an organization may reduce the risk of political campaign intervention by monitoring the linked content and adjusting the links accordingly.

COMMENT

An audit would likely cover a return from two years ago. The exempt organization may encounter difficulty in recreating its website from two years ago. The challenge is made more difficult if the exempt organization had links to other websites. The content of the other websites likely would have changed during the two-year period.

Voter Education

Voter education, voter registration, and "get-out-the-vote" drives by Code Sec. 501(c)(3) organizations are permitted if they are carried out in a nonpartisan manner. Voter education or voter registration activities conducted in a biased manner that favors or opposes one or more candidates are prohibited.

EXAMPLE

A Code Sec. 501(c)(3) sets up a booth at the county fair where citizens can register to vote. The signs and banners in and around the booth give only the name of the organization, the date of the next upcoming statewide election, and notice of the opportunity to register. No reference to any candidate or political party is made by the volunteers staffing the booth or in the materials available at the booth, other than the official voter registration forms that allow registrants to select a party affiliation. The IRS has explained on its website that the Code Sec. 501(c)(3) is not engaged in political campaign intervention when it operates this voter registration booth.

Voter Guides

The IRS has cautioned that preparing or distributing a voter guide may violate the prohibition against political campaign intervention if the guide focuses on a single issue or narrow range of issues, or if the questions are structured to reflect bias. Any document that identifies candidates and their positions close in time to an election has the potential to result in political campaign intervention. Preparation or distribution of voter guides, because of their nature, present a particular risk for noncompliance.

Candidate Appearances

An exempt organization may invite political candidates to speak at its events without jeopardizing its tax-exempt status. Political candidates may be invited in their capacity as candidates, or in their individual capacity (not as a candidate). Candidates may also appear without an invitation at organization events that are open to the public.

When a political candidate is scheduled to speak at its event, the Code Sec. 501(c)(3) organization should ensure that it:

- Provides an equal opportunity to political candidates seeking the same office;
- Does not indicate any support for or opposition to the candidate; and
- Does no political fundraising.

A candidate may appear at an event of the Code Sec. 501(c)(3) organization in a noncandidate capacity. The candidate's presence at an organization-sponsored event, in itself, does not cause the organization to be engaged in political campaign intervention. However, if the candidate is publicly recognized by the organization, or if the candidate is invited to speak, the organization must ensure that:

- The individual is chosen to speak solely for reasons other than candidacy for public office;
- The individual speaks only in a noncandidate capacity;
- Neither the individual nor any representative of the organization makes any mention of his or her candidacy or the election;
- No campaign activity occurs in connection with the candidate's attendance; and
- The organization maintains a nonpartisan atmosphere on the premises or at the event where the candidate is present.

Social Welfare Organizations

Recently, Congress has raised questions about the IRS's oversight of Code Sec. 501(c)(4) organizations (social welfare organizations). Congressional hearings were held after learning, in a report by the Treasury Inspector General for Tax Administration (TIGTA), that the IRS used inappropriate criteria to identify specific groups applying for tax-exempt status (Reference Number: 2013-10-053).

COMMENT

Social welfare organizations were first exempted from paying federal income tax by the *Revenue Act of 1913*. The legislative history does not explain the rationale of this exemption in any detail. In practice, Code Sec. 501(c)(4) status has sometimes been used by both the courts and the Service as a "catch all" exemption provision for organizations that lack the accepted essential characteristics of taxable entities, but elude classification under other subparagraphs of Code Sec. 501(c).

COMMENT

The issue of tax-exempt organizations participating in political campaign activities became much more of a concern after the Supreme Court's 2010 decision in ***Citizens United v. FEC*** (130 SCT 876). Previously, it was illegal for any corporation to expressly advocate for the election of defeat of candidates for federal office. ***Citizens United*** overturned the law. Now, corporations, including tax-exempt organizations, can advocate for the election or defeat of candidates for federal office.

Code Sec. 501(c)(4) organizations are entitled to federal tax exemption if they are operated exclusively for the promotion of social welfare, not organized for profit. Also exempt under Code Sec. 501(c)(4) are local associations of employees, whose membership is limited to the employees of a designated person or persons in a particular municipality, and the net earnings are devoted exclusively to charitable, educational, or recreational purposes.

An organization is operated exclusively for the promotion of social welfare if it is primarily engaged in promoting, in some way, the common good and general welfare of the people of a community.

There are two general concepts to remember:

- Organizations that promote social welfare should primarily promote the common good and general welfare of the people of the community as a whole. That is, they should exist primarily for bringing about civic betterment and social improvements; and
- An organization that primarily benefits a *private* group of citizens cannot qualify for Code Sec. 501(c)(4) tax-exempt status.

COMMENT

Common examples of Code Sec. 501(c)(4) organizations are the Jaycees, National Rifle Association, Sierra Club, and AARP.

Whether an organization is "primarily" engaged in promoting social welfare is determined by a facts and circumstances test. Relevant factors include:

- The amount of funds received from and devoted to particular activities;
- Other resources used in conducting these activities, such as buildings and equipment;
- The time devoted to activities (by volunteers as well as employees);
- The way the organization's activities are conducted; and
- The purposes furthered by various activities.

Promotion of social welfare does *not* include direct or indirect participation or intervention in political campaigns of any candidate for public office. However, a Code Sec. 501(c)(4) organization may engage in political campaigns on behalf of or in opposition to candidates for public office as long as the intervention is not the organization's primary activity.

It can be hard to determine whether a political activity has crossed the line into campaign intervention. This is because there are many political activities (for example, issue advocacy, distributing voter guides, and conducting get-out-the-vote drives) that are not considered campaign intervention if they do not show a bias towards or against a candidate. Whether an activity is campaign intervention will depend, again, on the facts and circumstances of each case. The tax code and regulations also do not address how to determine whether a Code Sec. 501(c)(4) organization's campaign activity is its primary activity.

All of a Code Sec. 501(c)(4) organization's activities, however, can be *lobbying*. The organization will be a social welfare organization as long as the lobbying is directed toward its social welfare purpose.

If a Code Sec. 501(c)(4) organization wants to engage in campaign activities, it has two choices—do so directly through its own organization or set up a separate fund under Code Sec. 527. Campaign activities performed in a separate, segregated fund attached to a Code Sec. 501(c)(4) organization will not be attributed back to the organization. If the Code Sec. 501(c) organization conducts the activity itself, it is subject to tax, but is not required to file Form 8871, *Political Organization Notice of Section 527 Status,* to be tax-exempt. If the Code Sec. 501(c) organization establishes a separate segregated fund, the fund is treated as a separate political organization and does not qualify for the exception from filing Form 8871.

COMMENT

Code Sec. 527(k) requires Code Sec. 527 political organizations to publicly disclose the name of anyone who contributes $200 or more in a calendar year. Code Sec 501(c)(3) and (4) organizations are not required to disclose the names of their contributors or the nature of their expenditures.

COMMENT

Determination of whether an organization has violated its tax-exempt status by engaging in too much campaign activity is made by looking at its activities during the *entire* year. Therefore, it would not seem possible to determine whether an organization should have its Code Sec. 501(c)(4) status revoked by looking only at its activities during the period immediately prior to an election.

COMMENT

Code Sec. 501(c)(4) organizations must also follow the federal campaign finance laws.

RULES FOR CHARITABLE HOSPITAL COMPLIANCE WITH PPACA PROPOSED

The IRS has proposed regulations that provide guidance for charitable hospital organizations relating to financial assistance and emergency medical care policies, charges for certain care provided to individuals eligible for financial assistance, and billing and collections (NPRM REG-130266-11). The regulations reflect changes to the law made by the *Patient Protection and Affordable Care Act of 2010* (PPACA) (P.L. 111-148). The proposed regulations also contain a section that defines *hospital organization, hospital facility,* and other key terms used in the regulations.

Background

PPACA enacted Code Sec. 501(r), which applies to tax-exempt hospital organizations and their facilities. The proposed regulations address Code Sec. 501(r)(4)–(6) and set forth certain requirements, including:

- A tax-exempt hospital must create a financial assistance policy (FAP) that, among other things, sets forth the hospital's criteria for determining an individual's eligibility for financial assistance and the basis for calculating charges for medical services;
- A hospital organization must limit the amounts it charges eligible individuals for emergency care to no more than the amount generally billed (AGB) to individuals who have insurance covering such care;
- A hospital organization must engage in "reasonable efforts" to determine an individual's eligibility for financial assistance under its FAP prior to engaging in extraordinary collection actions (ECA); and
- A hospital facility must use certain methods to widely publicize its FAP.

The proposed regulations under Code Sec. 501(r)(5) describe how a hospital facility determines the maximum amounts it can charge individuals eligible for financial assistance for emergency and other medically necessary care.

If an eligible individual has not applied for financial assistance at the time charges are made, the proposed regulations provide that a hospital facility will not fail to satisfy Code Sec. 501(r)(5) if it charges the individual more than the insurance rate. However, the hospital facility must comply with all the requirements regarding notifying individuals about the FAP and respond to applications submitted, including correcting the amount charged and seeking to reverse any ECA previously initiated if an individual is later found to be eligible for assistance.

Extraordinary Collection Actions

The proposed regulations under Code Sec. 501(r)(6) describe the actions that are considered "extraordinary collection actions" and the "reasonable efforts" a hospital facility must make to determine assistance eligibility before engaging in these actions. In general, to have made reasonable efforts under the proposed regulations a hospital facility must determine whether an individual is assistance-eligible or provide required notices during a period ending 120 days after the date of the first billing statement.

The proposed regulations state that ECAs include any actions taken by a hospital facility against an individual related to obtaining payment of a bill for care covered under the hospital facility's FAP that require a legal or judicial process. ECAs that require a legal or judicial process include, but are not limited to, actions to:

- Place a lien on an individual's property;
- Foreclose on an individual's real property;
- Attach or seize an individual's bank account or any other personal property;
- Commence a civil action against an individual;
- Cause an individual's arrest;
- Cause an individual to be subject to a writ of body attachment; and
- Garnish an individual's wages.

Although a hospital facility may undertake extraordinary collection actions after this 120-day notification period, a hospital facility that has not determined whether an individual is assistance-eligible must still accept and process a financial assistance application from the individual for an additional 120 days. Accordingly, the total period during which a hospital facility must accept and process FAP applications is 240 days from the date of the first billing statement.

If a hospital facility receives a financial assistance application during the application period, it must suspend any ECAs until it has processed the application and, if it determines the individual is assistance-eligible, must seek to reverse the ECAs and promptly refund any overpaid amounts. While debts may be referred to third parties to assist with collection actions at any time (except to the extent collection is considered extraordinary), including during the initial 120-day notification period, they may not be sold to third parties during the notification period unless and until an eligibility determination has been made.

Public Hearing

At a public hearing following the release of the proposed regulations, speakers expressed a need for greater flexibility, transparency, and clarity from the regulations.

COMMENT

"The message we uniformly heard from [hospitals of all types, sizes, and locations] was one size does not fit all; do not interrupt what is working; focus on transparency and disclosure to the community," said Andreanna Ksidakis, president, Sutter Ventures, Ltd., who represented the American Hospital Association.

Speakers also expressed concern that the proposed regulations might interfere with or preempt current state regulations or an organization's preexisting efforts and create a duplicative and unnecessary administrative burden. Some speakers suggested that the IRS introduce additional methods by which organizations may calculate AGBs to individuals eligible under its FAP. Other speakers stated that the IRS should allow a hospital organization more than one procedure to show that it made reasonable efforts to determine an individual's eligibility under an FAP.

FAP Eligibility

Under the proposed regulations, a hospital organization must use reasonable efforts to determine eligibility for assistance under an FAP. Some speakers expressed concern that patients may not be cooperative or responsive as hospitals attempt to determine eligibility, which could delay the determination process.

One practitioner recommended that the final regulations specify that a hospital will have made reasonable efforts if it relies on the financial assistance application or "other trustworthy methods," which would be described and disclosed annually on its Form 990, *Return of Organization Exempt From Income Tax*.

Some of the presumptive eligibility standards require looking at local demographics and using service providers to see whether a particular individual has given an address that may not even exist or may be in an underserved area, the practitioner said. She stated that hospitals do not want to send bills to collections if they know they are uncollectible. "We would rather find out [about eligibility] sooner rather than later and use our systems and databases to figure that out. But, by using those same systems, hospitals may discover that someone does indeed have an ability to pay," she said.

EXAMPLE

The Care in Faith Hospital considers whether Jeffrey Towne is eligible for assistance under an FAP. He is a taxpayer who resides in an area of high wealth and whose zip code has many luxury dwellings. However, after appearing in the hospital's database as a previous recipient of charity care, it may be unlikely Jeffrey has the ability to pay for his services.

Another practitioner cautioned that an individual's zip code would not always be a good standard for determining ability to pay. She stated concern over the use of soft credit checks to determine a person's ability to pay.

EXAMPLE

Janice Jensen resides in a wealthy area of New York City and has not had her credit score updated recently, but in fact she has recently lost her job and is arrears in credit card and rent payments.

Billings and Collections

Hospitals generally support the intent of the PPACA and the proposed regulations to impose an obligation on hospitals to determine whether an individual is eligible for financial assistance before undertaking collection action. Many hospitals already had procedures in place to ensure collection action would not be taken until eligibility had been determined. The proposed regulations may be placing unnecessary limitations on hospitals. The proposed regulations create an eight-month process with a very prescriptive and extremely detailed set of procedures that, when combined with other provisions, effectively applies to every patient, said a speaker at the hearing. "From a practical perspective, the 120-day notification and the 120-day application procedures will require a new set of hospital policies with parallel tracking and no commensurate benefit," the speaker cautioned.

The proposed regulations also make it possible for patients to delay payment. Regardless of whether he or she has insurance or the ability to pay, a patient might simply refuse to engage in meaningful discussion with the hospital regarding payment options. Practitioners stated that the two 120-day periods are too long and that it is unnecessary to ask hospitals to wait for 240 days to begin enforcement action. Unnecessary paperwork or delay in determining eligibility for assistance may not be good for the patients or the hospitals. An early review of demographics and other factors may indicate whether a patient has the ability to pay. Waiting more than 240 days to undertake significant collection action may be unjustified, especially because the longer the bill remains outstanding generally, the more difficult funds tend to be to collect.

STUDY QUESTIONS

3. Caution is advisable for Code Sec. 501(c)(3) organizations using websites and social media because:

a. Links outdate quickly and users of the organizations' websites may be frustrated when they are directed to dead links
b. Content of the sites linked to is readily available to the IRS in the event the 501(c)(3) organizations are audited
c. The organizations are responsible for consequences of maintaining links to sites that may subsequently intervene in political campaigns
d. Internet fundraising is not subject to the same rules as 501(c)(3) organizations by the Federal Election Commission

4. Which activity is allowed for Code Sec. 501(c)(4) organizations having tax-exempt status?

a. Lobbying legislators for an issue related to the organizations' social welfare purpose
b. Political advocacy managed by employees of the organizations, not volunteers
c. Political campaigning to benefit a specific, private group of citizens such as existing city council members
d. Political opposition to certain candidates as long as the names of supporters are registered with the IRS prior to the election

STARTING CHARITABLE DISASTER RELIEF ORGANIZATIONS

No one can predict what the future holds but, with hurricane and tornado seasons, drought conditions, and annual wildfires, Americans may certainly experience many future disasters. One response to a disaster is to establish a new charitable organization to assist victims. The tax code provides tax-exempt treatment for many of these startups, but organizers should be aware of the host of complex compliance rules.

The IRS established new procedures partly in response to the massive outpouring of charitable support following the September 11, 2001, terrorist attacks and the widespread destruction left by Hurricane Katrina in 2005. The basic procedures, requirements, and developments related to tax-exempt disaster relief charities are addressed here.

Tax Advantages of 501(c)(3) Organizations

Tax-exempt status is meant to incentivize donations, and therefore it provides benefits to the charitable organization, the donors, and the relief recipients, as the table summarizes.

Table 1. Tax Advantages for Charitable Giving

For Organizations	For Donors	For Recipients
Ability to attract donors with the promise of a tax deduction for their contributions under Code Sec. 170	Eligibility to deduct some or the entire amount of the charitable contributions from their adjusted gross income	Broader eligibility to exclude from gross income qualified payments received from a charitable organization
Exemption from federal employment taxes and often from state, local, and property taxes		
Reduced U.S. postal rates		

What Is a Tax-Exempt Organization?

An organization qualifies as an exempt charity if it:

- Is organized and operated exclusively for charitable purposes;
- Serves public, rather than private, interests; and
- Refrains from participating or intervening in any political campaign or engaging in substantial amounts of lobbying activity.

Most disaster relief should easily fall into one of the exempt purposes listed under Code Sec. 501(c)(3). The kinds of aid that charitable organizations can provide are numerous. These include providing food, clothing, and shelter to individuals and businesses, so long as assistance is a reasonable means of accomplishing a charitable purpose. In addition, there must be no, or only incidental, benefit to a private interest.

Applying for Tax-Exempt Status

With some exceptions for religious organizations such as churches, temples, and mosques, the tax code requires that a new charity with actual or anticipated annual gross receipts of more than $5,000 must submit an application for tax-exempt status to the IRS. An organization applies by submitting Form 1023, *Application for Recognition of Exemption Under Section 501(c)(3) of the Internal Revenue Code.*

The completed Form 1023 must contain or be accompanied by:

- An employer identification number (EIN), obtained by filing Form SS-4;
- Checklist for Form 1023 and Form 1023 Schedules A through H, as needed;
- Copies of the organizing documents, for example a certified copy of the articles of incorporation and bylaws;
- Any request for expedited review of the application;
- Form 2848, *Power of Attorney and Declaration of Representative*;
- Form 8821, *Tax Information Authorization*, or 5768, *Election/Revocation of Election by an Eligible Section 501(c)(3) Organization To Make Expenditures To Influence Legislation*, if required; and
- The appropriate user fee.

COMMENT

Because of the complexities involved with starting a new charity, potential contributors may want to consider using an existing charity to provide relief to disaster victims. When disasters strike, new charities spring up to help the victims, and existing charities want to expand their activities to provide disaster relief. However, often these organizations do not understand the complexities of starting and operating an organization to provide disaster relief.

Private foundation versus public charity. In its application, an organization must specify whether it wants to be classified as a private foundation or a public charity. The distinction is important because the rules for private foundations differ from those for public charities. The distinction between private foundation and public charity classification is important. Public charity status is the more advantageous category. The principal reason is that private foundations must:

- Refrain from acts of self dealing (Code Sec. 4941);
- Meet minimum distribution requirements (Code Sec. 4942);
- Abstain from excess business holdings (Code Sec. 4943);
- Abstain from jeopardizing investments (Code Sec. 4944); and
- Refrain from making certain expenditures (Code Sec. 4945).

An additional advantage from public charity status is the exemption from the Code Sec. 4940 tax on net investment income to which most private foundations are subject.

COMMENT

After September 11, Congress passed the *Victims of Terrorism Tax Relief Act of 2001* (P.L. 107-134), which provided more relaxed rules for employer-sponsored private foundations that provide disaster relief to eligible victims affected by a qualified disaster.

While application is pending. New charities whose organizers want to provide relief to victims as quickly as possible may operate as tax-exempt pending the IRS's approval. However, donors cannot rely upon an organization holding itself out as tax-exempt to deduct their contributions until the charitable organization receives its official determination letter from the IRS granting it tax-exempt status.

Expedited reviews of Form 1023 are possible if a compelling reason is provided for the IRS to process the application ahead of others. IRS procedures require that applicants for expedited review provide the compelling reason:

- A brief description of the disaster and details of how the organization will provide relief;

- An explanation of the immediate need for the organization's specific disaster relief services;
- Any other anticipated consequences of denial of expedited review; and
- The date on which an exemption letter is required.

COMMENT

Expedited review may be necessary when a new organization has a grant pending and a short window of time in which to obtain the grant.

Charitable Class

The group of individuals that may properly receive assistance from a tax-exempt charity is a "charitable class." A charitable class must be large enough or sufficiently indefinite that the community as a whole, rather than a preselected group of people, receives benefits when a charity provides assistance.

Basis of charitable class. A tax-exempt organization cannot target and limit its disaster assistance to specific individuals. Nor can donors earmark contributions for a particular individual or family. When a disaster or emergency occurs, a charitable organization may help individuals who are in need or otherwise distressed because they are part of a general class of charitable beneficiaries, provided the organization selects who gets the assistance based upon general charitable standards.

Needy or distressed test. Charitable funds may not be distributed to individuals simply because they are disaster victims. An organization must generally assess the financial and other needs of its intended aid recipients. The severe and immediate nature of a disaster generally means that organizations may provide services such as rescue services, food, shelter, and counseling without a needs test.

Documentation

Charities that provide short-term emergency aid must document the:

- Type of assistance provided;
- Criteria for disbursing the aid;
- Date;
- Location;
- Estimated number of disaster victims assisted;
- Charitable purpose accomplished; and
- Cost of the aid.

Longer-term aid necessitates more detailed records that include an assessment of needs to determine the recipients' financial resources and their physical, mental, and emotional well-being. Additionally, records should include:

- A complete description of the assistance provided;
- Costs;
- Purpose for which the aid was given;
- The charity's criteria for disbursing assistance under each program;
- How the recipients were selected; and
- The name, address, and amount distributed to each recipient.

Reporting Requirements

Most charitable organizations are required to file annual return information (Form 990 series). Public charities file Form 990, *Return of Organization Exempt From Income Tax,* or the short version (Form 990-EZ). Form 990-N, *Electronic Notice (e-Postcard) for Tax-Exempt Organizations Not Required To File Form 990 or 990-PF,* is available to many small charities.

Charitable Contribution Deductions

A donor to a qualified tax-exempt organization must substantiate contributions of $250 or more to claim a tax deduction by providing the IRS with a contemporaneous written acknowledgment of the contribution from the donee organization. An organization that does not acknowledge a contribution incurs no penalty; but, without a written acknowledgment, the donor cannot claim the tax deduction.

COMMENT

Organizations can assist a donor by providing a timely, written statement with the name of the recipient organization, the amount of cash, and a description (but not value) of any property other than cash contributed.

If the organization provided the donor with some benefit in return for its contribution, it must give a description and good faith estimate of the value of goods or services it provided in return for the contribution in its acknowledgment. If the organization did not provide goods or services in return for the contribution, it must also provide a statement to that effect. Failure to provide such a statement may preclude the donor from deducting the amount as a charitable contribution.

Working with volunteers. Because so much work done by tax-exempt organizations is generally performed by volunteers, organizations must understand the rules regarding tax treatment of volunteer services. There is no tax deduction available for the value of a volunteer's time and services.

EXAMPLE

Deborah Grisse, a volunteer for her town's youth soccer league, is an expert grant writer who generally charges $50 per hour. She has worked four hours writing press releases and a feature story for the tax-exempt league. Deborah cannot claim an itemized deduction of the $200 value of her services provided to the organization.

However, a volunteer may claim a deduction for certain out-of-pocket costs, including:

- Unreimbursed supplies purchased in performance of volunteer work, such as stamps and stationery;
- The purchase cost and upkeep of a required uniform not suitable for everyday use;
- Unreimbursed telephone/cell expenses; and
- Car expenses such as parking fees, tolls, and the cost of gas and oil for miles traveled on the charity's behalf.

COMMENT

The 2013 standard mileage rate for charitable purposes is 14 cents per mile, as set without inflation adjustment under Code Sec. 170(i).

EXAMPLE

Although Deborah Grisse may not deduct her usual charges for writing, she may deduct $28 for the 200 miles she drove to interview players for the feature story, plus the $35 she spent printing and mailing the press releases.

REGULATIONS ISSUED FOR TYPE III SUPPORTING ORGANIZATIONS

Supporting organizations are public charities that carry out their exempt purposes by supporting other exempt organizations, usually other public charities. The classification is important because it is one way a charity can avoid classification as a private foundation, a status that is subject to a much more restrictive regulatory regime. The key feature of a supporting organization is a strong relationship with an organization it supports. The strong relationship enables the supported organization to oversee the operations of the supporting organization.

Because the legal and regulatory requirements are much more stringent for private foundations than for public charities, many organizations that might otherwise be private foundations seek to be supporting organizations.

There are three types of supporting organizations. To qualify as one of them, an organization must meet three tests and requirements. The three types of supporting organizations, as defined under the *Pension Protection Act of 2006* (PPA) (P.L. 109-280), are:

- Type I: The *parent-subsidiary type* in which the supported organization operates, supervises, or controls the supporting organization;
- Type II: The *brother-sister type* involving a supported organization and supporting organization that are both "supervised or controlled in connection with" a parent; and
- Type III: A type in which the supported and supporting organizations are merely *operated in connection* with one another and are not otherwise related to each other.

Type III is further divided into categories of *functionally integrated* and *nonfunctionally integrated* (NFI) supporting organizations. The temporary regulations address the amount that a Type III supporting organization that is not functionally integrated must annually distribute and explain how assets are valued for purposes of this distribution requirement. The final regulations describe all of the other requirements of the relationship test for Type III supporting organizations.

The IRS has released final, temporary, and proposed regulations for Type III supporting organizations under Code Sec. 509(a)(3) (T.D. 9605, REG 155929-06). The final regulations generally track the proposed regulations issued in 2009 with modifications to the rules for payout requirements for nonfunctionally integrated Type III supporting organizations (NFI Type III supporting organizations). The final regulations added a few changes that provide important clarifications.

Notably, the final regulations clarify that:

- All supporting organizations must meet the "significant voice responsiveness" test of Reg. § 1.509(a)-4(i)(3)(iii);
- There will be future guidance on the meaning of *control* for purposes of the prohibition on supported organizations from receiving contributions from donors that control a supported organization; and
- Certain transitional relief is provided with respect to the notification requirement and the integral-part test for Type III supporting organizations.
- Finally, the Treasury and the IRS plan additional guidance on how supporting organizations can qualify as functionally integrated by supporting a governmental entity.

COMMENT

The regulations also describe functionally integrated Type III supporting organizations, which are generally not subject to a distribution requirement if the organizations either:

- Engage in activities substantially all of which directly further the exempt purposes of the supported organization(s) to which it is responsive; or
- Are the parents of each of their supported organizations.

Tests

To qualify as Type I, II, or III, the supporting organization must pass three tests:

- The notification requirement;
- The responsiveness test; and
- The integral-part test.

Each of these tests has been altered from its original form by the 2009 proposed and final regulations.

NFI Type III Supporting Organizations

Proposed regulations issued in 2009 generally provided that a NFI Type III supporting organization must annually distribute a "distributable amount" equal to at least 5 percent of the fair market value of its nonexempt-use assets. The distribution requirement was based on non-exempt-use assets, rather than on income. The IRS took this approach out of concerns that the income-based payout test could result in little or nothing being paid to charity if the supporting organization's assets produced little or no income.

Revised Distribution Requirements

The final regulations modify this approach. The IRS observed that the restrictions on NFI Type III supporting organizations reduce the likelihood that substantial contributors to a NFI Type III supporting organization would be able to use the supporting organization's assets to further their own interests. Therefore, the IRS has decided that a NFI Type III supporting organization should annually distribute a distributable amount equal to the greater of 85 percent of adjusted net income or 3.5 percent of the fair market value of the supporting organization's non-exempt-use assets.

COMMENT

Because there is an asset-based component, there is also a valuation required of the fair market value of the organization's assets.

Definition of *supported organization*. The final regulations maintain the term *publicly supported organization* and continue to use it in every paragraph of Reg. § 1.509(a)-4 other than Reg. § 1.509(a)-4(i). The final regulations also revise the definition of "supported organization" in the 2009 proposed regulations and apply the term only in newly amended Reg. § 1.509(a)-4(i).

For purposes of Reg. § 1.509(a)-4(i), a supported organization of a Type III supporting organization is any publicly supported organization designated by name in the supporting organization's articles of organization.

In addition, a supported organization of a Type III supporting organization can include a publicly supported organization that is not designated by name in the supporting organization's articles. There has to be a historic and continuing relationship between the supporting organization and the publicly supported organization and, because of this relationship, a substantial identity of interests has developed between the organizations.

Requirement to notify supported organizations. The final regulations clarify the relationship between the filing date of the Form 990 and the date notification is provided by referring to the Form 990, *Return of Organization Exempt From Income Tax,* "that was most recently filed as of the date the notification is provided" rather than simply the "most recently filed Form 990."

EXAMPLE

Run for Health, a Type III supporting organization reporting on a calendar year basis, has not filed its 2013 Form 990 by May 31, 2014. Because it requested an extension, Run for Health can satisfy the Form 990 portion of its notification requirement for 2013 (which it needs to meet by May 31, 2014) by providing a copy of the 2012 Form 990 that it filed in 2013.

Responsiveness test. The Treasury Department and the IRS have concluded that the term *significant voice* makes clear that the responsiveness test requires only that the officers, directors, or trustees of a supported organization have the *ability to influence* the supporting organization's decisions regarding the supporting organization's use of its income or assets. The test is not whether the officers, directors, or trustees of the supported organization have *control* over such decisions.

The IRS intends to require that all the supported organizations meet the responsiveness test with the supporting organization instead of just some organizations.

COMMENT

The relationship between the supporting organization and the supported organization is a fundamental basis for the supported organization's tax status and for several other decisions that the IRS makes regarding the tests that they are required to do. Therefore, ensuring that there really is a strong relationship between the supported and supporting organizations is important.

The final and proposed regulations also include an example of how a trust might have a close and continuous working relationship with a supported organization.

The IRS received several panicked comments because an example in the 2009 regulations involved an organization that held quarterly face-to-face meetings. The preamble to the final regulations clarifies that the example is not the only way to meet the significant voice responsiveness test. To better illustrate options for satisfying the significant voice responsiveness test, the example has been amended in the final regulations to refer to "quarterly face-to-face or telephonic meetings" rather than only face-to-face meetings.

Integral-part test. The integral-part test has also been changed. In the older regulations, two tests were part of the integral-part test: a "but-for" test and a "pay substantially all" test. These have been transformed by the final regulations into a *functionally integrated test* and a *nonfunctionally integrated test,* which were the terms that the PPA introduced. The new functionally integrated test has components of the old but-for test. The nonfunctionally integrated test has components of the old "pay out substantially all income" test.

The Treasury Department and the IRS agree that the meaning of the phrase "directly further the exempt purposes," as used in the functionally integrated test, is similar to the meaning of the phrase "directly for the active conduct of activities constituting" the exempt purposes, as used in the definition of a private operating foundation and as described in detail in Reg. § 53.4942(b)-1(b)(1).

Consequently, in defining direct furtherance activities, the final regulations use language similar to that used in Reg. § 53.4942(b)-1(b)(1) by clarifying that direct furtherance activities are activities conducted by the supporting organization itself, rather than by a supported organization.

Transitional relief. The final regulations added a requirement that supporting organizations must notify their supported organizations of certain information. Essentially, the supporting organization needs to give notice to all of its supported organizations that contain a description of the support from the prior year and the most recently filed Form 990. That notice is due the last day of the fifth month following the close of the supporting organization's tax year.

The temporary regulations provide transition relief for the first year in which notification is required from a supporting organization whose tax year includes December 28, 2012 (the date on which the final and temporary regulations became effective). That notification is due the later of the last day of the fifth month following the close of the tax year or the day the Form 990 is due for that tax year, including extensions.

EXAMPLE

Rapid City Disaster Response, a supporting organization, reports on the calendar year and files a Form 8868, *Application for Extension of Time To File an Exempt Organization Return,* for 2012. The organization gets a three-month extension so that its Form 990 for 2012 is not due until August 15, 2013. Disaster Response would have until August 15, 2013, to provide its notice for 2012.

The IRS recognizes that many supporting organizations do not have counsel on staff or may not be in contact with their advisors at regular intervals during the year, and they may come to a practitioner only right before the Form 990 is due, or they might not file the extension request until after May 31.

The final regulations have provided additional transition relief for Type III supporting organizations that meet and continue to meet the but-for portion of the integral-part test under existing Reg. § 1.509(a)-4(i)(3)(ii). Those supporting organizations will be treated as meeting the requirements of a functionally integrated Type III supporting organization until the first day of the organization's second tax year beginning after December 28, 2012.

STUDY QUESTIONS

5. A charitable class of a tax-exempt disaster relief charity:

a. Includes targeted and limited individuals receiving assistance
b. Is based on general charitable standards
c. Includes any disaster victim
d. Is based on a percentage of individuals requiring assistance

6. Types I, II, and III supporting organizations include all of the following ***except:***

a. Supporting and supported organizations operated in connection with one another

b. Functionally nonintegrated type

c. Brother-sister type

d. Parent-subsidiary type

CONCLUSION

The IRS is responsible for ensuring that organizations are not abusing their tax exemptions, and for providing exempt organizations with clear guidance and details regarding the specific compliance requirements that each of the many exempt organization varieties must follow. Legislative and regulatory changes to the tax code provisions keep the IRS busy on one hand, whereas ever-inventive individuals and organizations challenge the IRS oversight abilities on the other hand. As a result, constant attention to change is essential for any practitioner in the exempt organizations area.

CPE NOTE: When you have completed your study and review of chapters 8–9, which comprise Module 4, you may wish to take the Quizzer for this Module.

Go to **CCHGroup.com/PrintCPE** to take this Quizzer online.

TOP FEDERAL TAX ISSUES FOR 2014 CPE COURSE

Answers to Study Questions

MODULE 1 — CHAPTER 1

1. a. *Incorrect.* Medicare supplemental health insurance (a Medigap policy) is not included in MEC but is an excepted benefit.
b. *Incorrect.* Such coverage is an excepted benefit and not included in MEC.
c. *Correct.* Minimum essential coverage includes COBRA continuation coverage of an employer-sponsored plan.
d. *Incorrect.* Such specific coverage is an excepted benefit not included in MEC.

2. a. *Incorrect.* The tax credit applies to taxpayers who apply through exchanges, a necessary feature of the exchange provisions.
b. *Incorrect.* The employer mandate is a key provision of the PPACA pertaining to penalties on employers who fail to notify employees about the availability of health insurance exchanges and other benefits of the exchanges.
c. *Correct.* Wellness programs and premium discounts are not provided by the government and are not related to federal revenue.
d. *Incorrect.* The individual mandate (individual shared responsibility payment) is a revenue-generating provision of the reform law.

3. a. *Incorrect.* These revenue sources are included in MAGI in calculating eligibility for the credit.
b. *Correct.* Dependents are ineligible for the credit.
c. *Incorrect.* Household income factors MAGI in the formula for eligibility.
d. *Incorrect.* The credit is available for household incomes between 100 and 400 percent of the FPL.

4. a. *Incorrect.* Employer plans must be equivalent to average bronze, not silver, levels of coverage.
b. *Correct.* Code Sec. 4980H(a) requirements are satisfied if MEC is offered to at least 95 percent of FTEs.
c. *Incorrect.* Dependents must be covered up to age 26, not 23.
d. *Incorrect.* The unaffordability of the group coverage does not exempt ALEs from the assessable payments.

5. a. *Correct.* The primary amendments to HIPAA incorporate nondiscrimination and wellness provisions that were issued in 2006 regulations for HIPAA.

b. *Incorrect.* The eight factors devised for HIPAA remain the same.
c. *Incorrect.* HIPAA's discounts, rebates, and modifications for cost-sharing amounts were further supported in the PPACA amendments to HIPAA, as long as those incentives are nondiscriminatory.
d. *Incorrect.* The intent of the PPACA wellness program is to encourage flexibility in program design.

6. a. *Incorrect.* The credit increases to 50 percent in 2014.
b. *Correct.* The 50 percent credit applies for both 2014 and 2015, after which the credit will no longer be offered.
c. *Incorrect.* The credit will not be offered to nonprofit employers in 2016.
d. *Incorrect.* The credit is scheduled to be discontinued after 2015.

MODULE 1—CHAPTER 2

1. a. *Incorrect.* Reporting the NII liability is not postponed until the following tax period.
b. *Correct.* When the taxpayer changes the annual accounting period or otherwise has a short tax year, the threshold for the NII tax is reduced proportionately for the number of months in the short tax year.
c. *Incorrect.* Form 8960 is always submitted with the taxpayer's Form 1040 or 1041.
d. *Incorrect.* Reporting the NII tax does not require filing an amended return for the period prior to the short tax year.

2. a. *Correct.* Only the citizen's income is used to determine NII tax liability and he or she must file separately unless the couple has elected to treat the nonresident alien as a resident.
b. *Incorrect.* The nonresident alien's income is not measured for the NII tax unless the spouses elect under Code Sec. 6013(g) to treat the nonresident alien as a resident for joint filing.
c. *Incorrect.* The nonresident spouse's income is not figured for NII tax liability using the $125,000 threshold.
d. *Incorrect.* Code Sec. 1411 rules do not assess NII tax liability for the couple using a $250,000 threshold for each spouse.

3. a. *Correct.* If the trading is infrequent and noncontinuous, it does not rise to the level of a Section 162 trade or business.
b. *Incorrect.* Although determination of the nature of the activity must consider the facts in each case, prior court rulings are a general basis for judging whether the activity is conducted in the ordinary course of a trade or business.

c. *Incorrect.* For-profit and income-generating activities are general indicators that an activity is being conducted as a trade or business.
d. *Incorrect.* The factors used to determine whether an activity is a trade or business generally follow the Code Sec. 162 business expense rules.

4. a. *Incorrect.* The adjustment is available in disposition of the interest in an installment sale.
b. *Correct.* Just as the installment sale provisions of Code Sec. 453 dictate accounting for gains, the adjustment for NII uses the same proportion of the net gain.
c. *Incorrect.* No acceleration occurs due to the nature of the income from installment payments.
d. *Incorrect.* A portion of the adjustment is taken each year.

5. a. *Incorrect.* Under the qualified plan distribution exception, Code Sec. 457(b) distributions are not included in NII.
b. *Incorrect.* Distributions from qualified plans used to purchase life insurance policies are not included in NII.
c. *Incorrect.* Under the proposed regs, NII does not include qualified retirement plan distributions.
d. *Correct.* Distributions that are not included in NII may be included in gross income under Chapter 1 rules.

6. a. *Correct.* Losses remaining in a taxable transaction after the losses are applied against passive activity net income or gain may be classified as nonpassive and thus used to offset nonpassive activity income.
b. *Incorrect.* The suspended passive activity losses may be so applied in certain circumstances.
c. *Incorrect.* In some situations, suspended passive losses may be netted against income from nonpassive activities.
d. *Incorrect.* The Code Sec. 469(g) provision applies only to disposition of the entire interest in a taxable transaction.

MODULE 2 — CHAPTER 3

1. a. *Incorrect.* Voluntary accounting method changes do not require appeal to either the IRS Appeals Office or a decision by government counsel.
b. *Correct.* Procedures in Rev. Proc. 97-27 details voluntary *advance* consent procedures, whereas Rev. Proc. 2011-14 provides *automatic* voluntary consent procedures.
c. *Incorrect.* Form 3115 is filed whether a change in accounting method is effected through the advance or automatic consent procedure.

d. *Incorrect.* Audit protection applies whether a voluntary accounting method change is effected through the automatic or advance consent procedure.

2. a. *Incorrect.* Audit protection does not apply with respect to a method change that is an issue before the Appeals Office or in federal court.
b. *Incorrect.* Although a taxpayer may file an accounting method change within 120 days of the close of an examination even though another examination has begun, audit protection does not apply if the accounting method change is the subject of the second examination.
c. *Incorrect.* Although a taxpayer may file an accounting method change with respect to a pending issue, audit protection does not apply.
d. *Correct.* A taxpayer under continuous examination (i.e., an examination that has lasted at least 12 months) will receive audit protection with respect to an accounting method change if Form 3115 is filed within the first 90 days of the tax year of change, and the change is not related to the issue under examination.

3. a. *Correct.* A net negative adjustment period for a voluntary change is one year, taken into account entirely in the year of change, whereas a net positive adjustment period is applied ratably over a four-year adjustment period.
b. *Incorrect.* A net negative adjustment has a different adjustment period, and the two periods are set at a different range for voluntary changes.
c. *Incorrect.* The Code Sec. 481(a) taxpayer-favorable and net positive adjustment periods have different durations.
d. *Incorrect.* Both of the Code Sec. 481(a) adjustment periods for voluntary changes are of shorter duration.

4. a. *Incorrect.* The National Office notifies the taxpayer that, upon review, the change was noncompliant and consent is not granted.
b. *Incorrect.* The IRS has the discretion to allow the taxpayer to conform the accounting method reviewed with amended returns for the year of change and any later affected years. Taxable income will be computed on each amended return as if the proper accounting method had been adopted.
c. *Correct.* The National Office will not grant consent to change to an improper method of accounting.
d. *Incorrect.* The taxpayer must check box 16 on Form 3115 in order to be assured that a conference of right will be held before formal rejection.

5. a. *Incorrect.* For an advance consent request, Form 3115 must be filed by the last day of the tax year for the change.

b. *Correct.* No filing fee applies to automatic consent filings. However, a fee in the amount of $1,000, $4,000, or $7,000 applies to advance consent filings, depending upon the taxpayer's gross income.
c. *Incorrect.* If the IRS reviews an incomplete automatic consent application a taxpayer will be given 30 days to provide the National Office with the additional information.
d. *Incorrect.* A six-month filing extension, measured from the original due date of the return without regard to extensions, only applies to automatic consent requests.

6. a. *Incorrect.* If the examiner cannot determine or reasonably estimate the adjustment and a cutoff method is inappropriate, the year of change may be deferred.
b. *Incorrect.* A deferral may be made if the improper method of accounting has no material effect in the year of the change.
c. *Correct.* Only the Office of Appeals or government counsel can change the otherwise-applicable year of change to reflect the hazards of litigation.
d. *Incorrect.* If the limitations period has expired for tax years after the year in which the change would have been imposed, the agent may defer the year of the change.

MODULE 2 — CHAPTER 4

1. a. *Incorrect.* Deferring the tax liability does not increase the total taxes due.
b. *Incorrect.* Deferring a tax liability uses the asset/liability method to significantly defer taxes.
c. *Correct.* The deferral in paying taxes is an effect of a deferred tax liability, and a net deferred tax asset results in paying more tax currently.
d. *Incorrect.* If a company has a net deferred tax asset, the company recognizes the tax due currently.

2. a. *Incorrect.* Traditional IRA owners must stop making contributions to their accounts in the year they reach age 70½.
b. *Incorrect.* Annual RMDs from traditional IRAs must begin when the owner reaches age 70½.
c. *Incorrect.* Owners taking distributions from a deductible IRA pay taxes on both the original contribution amounts plus earnings, whereas distributions from a nondeductible traditional IRA are taxed on just the earnings because the original contribution amounts were not tax-free.
d. *Correct.* Distributions of both the contributions and earnings in Roth IRAs are tax-free.

3. a. *Incorrect.* Unlike other types of IRA, for which the total contribution for 2013 is $5,500 ($6,500 for those older than age 50), SEP-IRAs allow contributions by employers for 2013 of the much more generous lesser of 25 percent of the employee's wages or $51,000.
b. *Incorrect.* Unlike other IRAs, the deadline for contributions is not April 15 of the following tax year but the filing date of the employer's income tax return, which differs for companies using a fiscal year.
c. *Correct.* Like other types of traditional IRAs, distributions from SEP-IRAs are taxable. Only Roth IRA distributions are not taxed upon withdrawal.
d. *Incorrect.* Employers may continue to contribute to a SEP-IRA of an employee who has reached age 70½.

4. a. *Incorrect.* There are no tax consequences to the employer in granting the ISO.
b. *Incorrect.* The employee is not taxed on the award when he or she receives it.
c. *Correct.* Taxation of the award is deferred until the employee sells the stock purchased with the option.
d. *Incorrect.* If the employee does not purchase the option, he or she has no basis in the option and cannot claim a loss after the option is exercised.

5. a. *Incorrect.* The savings component is the portion of permanent life insurance premiums that enable policies to accrue cash value.
b. *Correct.* This test prohibits the cash surrender value of the contract from exceeding the net single premium necessary to fund future benefits under the contract.
c. *Incorrect.* This test disqualifies contracts that permit excessive amounts of cash value buildup.
d. *Incorrect.* The loading component is the portion of life insurance premiums that covers expenses and ensures profits to the insurance company.

6. a. *Incorrect.* Interests in a partnership are excluded from like-kind exchange transactions.
b. *Correct.* Trading a used vehicle for a new one constitutes a like-kind exchange.
c. *Incorrect.* Like-kind exchanges do not include monetary transactions, and issuance of a loan is not akin to ownership of real property.
d. *Incorrect.* Transfers of stocks, bonds, and notes are property types excluded from treatment as like-kind exchanges.

MODULE 3 — CHAPTER 5

1. a. *Correct.* Unlike innocent spouse relief, injured spouse relief applies to a spouse's share of an overpayment of a qualified past-due debt.
b. *Incorrect.* Injured spouse relief is not applied prospectively to estimated taxes that will become due in subsequent quarters.
c. *Incorrect.* Injured spouse relief is only available for joint overpayments, in cases when an injured spouse's share of a joint overpayment is applied to the other spouse's qualified past-due debt .
d. *Incorrect.* Injured spouse relief is not related to whether property is a separate or community asset.

2. a. *Incorrect.* Whether assets that could be used to pay the assessment are jointly or separately held is not a determining factor in obtaining relief.
b. *Correct.* A spouse who establishes that he or she signed the return under duress is not considered to be jointly and severally liable for the deficiency.
c. *Incorrect.* A spouse may not qualify for relief if he or she had actual knowledge of the item even if that spouse is unaware of the asset's source.
d. *Incorrect.* If a requesting spouse had actual knowledge of only a portion of an erroneous item, then relief is not available for that portion of the erroneous item.

3. a. *Incorrect.* The requesting spouse may obtain relief from IRS penalties if eligible for any type of innocent spouse relief.
b. *Incorrect.* Relief from interest charges is available under any type of innocent spouse relief.
c. *Incorrect.* Actual knowledge of an erroneous item will not preclude general innocent spouse relief or separation of liability relief, or weigh against equitable relief, in cases of abuse or if the requesting spouse signed the return under duress.
d. *Correct.* Only equitable innocent spouse relief can provide relief from underpayments.

4. a. *Incorrect.* The legal obligation to pay the liability is a separate factor in determining whether to grant equitable relief.
b. *Correct.* If denying relief will cause the requesting spouse to suffer economic hardship, this factor will weigh in favor of relief. Economic hardship exists if paying the tax liability in whole or in part will cause the requesting spouse to be unable to pay reasonable basic living expenses.
c. *Incorrect.* The resources of the nonrequesting spouse are not a factor in determining economic hardship of the requesting spouse.

d. ***Incorrect.*** The requesting spouse's marital status is not a factor in determining economic hardship.

5. a. ***Incorrect.*** Ownership percentages are not dictated by filing status.
b. ***Correct.*** **Spouses each report half of the community income on their separate federal returns.**
c. ***Incorrect.*** Although community income may be recharacterized as separate income in certain situations, it is not required.
d. ***Incorrect.*** Spouses in community property states may file joint or separate tax returns.

6. a. ***Correct.*** **The requesting spouse may not file a joint return for the tax year for which he or she is requesting relief.**
b. ***Incorrect.*** The requesting spouse must establish that he or she had no knowledge or reason to know of the unreported community income.
c. ***Incorrect.*** Whether the requesting spouse benefitted from the omitted item is a factor in determining whether it would be inequitable to hold a requesting spouse liable for a deficiency attributable to an item of community income but is not required to request traditional relief.
d. ***Incorrect.*** The requesting spouse is considered to have knowledge of the income if he or she is aware of the activity that produced the income and thus does not qualify for traditional relief.

MODULE 3 — CHAPTER 6

1. a. ***Incorrect.*** Return preparers are not likely to learn of stolen SSN information sooner than taxpayers themselves.
b. ***Correct.*** **Identity thieves tend to file earlier than the taxpayers, whose returns then are rejected by the IRS.**
c. ***Incorrect.*** Victims of identity theft generally must inform their banks and credit card issuers about the crime.
d. ***Incorrect.*** The IRS uses employer- and investment broker-supplied forms to notify the IRS of taxpayer income; the IRS does not use SSN tracking with taxpayer-supplied income.

2. a. ***Incorrect.*** Online users should change their passwords regularly and not use the same password to access various accounts.
b. ***Incorrect.*** Hackers and other identity thieves often try first to access accounts using familiar names and dates for their victims.
c. ***Correct.*** **Complicated passwords that mix digits, letters, and special characters are the most difficult for thieves to guess.**

d. *Incorrect.* Using SSNs poses the triple threat of being all one type of character, being accessible from other stolen sources, and revealing the victim's SSN if it is already not known by the thief.

3. a. *Correct.* Businesses actually file more, different types of returns than do individuals but receive less attention for identity theft than do cases of stolen identities of individuals.
b. *Incorrect.* Because public issuers have extensive tax-related information filed publicly and employers disseminate tax-related information such as EINs, business information is more easily accessed than individuals' tax data.
c. *Incorrect.* Less information is required to establish credit by a business, so that business targets may be victimized more easily than individuals.
d. *Incorrect.* The EINs of business entities are included in SEC filings, IRS forms, and website postings, making businesses an easier target.

4. a. *Incorrect.* Saving computer files in one location is not in and of itself a good protection measure, especially if the computer hard drive is stolen or lost. Using encrypted files and locking up sensitive information is a better strategy.
b. *Correct.* Thieves are often able to steal personal information from discarded documents and correspondence. Redacting SSNs and other important numbers can prevent them from falling into the wrong hands.
c. *Incorrect.* Identity thieves generally file returns earlier in the season to ensure the IRS processes its fraudulent return first.
d. *Incorrect.* The IRS will not provide tax return information absent a power of attorney form signed by the taxpayer. It is also not a means of protecting client information stored in your own files.

5. a. *Incorrect.* Taxpayers prepare and submit Form 14039 before receiving IP PINs.
b. *Incorrect.* Receipt of IP PINs does not mean that these agencies have been informed of the fraudulent activities.
c. *Incorrect.* The IRS does not resolve issues associated with identity theft; only the victims' tax issues are the concern of the IRS.
d. *Correct.* Taxpayers list the IP PINs on their properly filed returns so they are not rejected by the IRS, which may have received earlier, fraudulent returns filed using the victims' SSNs.

6. a. *Incorrect.* Partners in crime employed or owned by check-cashing businesses may help thieves cash fraudulent refunds.
b. *Incorrect.* Thieves may target check-cashing businesses rather than financial institutions at which victims may have actual accounts.

c. *Correct.* The amount of the refund is not the determining factor for why thieves target check-cashing businesses.
d. *Incorrect.* Check-cashing entities generally do not practice the same due diligence as financial institutions in checking for fraudulent refund checks.

MODULE 3 — CHAPTER 7

1. a. *Incorrect.* Although people approaching retirement may decrease the percentage of equities they hold, boomers may retain part of the portfolio in stocks and bonds to protect future income from inflation.
b. *Correct.* Prospective retirees often wish to lower the risk level of their investments yet allow for growth of funds to minimize the effects of inflation.
c. *Incorrect.* Ordinary income is taxed at a greater rate than capital gains, regardless of whether investors sell the taxable investment before or after they retire.
d. *Incorrect.* Exchanges of mutual funds within the same fund family are taxable (unless the investment is held in an IRA or other nontaxable account).

2. a. *Incorrect.* The surviving spouse may opt to be treated as the deceased's beneficiary rather than treating the IRA as his or her own.
b. *Correct.* Transfers of funds from a traditional IRA to a Roth account are never tax-free, whether by the account owner or a beneficiary.
c. *Incorrect.* The surviving spouse can roll the account balance into a traditional IRA or another qualified retirement plan account.
d. *Incorrect.* The owner's spouse may be designated as the account owner upon the death of the traditional IRA's owner.

3. a. *Incorrect.* Transportation for medical care by car, bus, train, or plane is a deductible medical expense, as are related expenses such as parking fees or tolls.
b. *Incorrect.* Lodging costs are deductible up to a maximum of $50 per person per night.
c. *Incorrect.* Medical insurance premium costs are deductible medical expenses.
d. *Correct.* Meals taken at the medical facility are deductible, but ones eaten outside of the hospital are not.

4. a. *Incorrect.* Retirement benefits are taxable if the taxpayer's income exceeds the base amount.
b. *Incorrect.* Survivor benefits to widow(er)s older than age 60 or ones with children younger than 18 may be taxable if the taxpayer's income exceeds the base amount.

c. *Correct.* SSI payments to disabled adults or for disabled children are never subject to tax.
d. *Incorrect.* One type of payment is not subject to federal tax.

5. a. *Incorrect.* Because partnerships are passthrough entities, proceeds are not taxed at an entity level.
b. *Incorrect.* Gain on the partnership assets is taxed.
c. *Correct.* The proceeds of the liquidating sale pass through to partners, who are taxed on an individual level on their Form 1040 tax returns.
d. *Incorrect.* Partnership interests are figured according to the partners' basis in the entity, and proceeds of the sale are allocated according to their relative percentages for recognition on individual tax returns.

6. a. *Correct.* Unlimited gifts may be made tax-free to directly pay for the recipient's medical expenses or qualified tuition costs. Donors may make additional tax-free gifts of up to $14,000 per recipient.
b. *Incorrect.* The maximum of $14,000 for a gift per recipient applies regardless of the frequency of payments within the year.
c. *Incorrect.* The $14,000 maximum for gifting rules applies regardless of whether the donor is expected to die within the tax year.
d. *Incorrect.* One method may be used to gift tax-free more than the $14,000 annual limit for a recipient.

MODULE 4 — CHAPTER 8

1. a. *Incorrect.* Deirdre has different U.S. reporting requirements for her account in Ireland.
b. *Incorrect.* Her reporting requirements for the account in Ireland are not met by attaching Form 8938 to her return.
c. *Correct.* Deirdre must file both Form 90-22-1 for receipt by the IRS by June 30 and attached Form 8938 to her return Form 1040 tax return by April 15 in 2015.
d. *Incorrect.* Deirdre's foreign account balance exceeds the filing threshold.

2. a. *Incorrect.* The $10,000 penalty applies only if the failure to report is corrected within 90 days after the IRS mails a notice of the failure to the taxpayer.
b. *Incorrect.* The $50,000 penalty is the maximum penalty for failure to correct the submission of Form 8938 for the remainder of the calendar tax year.

c. *Correct.* The maximum penalty for failure to submit Form 8938 during 2015 for the 2014 calendar year will equal the $10,000 failure to submit the form and a total of $50,000 if the form is not submitted by the end of 2015 ($10,000 per month × 6 months).
d. *Incorrect.* The maximum annual penalty for failure to file Form 8938 is not figured using percentages of the foreign holdings' value.

3. a. *Incorrect.* Investment entities such as brokerages are considered FFIs under FATCA.
b. *Correct.* Substantial United States direct or indirect owners of more than 10 percent of corporate stock by vote or value are considered *nonfinancial* foreign entities.
c. *Incorrect.* Insurance or holding companies in expanded affiliated groups are FFIs under FATCA.
d. *Incorrect.* Any entity whose business is constituted substantially or holding financial assets for others is considered an FFI under FATCA

4. a. *Incorrect.* Proceeds from the disposition of a grandfathered obligation are themselves grandfathered under FATCA requirements.
b. *Incorrect.* If the withholding agent can associate the payment with valid documentation that allows the payment reliably, the payment is excluded from withholding.
c. *Correct.* Unless an exemption applies, withholding agents must withhold the tax regardless of whether the FFI is a beneficial owner or intermediary for the payment.
d. *Incorrect.* Such outstanding obligations as of January 1, 2014, are grandfathered and thus excluded from withholding.

5. a. *Correct.* Insurance or annuity contracts whose value is less than $250,000 are exempt from the due diligence requirements of an FFI agreement.
b. *Incorrect.* The electronic search focuses on indicia of U.S. status such as a U.S. birthplace, address, or telephone number of the account owner.
c. *Incorrect.* Preexisting accounts with a balance exceeding $1 million as of the effective date of the FFI agreement and subsequent years are subject to an enhanced review seeking U.S. indicia for the account.
d. *Incorrect.* Bank or investment accounts having aggregated values of less than $50,000 are exempt from due diligence reviews by participating FFIs.

6. a. *Correct.* At least 98 percent of a local FFI's accounts must be held by residents (not necessarily citizens) of its country of organization.

b. *Incorrect.* Such procedures are required for a local FFI to exclude accounts for specified U.S. persons that are not residents of its country of organization.
c. *Incorrect.* A local FFI must comply with its country's withholding and reporting rules for resident accounts.
d. *Incorrect.* A local FFI is prohibited from soliciting customers from outside of its country of organization.

7. a. *Correct.* This category of FFI also included qualifying qualified collective investment vehicles, some restricted funds, and certain sponsored investment entities and controlled foreign corporations.
b. *Incorrect.* Certified deemed-compliant FFI status applies only to institutions such as qualifying nonregistering local banks, institutions having only low-value accounts, and sponsored, closely held investment vehicles.
c. *Incorrect.* There is no category of deemed-compliant FFI for individual institutions, although some depository FFIs that are part of an expanded affiliated group are owner-documented FFIs.
d. *Incorrect.* Credit card issuers are treated as a different category of deemed-compliant FFI.

8. a. *Incorrect.* The withholding agent does not establish an escrow account for the excess withholding.
b. *Correct.* The excess withholding is returned to the owner or payee and reduces the tax deposit in a subsequent period.
c. *Incorrect.* Reg. § 1.1461-2(b) rules apply to underwithholding, not overwithholding.
d. *Incorrect.* No penalty is imposed on the withholding agent.

9. a. *Incorrect.* The withholding agent may credit Chapter 4 withholding against payments due under Code Sec. 1441, 1442, or 1443.
b. *Incorrect.* Amounts withheld under Code Sec. 1445 generally are not subject to Chapter 4 withholding except in certain instances for distributions by qualified investment entities and USRPHCs.
c. *Incorrect.* Withholding and foreign passthrough payments subject to Code Sec. 1446 withholding generally are not subject to Chapter 4 withholding as well.
d. *Correct.* Chapter 4 withholding is generally not applied in addition to withholding payments mandated under provisions of these sections.

MODULE 4 — CHAPTER 9

1. a. *Incorrect.* Grants for travel or study must meet certain requirements to avoid payment of excise tax on the funds awarded.

b. *Correct.* Private foundations are required to make qualifying distributions of at least a minimum distributable amount each tax year.
c. ***Incorrect.*** Private foundations that influence the outcome of such an election are subject to paying excise tax on the funds spent.
d. ***Incorrect.*** Funds spent by private foundations to influence legislation are subject to excise taxes.

2. a. *Correct.* Broadening the class of practitioners may prove more cost effective and promote the quality of determinations made.
b. ***Incorrect.*** The situs of the foundations is not an issue in regulations for good faith determinations.
c. ***Incorrect.*** Timely filings of information returns are not a direct issue in broadening the class of qualified tax practitioners consulted by private foundations.
d. ***Incorrect.*** The expanded class of qualified tax practitioners does not include foreign counsel unless those advisors are CPAs, EAs, or attorneys.

3. a. ***Incorrect.*** Dead links are not the concern in the IRS caution about use of websites and links in social media.
b. ***Incorrect.*** Linked content may have changed in the interim between the original posts and the date of an IRS audit, and such content may be challenging to recreate.
c. *Correct.* If sites linked to by the Code Sec. 501(c)(3) organizations change the sites' content to advocate certain candidates or political positions, the organizations risk their tax-exempt status.
d. ***Incorrect.*** Internet communications are treated the same as distributed printed material by 501(c)(3) organizations.

4. a. *Correct.* Lobbying is permitted for 501(c)(4) organizations if done to promote their social welfare purpose.
b. ***Incorrect.*** Actions of both employees and volunteers are considered in examining whether the organizations' primary purpose is political rather than promoting the social welfare.
c. ***Incorrect.*** Organizations that primarily benefit or campaign for a private group may not hold tax-exempt status under Code Sec. 501(c)(4).
d. ***Incorrect.*** Code Sec. 501(c)(4) organizations are not required to disclose contributors' names before or after elections, nor must they disclose the nature of their expenditures.

5. a. ***Incorrect.*** A tax-exempt charity may not target and limit assistance to a group of individuals; the charitable class must be sufficiently indefinite so as not to be selective among the community requesting aid.

b. *Correct.* The charity may help individuals in need provided it selects recipients based on general charitable standards.

c. *Incorrect.* Disaster victims are assessed using the needy or distressed test to determine which victims require food, shelter, counseling, and rescue services.

d. *Incorrect.* Selection of recipients of disaster relief services is not based on percentages of the victims.

6. a. *Incorrect.* Type III supporting organizations are merely operated in connection and are not related otherwise.

b. *Correct.* Supporting organizations may be nonfunctionally or functionally integrated, but they must feature integration with the supported organization to qualify as Type III supporting organizations.

c. *Incorrect.* Type II brother-sister supported and supporting organizations are both supervised or controlled by a parent organization.

d. *Incorrect.* As a Type I supporting organization, the supported organization (parent) supervises or controls the supporting (subsidiary) organization.

TOP FEDERAL TAX ISSUES FOR 2014 CPE COURSE

Index

D

N

P

T

U

V

W

TOP FEDERAL TAX ISSUES FOR 2014 CPE COURSE

CPE Quizzer Instructions

This CPE Quizzer is divided into four Modules. To obtain CPE Credit, go to **CCHGroup.com/PrintCPE** to complete your Quizzers online for immediate results and no Express Grading Fee. There is a grading fee for each Quizzer submission.

Processing Fee:
$56.00 for Module 1
$56.00 for Module 2
$70.00 for Module 3
$70.00 for Module 4
$252.00 for all Modules

Recommended CPE:
4 hours for Module 1
4 hours for Module 2
5 hours for Module 3
5 hours for Module 4
18 hours for all Modules

Recommended CFP:
2 hours for Module 1
2 hours for Module 2
2 hours for Module 3
2 hours for Module 4
8 hours for all Modules

CTEC Course Number:
1075-CE-0159 for Module 1
1075-CE-0160 for Module 2
1075-CE-0161 for Module 3
1075-CE-0162 for Module 4

IRS Program Number:
4VRWB-T-00643-13-S for Module 1
4VRWB-T-00644-13-S for Module 2
4VRWB-T-00645-13-S for Module 3
4VRWB-T-00646-13-S for Module 4

Federal Tax Law Hours:
4 hours for Module 1
4 hours for Module 2
5 hours for Module 3
5 hours for Module 4
18 hours for all Modules

Ordering online is easy as 1 – 2 – 3!

1. Select your courses at CCHGroup.com/PrintCPE
2. Login to CCHGroup.com
3. Check out and link to your exams

SPECIAL OFFER: Save money if you purchase the bundle of all four Modules online by Dec. 31, 2013. You can complete the exams when it's most convenient for you.

Full details of the offer and instructions for purchasing your CPE Tests and accessing them after purchase are provided on the **CCHGroup.com/PrintCPE** website.

To mail or fax your Quizzer, send your completed Answer Sheet for each Quizzer Module to **CCH Continuing Education Department, 4025 W. Peterson Ave., Chicago, IL 60646**, or fax it to (773) 866-3084. Each Quizzer Answer Sheet will be graded and a CPE Certificate of Completion awarded for achieving a grade of 70 percent or greater. The Quizzer Answer Sheets are located at the back of this book.

Express Grading: Processing time for your mailed or faxed Answer Sheet is generally 8-12 business days. To use our Express Grading Service, at an additional $19 per Module, please check the "Express Grading" box on your Answer Sheet and provide your CCH account or credit card number **and your fax number.** CCH will fax your results and a Certificate of Completion (upon achieving a passing grade) to you by 5:00 p.m. the business day following our receipt of your Answer Sheet. **If you mail your Answer Sheet for Express Grading, please write "ATTN: CPE OVERNIGHT" on the envelope.** NOTE: CCH will not Federal Express Quizzer results under any circumstances.

> Recommended CPE credit is based on a 50-minute hour. Participants earning credits for states that require self-study to be based on a 100-minute hour will receive ½ the CPE credits for successful completion of this course. Because CPE requirements vary from state to state and among different licensing agencies, please contact your CPE governing body for information on your CPE requirements and the applicability of a particular course for your requirements.

Date of Completion: If you mail or fax your Quizzer to CCH, the date of completion on your Certificate will be the date that you put on your Answer Sheet. However, you must submit your Answer Sheet to CCH for grading within two weeks of completing it.

Expiration Date: December 31, 2014

Evaluation: To help us provide you with the best possible products, please take a moment to fill out the course Evaluation located after your Quizzer. A copy is also provided at the back of this course if you choose to mail or fax your Quizzer Answer Sheets.

CCH is registered with the National Association of State Boards of Accountancy (NASBA) as a sponsor of continuing professional education on the National Registry of CPE Sponsors. State boards of accountancy have final authority on the acceptance of individual courses for CPE credit. Complaints regarding registered sponsors may be addressed to the National Registry of CPE Sponsors, 150 Fourth Avenue North, Suite 700, Nashville, TN 37219-2417. Web site: www.nasba.org.

CCH is registered with the National Association of State Boards of Accountancy (NASBA) as a Quality Assurance Service (QAS) sponsor of continuing professional education. State boards of accountancy have final authority on the acceptance of individual courses for CPE credit. Complaints regarding registered sponsors may be addressed to NASBA, 150 Fourth Avenue North, Suite 700, Nashville, TN 37219-2417. Web site: www.nasba.org.

CCH has been approved by the California Tax Education Council to offer courses that provide federal and state credit towards the annual "continuing education" requirement imposed by the State of California. A listing of additional requirements to register as a tax preparer may be obtained by contacting CTEC at P.O. Box 2890, Sacramento, CA, 95812-2890, toll-free by phone at (877) 850-2832, or on the Internet at www.ctec.org.

> One **complimentary copy** of this course is provided with certain copies of CCH publications. Additional copies of this course may be downloaded for free from **CCHGroup.com/PrintCPE** or ordered by calling 1-800-248-3248 (ask for product 10024491-0001).

Quizzer Questions: Module 1

1. Under the individual mandate program, an individual is responsible for a payment if the individual:

   a. Qualifies for an exemption from the coverage requirement
   b. Has health insurance that qualifies as minimum essential coverage
   c. Is divorced
   d. Has coverage for him- or herself and dependents

2. The individual affordability exemption applies when annual contributions exceed _____ of the taxpayer's household income.

   a. 5 percent
   b. 8 percent
   c. 9.5 percent
   d. 10 percent

3. The PPACA exempts all of the following from the requirement for coverage or imposition of monthly penalty amounts ***except:***

   a. Taxpayers younger than 18
   b. Individuals lacking coverage for three consecutive months or fewer
   c. Incarcerated individuals
   d. Individuals who are not lawfully present in the United States

4. Small businesses seeking assistance in initiating group health plans can use:

   a. American Health Benefit Exchanges
   b. SHOP Exchange
   c. Employer mandate exchange
   d. Health insurance premium assistance

5. A family with an income of 400 percent of the federal poverty level may qualify for the premium assistance tax credit if their health premiums exceed at least ____ of their household income.

   a. 2 percent
   b. 5 percent
   c. 8 percent
   d. 9.5 percent

6. Under PPACA, an applicable large employer subject to employer mandate requirements is one that employs ____ or more full-time or full-time equivalent employees.

   a. 25
   b. 50
   c. 75
   d. 100

7. Which of the following is ***not*** a category of wellness program under the final regulations for plan years as of January 1, 2014?

   a. Incentivized wellness programs
   b. Participatory wellness programs
   c. Activity-only wellness programs
   d. Outcome-based wellness programs

8. The IRS has postponed the ____ until January 1, 2015:

   a. Individual shared responsibility payment
   b. Health insurance premium assistance tax credit
   c. Employer shared responsibility payment
   d. None of the above was postponed

9. Which of the following taxes/fees under PPACA is scheduled to take effect in 2014?

   a. Branded prescription drug fee
   b. Medical device excise tax
   c. Annual health insurance provider fee
   d. Indoor tanning service tax

10. The Supreme Court upheld the constitutionality of the PPACA under which of the following?

    a. Congress's power to establish due process
    b. Congress's powers over interstate commerce
    c. Congress's taxing power
    d. Congress's power to expand federal health care systems such as Medicare

11. The net investment income (NII) tax is effective for tax years beginning:

a. January 1, 2012
b. After December 31, 2012
c. July 1, 2013
d. After December 31, 2013

12. The NII tax is imposed at a rate of:

a. 2.5 percent
b. 3 percent
c. 3.8 percent
d. 4.5 percent

13. The threshold for NII tax liability for joint filers is MAGI of:

a. $125,000
b. $200,000
c. $250,000
d. $350,000

14. The threshold for the NII tax for 2013 returns of estates and trusts is:

a. $10,500
b. $11,950
c. $12,800
d. $14,100

15. Net investment income includes:

a. Capital gains distributions from mutual funds
b. Alimony
c. Self-employment income
d. Qualified retirement plan distributions

16. Net investment income does ***not*** include:

a. Operating income from an active business
b. Income passed through to a non-active S corporation shareholder
c. Income from working capital of an active business
d. Gain from the sale of second homes

17. Which of the following is ***not*** an exception or recharacterization of income as nonpassive?

   a. Developer rule
   b. Portfolio income exception
   c. Self-rented property recharacterization
   d. Real estate professional exception

18. The Code Sec. 1411 exception for including gain from transfers of partnership interests or S corp stock sale in NII is implemented under the regulations through:

   a. A transfer exclusion
   b. A dissolution tax-free sale
   c. A safe harbor
   d. An adjustment

19. Which category of NII can never be a negative amount for use in netting gains and deductions?

   a. Category (i)
   b. Category (ii)
   c. Category (iii)
   d. None of the category deductions can be netted

20. Under the proposed regulations, net operating loss deductions:

   a. May not be applied against net investment income
   b. May be applied if the NII exceeds the NOL
   c. May be applied if the NOL will have a balance to carry forward
   d. May be applied if the NOL has already been carried over from a previous tax year

Quizzer Questions: Module 2

21. An accounting method is ***not*** permissible unless:

- **a.** It was implemented following issuance of Rev. Proc. 2011-14
- **b.** It clearly reflects the entity's income
- **c.** It is implemented following automatic adoption
- **d.** It has been used since the inception of the entity

22. A taxpayer's treatment of an item involves an accounting method if it:

- **a.** Is a budgeted expense of doing business
- **b.** Is a non-GAAP item
- **c.** Affects lifetime income
- **d.** Involves the proper time for including the item in income or claiming the item as a deduction

23. An amended return may not be used to correct improper treatment of items that have been claimed on ______ or more consecutively filed returns.

- **a.** Two
- **b.** Three
- **c.** Four
- **d.** Five

24. Audit protection:

- **a.** Does not apply to advance consent changes
- **b.** Does not apply to automatic consent changes
- **c.** Offers the benefit that interest and penalties are not imposed for tax years prior to the year of change
- **d.** Begins to apply on the date the tax return for the year of change is filed

25. A taxpayer under continuous examination may file an accounting method change unrelated to the audit issue within _____ of the beginning of the tax year of change and receive audit protection.

   a. 30 days
   b. 60 days
   c. 90 days
   d. 120 days

26. Duplication or omission of deductions and income resulting from an accounting method change is prevented with a:

   a. Change in overall accounting method
   b. Code Sec. 481(a) adjustment
   c. Change in tax year used by the entity
   d. Code Sec. 381(a) reorganization

27. The IRS responds to a request for a change in accounting method under the advance consent procedure:

   a. With a letter ruling
   b. With an order for an examination
   c. By suspending accumulation of interest and penalties for the item at issue
   d. With a referral to the Office of Appeals

28. A taxpayer preserves the opportunity for a conference of right prior to receiving a final adverse decision on a proposed accounting method change by:

   a. Filing an amended return for each year the improper method was used
   b. Rejecting the consent agreement with the original ruling
   c. Checking box 16 of Form 3315 in applying for the change
   d. Switching from use of an advance consent to an automatic consent procedure

29. The Code Sec. 481(a) adjustment period for a positive (unfavorable) adjustment in the case of an involuntary change is.

   a. One year
   b. Two years
   c. Three years
   d. Four years

30. The time value of money resolution to an accounting change issue:

a. May result in the payment of a refund to the taxpayer
b. Excludes costs of the hazards of litigation
c. May be a capitalized or deductible payment by the taxpayer
d. May take into account the taxpayer's tax rates and tax attributes

31. All of the following are deductible temporary differences between financial and income tax accounting for assets ***except:***

a. Depreciable assets
b. Warranty liability
c. Accounts receivable
d. Allowances for doubtful accounts

32. What is the maximum IRA contribution a taxpayer aged 52 may make for 2013?

a. $5,000
b. $5,500
c. $6,000
d. $6,500

33. When are payments from installment sales generally taxed?

a. In the year the sale is made
b. In the year in which all payments are received
c. Starting in the year in which payments exceed tax basis in the property
d. Each year an installment payment is made, pro rata based on gross profit

34. Guaranteed benefits at a set amount are made from the ______ type of qualified retirement plan.

a. Profit-sharing
b. Pension
c. Money purchase
d. Stock bonus

35. A 401(k) plan may not require employees to complete more than _____ of service in order to participate.

a. One year
b. Two years
c. Three years
d. Five years

36. To qualify for long-term capital gain treatment, incentive stock options must be held for at least _____ from the date the option is granted.

a. One year
b. Two years
c. Three years
d. Five years

37. Life insurance contracts are disqualified under the _____ when excessive cash value builds up for the life insurance risk.

a. Loading component
b. Guideline premium requirement
c. Cash value corridor test
d. Cash value accumulation test

38. Which type of contract is payable in a single payment on an exchange with no gain recognition?

a. Life insurance contract
b. Annuity contract
c. Endowment contract
d. Gain is recognized in exchange for all of these contracts

39. Types of property considered in like-kind exchanges do ***not*** include:

a. Real property
b. Depreciable tangible personal property
c. Other personal property
d. Intangible business property

40. A shareholder may defer taxes using a stock purchase agreement with an investment bank in a(n):

a. Stock interest plan
b. Incentive stock option
c. Variable prepaid forward contract
d. Like-kind exchange

Quizzer Questions: Module 3

41. All of the following are types of innocent spouse relief ***except:***

a. Equitable
b. General
c. Compliant
d. Separation of liability

42. Innocent spouse relief typically applies when tax liabilities:

a. Exceed $10,000 in understated income items
b. Are generally attributable to only one of the spouses
c. Are incurred after spouses separate but are not yet divorced
d. Are incurred across multiple years' returns

43. Requests for relief under Code Sec. 6015(b) rules must be made within ______ after the IRS first attempts to collect the liability.

a. 12 months
b. 18 months
c. Two years
d. Five years

44. A requesting spouse receives a significant benefit from an unpaid tax liability or an item giving rise to a deficiency if the benefit is:

a. In excess of normal support
b. Shared disproportionately by the spouses
c. Awarded exclusively to the nonrequesting spouse
d. Awarded in excess of a settlement amount in divorce cases

45. The type of relief exclusively available to couples treated as no longer married is:

a. Equitable
b. General
c. Compliant
d. Separation of liability

46. The type of innocent spouse relief available for liabilities arising from underpayments is:

- **a.** Equitable
- **b.** General
- **c.** Compliant
- **d.** Separation of liability

47. Streamlined determinations apply to which type of innocent spouse relief?

- **a.** Equitable
- **b.** General
- **c.** Compliant
- **d.** Separation of liability

48. A married taxpayer in a community property state:

- **a.** Distinguishes between community and separate income on federal tax returns
- **b.** May be liable for tax on community income earned by a spouse, even when he or she files a separate return
- **c.** Must file a separate return if he or she has separate income
- **d.** May not apply for traditional relief under Code Sec. 66(a) if the spouses have different domiciles

49. The current rules for requesting equitable relief took effect on:

- **a.** January 31, 2011
- **b.** September 16, 2013
- **c.** December 15, 2012
- **d.** March 15, 2013

50. A request for innocent spouse relief may be:

- **a.** Canceled by the nonrequesting spouse
- **b.** Made for liabilities for which the statutory period for collection has expired
- **c.** Used to request a refund if the request is for separate liability relief
- **d.** Made before collection activity commences

51. Which of the following is ***not*** susceptible to having its identity stolen for the purpose of committing tax return fraud?

   a. An individual
   b. A for-profit business
   c. A tax-exempt organization
   d. Any person or entity is a potential victim of taxpayer identity fraud

52. Identity thieves *most commonly* obtain Social Security numbers of taxpayer victims in order to:

   a. File claims for survivor benefits with the SSA
   b. File tax returns claiming refunds
   c. Seek returns of quarterly estimated tax payments mid-year
   d. Start receiving retirement benefits early

53. To help mitigate taxpayer identity theft, the IRS has stated that it will request personal taxpayer identification information only through which mode of communication?

   a. U.S. postal mail
   b. E-mail
   c. Social media
   d. Text messaging

54. Best practices that individual taxpayers can adopt to avoid identity theft include all of the following ***except:***

   a. Having the post office hold their mail during vacations
   b. Never carrying their Social Security cards outside of home
   c. Delaying filing their tax returns until the due date
   d. Shredding documents containing personal information

55. Identity thieves have also impersonated the identities of tax return preparers by using which type of identification to electronically file fraudulent tax returns?

   a. TIN
   b. EIN
   c. EFIN
   d. IP PIN

56. A best practice suggested by a professional organization for CPAs and tax return preparers protecting their business from identity thieves is:

a. Preparing fewer tax returns
b. Thoroughly vetting all new clients
c. Pressing clients to file as soon as possible
d. Safeguarding all client information in locked file drawers and encrypted documents

57. Individuals and businesses should file Form 14039, *Identity Theft Affidavit,* with the _____ if they suspect or realize theft of personal information.

a. IRS
b. FTC
c. SSA
d. TAS

58. The IRS currently uses _____ effectively to detect potential indicators of fraud before tax refunds are issued.

a. The National Directory of New Hires
b. Early audits
c. Matching of Form 1099-K data with line items on small business tax returns
d. Filters

59. Identity protection personal identification numbers (IP PINs) are used by:

a. The IRS to accept returns with taxpayers' SSNs have been compromised
b. The FTC to track identification numbers of business victims of fraud
c. Payment settlement entities (PSEs) for third-party network transactions
d. The Taxpayer Advocate Service to track identity theft cases

60. The IRS has implemented all of the following to address taxpayer identity theft ***except:***

a. Joint enforcement with the Attorney General and Treasury Inspector General for Tax Administration
b. Using truncated SSNs on official notices
c. Collaboration with state and local law enforcement agencies
d. Sweeps of check-cashing businesses

61. Which of the following is ***not*** a major difference between boomer retirees and ones of previous generations?

a. Job skills and locations are more mobile for boomers
b. Boomers generally cannot rebalance their retirement investments
c. Boomers' life expectancy is longer
d. Boomers generally have no or limited employer pensions

62. Net investment income is taxed at an additional 3.8 percent to the extent that adjusted gross income exceeds ______ for married joint filers.

a. $125,000
b. $150,000
c. $200,000
d. $250,000

63. Gain from sale of a married couple's principal residence may be excludable from income up to certain limits if the property was their primary home for at least _____ of the _____ years before the sale.

a. Two; three
b. Two; five
c. Four; five
d. Five; seven

64. Annuity payments may be taxable income to recipients if the funds received are:

a. Also life insurance proceeds
b. Less than exclusion ratio amounts
c. In excess of return of capital
d. From investment amounts exceeding the annuity's current cash value

65. A phaseout of deductions for traditional IRA contributions by a couple having a spouse covered by an employer retirement plan apply if their income is between:

a. $95,000 and $115,000
b. $75,000 and $90,000
c. $59,000 and $69,000
d. $10,000 and $25,000

66. A beneficiary of an inherited IRA may:

a. Make a trustee-to-trustee transfer to an IRA maintained under the deceased's name
b. Make additional contributions to the IRA
c. Roll over the balance to his or her own Roth IRA tax-free
d. Rename the IRA in the name of his or her spouse

67. The threshold for claiming medical expenses for taxpayers ages 65 and older is ______ of adjusted gross income.

a. 5.5 percent
b. 7.5 percent
c. 10 percent
d. 15 percent

68. All of the following are advantages of the family limited partnership to transfer a family business to younger family members ***except:***

a. Avoidance of gift tax by limiting annuals transfers to $14,000 per recipient
b. Retention of control by the owner who receives a small general partnership interest
c. The ability to establish the FLP shortly before the owner's death
d. The ability to protect the business from outsiders using a buy-sell agreement

69. The *American Taxpayer Relief Act of 2012* set the exclusion amount for estate tax, subject to an annual inflation adjustment, at:

a. $1 million
b. $2 million
c. $3.5 million
d. $5 million

70. A _____ trust gives the trustee complete control in decisions about distributions for the beneficiary.

a. Spendthrift
b. Support
c. Discretionary
d. Grantor

TOP FEDERAL TAX ISSUES FOR 2014 CPE COURSE

Quizzer Questions: Module 4

71. Foreign Bank Account Report (FBAR) regulations mandate that taxpayers report foreign financial transactions that were initially instituted by:

    a. Chapter 4 of the tax code
    b. The *Bank Secrecy Act*
    c. Intergovernmental agreements
    d. The HIRE Act

72. FBARs must be received for the preceding year by ______ of the succeeding calendar year.

    a. April 15
    b. June 30
    c. September 30
    d. December 31

73. An FBAR is required when a U.S. Person has a financial interest in or signature authority over one or more foreign financial accounts with an aggregate value greater than $______.

    a. $1,000
    b. $2,500
    c. $10,000
    d. $25,000

74. FATCA discourages tax evasion using all of the following methods ***except:***

    a. Imposing withholding requirements on noncompliant FFIs and NFFEs
    b. Increasing disclosure obligations on high-risk NFFEs
    c. Subjecting U.S. business entities to penalties for failure to withhold taxes on foreign source revenues
    d. Extending information reporting to reach FFIs having U.S. accounts

75. A substantial U.S. owner of an NFFE holds more than _____ of corporate stock, partnership capital or profits, or beneficial trust interests.

- **a.** 10 percent
- **b.** 25 percent
- **c.** 51 percent
- **d.** 75 percent

76. Withholdable payments generally include:

- **a.** Payments to a deemed-compliant FFI
- **b.** U.S. source FDAP income
- **c.** Short-term original issue discounts
- **d.** Payments to a territory financial institution

77. Withholding agents must withhold _____ on withholdable payments.

- **a.** 10 percent
- **b.** 15 percent
- **c.** 30 percent
- **d.** 35 percent

78. FATCA implementation rules generally require an FFI, starting after _____, to withhold 30 percent of any passthrough payment made to recalcitrant account holders or to all account holders if the FFI neither entered an FFI agreement nor otherwise qualifies as a deemed-compliant entity.

- **a.** December 31, 2013
- **b.** April 15, 2014
- **c.** June 30, 2014
- **d.** December 31, 2014

79. All of the following are types of financial accounts that may be considered United States accounts ***except:***

- **a.** Custodial accounts
- **b.** Commercial accounts
- **c.** Certificates of deposit
- **d.** Interests traded on securities markets

80. Participating FFIs must report information about U.S. account balances as of the end of the:

a. Week
b. Month
c. Quarter
d. Year

81. Under the reporting rules, participating FFIs must report for calendar year 2014 by:

a. March 31, 2015
b. April 15, 2015
c. June 30, 2015
d. December 31, 2015

82. Local banks and FFIs that have low-value accounts and that are not required to register with the IRS may be:

a. Owner-documented FFIs
b. Certified deemed-compliant FFIs
c. Registered deemed-compliant FFIs
d. Designated deemed-compliant FFIs

83. To report to the IRS Chapter 4 reportable amounts paid to a recipient during the preceding calendar year, Form 1042-S, *Foreign Person's U.S. Source Income Subject to Withholding,* must be filed by ______ of the following calendar year.

a. March 15
b. April 15
c. September 30
d. December 31

84. Which of the following is ***not*** a responsibility of a withholding agent?

a. Reporting information regarding an indirect owner of its FFI
b. Filing a Form 1042-S information return
c. Remitting the tax withheld
d. Filing Form 1042 for aggregate Chapter 4 reportable amounts

85. An account's balance or value will be initially measured to determine whether it is exempt from review as of:

a. December 31, 2013
b. June 30, 2014
c. October 15, 2014
d. December 31, 2014

86. Under Code Sec. 4942, private foundations must make qualifying distributions equal to at least the:

a. Nontaxable expenditures
b. Distributable amount
c. Qualified amount
d. Charitable amount

87. Under the proposed regulations for grants to foreign organizations, qualified tax practitioners include all of the following ***except:***

a. Enrolled agents
b. IRS examiners
c. Certified public accountants
d. Attorneys

88. Which of the following is ***not*** considered a violation of the prohibition on political campaign interventions for Code Sec. 501(c)(3) organizations?

a. Public statements of positions by the organizations
b. Allowing only selected candidates to use the organizations' facilities
c. Sponsoring a get-out-the-vote campaign for elections
d. Distributing statements in favor of candidates for public office

89. Political activities by tax-exempt Code Sec. 501(c)(4) organizations are allowed if:

a. The events in which candidates participate are private
b. Only volunteers and not employees endorse the political candidate
c. Their activities involve candidates for local and state offices rather than federal positions
d. Their lobbying is directed toward a social welfare purpose

90. The basis used by tax-exempt hospital organizations to calculate charges for medical services is spelled out in:

a. The financial assistance policy
b. The amount generally billed amount for emergency care
c. The extraordinary collection actions document
d. Reasonable collection actions policy

91. All the following are reasonable efforts to determine eligibility for assistance under the proposed regulations for charitable hospitals under Code Sec. 501(r)(6) ***except:***

a. Checking pay stubs or unemployment compensation reports
b. Not accepting a patient's rough estimate of income
c. Checking local demographics for the area surrounding the patient's address
d. Using service providers that can check whether the patient's reported address exists

92. All of the following are benefits for organizations qualifying as disaster relief organizations ***except:***

a. Ability to promise prospective donors that contributions qualify as Code Sec. 170 deductions
b. Eligibility to use reduced postal rates for mailing solicitations
c. Exemption from supplying donors with substantiation for cash donations exceeding $250
d. Exemption from paying employment taxes

93. The 2013 standard mileage rate for deducting miles driven for charitable purposes is:

a. 14 cents per mile
b. 28 cents per mile
c. 34 cents per mile
d. Actual cost of fuel based on the vehicle's average miles per gallon

94. A Type I, II, or III supporting organization must pass all of the following tests ***except:***

a. The integral-part test
b. The notification requirements
c. The functional integration test
d. The responsiveness test

95. Under the responsiveness test, officers, directors, or trustees of supported organizations are required to:

a. Control the organization's use of its income or assets
b. Have the ability to influence the organization's use of its income or assets
c. Directly oversee the solicitation of the organization's income or assets
d. Make management assertions about the use of the organization's income or assets

TOP FEDERAL TAX ISSUES FOR 2014 CPE COURSE (10014583-0002)

Module 1: Answer Sheet

Save more by ordering online! Go to **CCHGroup.com/PrintCPE** for offer details and to complete your Quizzer online for instant results and no Express Grading Fee.

A $56.00 processing fee will be charged for each user submitting Module 1 for grading. If you prefer to mail or fax your Quizzer, remove both pages of the Answer Sheet from this book and return them with your completed Evaluation Form to: CCH Continuing Education Department, 4025 W. Peterson Ave., Chicago, IL 60646-6085 or fax your Answer Sheet to CCH at 773-866-3084. You must also select a method of payment below.

NAME ______________________________

COMPANY NAME ______________________________

STREET ______________________________

CITY, STATE, & ZIP CODE ______________________________

BUSINESS PHONE NUMBER ______________________________

E-MAIL ADDRESS ______________________________

DATE OF COMPLETION ______________________________

CFP REGISTRANT ID (for Certified Financial Planners) ______________________________

PTIN ID (for Enrolled Agents or RTRPs only) ______________________________

CRTP ID (for CTEC Credit only) ______________________________

METHOD OF PAYMENT:

☐ Check Enclosed ☐ Visa ☐ Master Card ☐ AmEx

☐ Discover ☐ CCH Account* ______________________________

Card No. ______________________________ Exp. Date ______________

Signature ______________________________

EXPRESS GRADING: Please fax my Course results to me by 5:00 p.m. the business day following your receipt of this Answer Sheet. By checking this box I authorize CCH to charge $19.00 for this service.

☐ Express Grading $19.00 Fax No. ______________________________

* Must provide CCH account number for this payment option

TOP FEDERAL TAX ISSUES FOR 2014 CPE COURSE (10014583-0002)

Module 1: Answer Sheet

Please answer the questions by indicating the appropriate letter next to the corresponding number.

1. ____	6. ____	11. ____	16. ____
2. ____	7. ____	12. ____	17. ____
3. ____	8. ____	13. ____	18. ____
4. ____	9. ____	14. ____	19. ____
5. ____	10. ____	15. ____	20. ____

Please complete the Evaluation Form (located after the Module 4 Answer Sheet) and return it with this Quizzer Answer Sheet to CCH at the address on the previous page. Thank you.

TOP FEDERAL TAX ISSUES FOR 2014 CPE COURSE (10014584-0002)

Module 2: Answer Sheet

Save more by ordering online! Go to **CCHGroup.com/PrintCPE** for offer details and to complete your Quizzer online for instant results and no Express Grading Fee.

A $56.00 processing fee will be charged for each user submitting Module 2 for grading. If you prefer to mail or fax your Quizzer, remove both pages of the Answer Sheet from this book and return them with your completed Evaluation Form to: CCH Continuing Education Department, 4025 W. Peterson Ave., Chicago, IL 60646-6085 or fax your Answer Sheet to CCH at 773-866-3084. You must also select a method of payment below.

NAME ______________________________

COMPANY NAME ______________________________

STREET ______________________________

CITY, STATE, & ZIP CODE ______________________________

BUSINESS PHONE NUMBER ______________________________

E-MAIL ADDRESS ______________________________

DATE OF COMPLETION ______________________________

CFP REGISTRANT ID (for Certified Financial Planners) ______________________________

PTIN ID (for Enrolled Agents or RTRPs only) ______________________________

CRTP ID (for CTEC Credit only) ______________________________

METHOD OF PAYMENT:

☐ Check Enclosed ☐ Visa ☐ Master Card ☐ AmEx

☐ Discover ☐ CCH Account* ______________________________

Card No. ______________________________ Exp. Date ______________

Signature ______________________________

EXPRESS GRADING: Please fax my Course results to me by 5:00 p.m. the business day following your receipt of this Answer Sheet. By checking this box I authorize CCH to charge $19.00 for this service.

☐ Express Grading $19.00 Fax No. ______________________________

* Must provide CCH account number for this payment option

TOP FEDERAL TAX ISSUES FOR 2014 CPE COURSE (10014584-0002)

Module 2: Answer Sheet

Please answer the questions by indicating the appropriate letter next to the corresponding number.

21. ____	26. ____	31. ____	36. ____
22. ____	27. ____	32. ____	37. ____
23. ____	28. ____	33. ____	38. ____
24. ____	29. ____	34. ____	39. ____
25. ____	30. ____	35. ____	40. ____

Please complete the Evaluation Form (located after the Module 4 Answer Sheet) and return it with this Quizzer Answer Sheet to CCH at the address on the previous page. Thank you.

TOP FEDERAL TAX ISSUES FOR 2014 CPE COURSE (10014585-0002)

Module 3: Answer Sheet

Save more by ordering online! Go to **CCHGroup.com/PrintCPE** for offer details and to complete your Quizzer online for instant results and no Express Grading Fee.

A $70.00 processing fee will be charged for each user submitting Module 3 for grading. If you prefer to mail or fax your Quizzer, remove both pages of the Answer Sheet from this book and return them with your completed Evaluation Form to: CCH Continuing Education Department, 4025 W. Peterson Ave., Chicago, IL 60646-6085 or fax your Answer Sheet to CCH at 773-866-3084. You must also select a method of payment below.

NAME ______________________________

COMPANY NAME ______________________________

STREET ______________________________

CITY, STATE, & ZIP CODE ______________________________

BUSINESS PHONE NUMBER ______________________________

E-MAIL ADDRESS ______________________________

DATE OF COMPLETION ______________________________

CFP REGISTRANT ID (for Certified Financial Planners) ______________________________

PTIN ID (for Enrolled Agents or RTRPs only) ______________________________

CRTP ID (for CTEC Credit only) ______________________________

METHOD OF PAYMENT:

☐ Check Enclosed ☐ Visa ☐ Master Card ☐ AmEx

☐ Discover ☐ CCH Account* ______________________________

Card No. ______________________________ Exp. Date ______________

Signature ______________________________

EXPRESS GRADING: Please fax my Course results to me by 5:00 p.m. the business day following your receipt of this Answer Sheet. By checking this box I authorize CCH to charge $19.00 for this service.

☐ Express Grading $19.00 Fax No. ______________________________

* Must provide CCH account number for this payment option

TOP FEDERAL TAX ISSUES FOR 2014 CPE COURSE (10014585-0002)

Module 3: Answer Sheet

Please answer the questions by indicating the appropriate letter next to the corresponding number.

41. ____	49. ____	57. ____	65. ____
42. ____	50. ____	58. ____	66. ____
43. ____	51. ____	59. ____	67. ____
44. ____	52. ____	60. ____	68. ____
45. ____	53. ____	61. ____	69. ____
46. ____	54. ____	62. ____	70. ____
47. ____	55. ____	63. ____	
48. ____	56. ____	64. ____	

Please complete the Evaluation Form (located after the Module 4 Answer Sheet) and return it with this Quizzer Answer Sheet to CCH at the address on the previous page. Thank you.

TOP FEDERAL TAX ISSUES FOR 2014 CPE COURSE (10014586-0002)

Module 4: Answer Sheet

Save more by ordering online! Go to **CCHGroup.com/PrintCPE** for offer details and to complete your Quizzer online for instant results and no Express Grading Fee.

A $70.00 processing fee will be charged for each user submitting Module 4 for grading. If you prefer to mail or fax your Quizzer, remove both pages of the Answer Sheet from this book and return them with your completed Evaluation Form to: CCH Continuing Education Department, 4025 W. Peterson Ave., Chicago, IL 60646-6085 or fax your Answer Sheet to CCH at 773-866-3084. You must also select a method of payment below.

NAME ____________________

COMPANY NAME ____________________

STREET ____________________

CITY, STATE, & ZIP CODE ____________________

BUSINESS PHONE NUMBER ____________________

E-MAIL ADDRESS ____________________

DATE OF COMPLETION ____________________

CFP REGISTRANT ID (for Certified Financial Planners) ____________________

PTIN ID (for Enrolled Agents or RTRPs only) ____________________

CRTP ID (for CTEC Credit only) ____________________

METHOD OF PAYMENT:

☐ Check Enclosed ☐ Visa ☐ Master Card ☐ AmEx

☐ Discover ☐ CCH Account* ____________________

Card No. ____________________ Exp. Date __________

Signature ____________________

EXPRESS GRADING: Please fax my Course results to me by 5:00 p.m. the business day following your receipt of this Answer Sheet. By checking this box I authorize CCH to charge $19.00 for this service.

☐ Express Grading $19.00 Fax No. ____________________

* Must provide CCH account number for this payment option

TOP FEDERAL TAX ISSUES FOR 2014 CPE COURSE (10014586-0002)

Module 4: Answer Sheet

Please answer the questions by indicating the appropriate letter next to the corresponding number.

71. ____	78. ____	85. ____	92. ____
72. ____	79. ____	86. ____	93. ____
73. ____	80. ____	87. ____	94. ____
74. ____	81. ____	88. ____	95. ____
75. ____	82. ____	89. ____	
76. ____	83. ____	90. ____	
77. ____	84. ____	91. ____	

Please complete the Evaluation Form (located after the Module 4 Answer Sheet) and return it with this Quizzer Answer Sheet to CCH at the address on the previous page. Thank you.

TOP FEDERAL TAX ISSUES FOR 2014 CPE COURSE (10024491-0001)

Evaluation Form

Please take a few moments to fill out and mail or fax this evaluation to CCH so that we can better provide you with the type of self-study programs you want and need. Thank you.

About This Program

1. Please circle the number that best reflects the extent of your agreement with the following statements:

	Strongly Agree				Strongly Disagree
a. The Course objectives were met.	5	4	3	2	1
b. This Course was comprehensive and organized.	5	4	3	2	1
c. The content was current and technically accurate.	5	4	3	2	1
d. This Course was timely and relevant.	5	4	3	2	1
e. The prerequisite requirements were appropriate.	5	4	3	2	1
f. This Course was a valuable learning experience.	5	4	3	2	1
g. The Course completion time was appropriate.	5	4	3	2	1

2. This Course was most valuable to me because of:

____ Continuing Education credit
____ Relevance to my practice/ employment
____ Price
____ Other (please specify) ____________________
____ Convenience of format
____ Timeliness of subject matter
____ Reputation of author

3. How long did it take to complete this Course? (Please include the total time spent reading or studying reference materials and completing CPE Quizzer).

Module 1 ____ Module 2 ____ Module 3 ____ Module 4 ____

4. What do you consider to be the strong points of this Course?

5. What improvements can we make to this Course?

TOP FEDERAL TAX ISSUES FOR 2014 CPE COURSE (10024491-0001)

Evaluation Form *cont'd*

General Interests

1. Preferred method of self-study instruction:
____ Text ____ Audio ____ Computer-based/Multimedia ____Video

2. What specific topics would you like CCH to develop as self-study CPE programs? ___
____
____
____

3. Please list other topics of interest to you ______________________
____
____

About You

1. Your profession:

____ CPA
____ Attorney
____ Financial Planner
____ Enrolled Agent
____ Tax Preparer
____ Other (please specify)
____

2. Your employment:

____ Self-employed
____ Service Industry
____ Banking/Finance
____ Education
____ Public Accounting Firm
____ Non-Service Industry
____ Government
____ Other ______________________

3. Size of firm/corporation:

____ 1 ____ 2-5 ____ 6-10 ____ 11-20 ____ 21-50 ____ 51+

4. Your Name ______________________________________
Firm/Company Name ______________________________
Address ____
City, State, Zip Code _____________________________
E-mail Address _____________________________________

THANK YOU FOR TAKING THE TIME TO COMPLETE THIS SURVEY!

NOTES

NOTES